CONTRIBUTIONS OF SELF PSYCHOLOGY TO GROUP PSYCHOTHERAPY

THE NEW INTERNATIONAL LIBRARY OF GROUP ANALYSIS SERIES

Series Editor: Earl Hopper

CONTRIBUTIONS OF SELF PSYCHOLOGY TO GROUP PSYCHOTHERAPY
Selected Papers

Walter Stone

KARNAC

visual narratives will be of particular interest to students of the social and collective unconscious.

Stone's work with narcissistic and borderline patients developed in parallel with his work with the chronically mentally ill, who are often institutionalised. He demonstrates that group therapy for such patients is not only a matter of containment and holding in the service of administrative control, but also involves interpretative work based on an understanding of the primary need for a good enough self-object. In general his clinical work is directed towards providing nurturing experience as a context for facilitating the achievement of insight in the service of the maturation of the self. Clearly, Stone has contributed to the development of an authentic relational perspective in psychoanalytical group therapy.

Group analysts will be able to connect these ideas with their own theories of ego training in action, the complementarity and reciprocity of transference and countertransference processes, the maintenance of an optimal balance of involvement and detachment in conducting and convening groups, and finding crucial areas of engagement between the group-as-a-whole and the members of it. I am especially interested in Stone's conceptualisation of envy, shame and helplessness, which is very similar to my own understanding of envy as a defence against the fear of annihilation rather than as a manifestation of the death instinct. This work locates aggression within the system of aggressive feelings, frustration and failures in empathy and care.

More personally, I very much appreciate Walter's colleagueship and friendship. He always finds time to listen with generosity and attention. These qualities are apparent in this selection of papers, which have contributed to the theoretical underpinning and clinical techniques of our profession.

Earl Hopper, Ph.D.
13 July 2009

PREFACE

In more than a century since Freud's monumental contributions
to understanding human behavior, the psychotherapeutic field is
replete with competing innovations in "how psychotherapy works."
This monograph follows my writings from 1977 until the present as I
have applied self psychology to group psychotherapy.

I was initially trained in a therapeutic paradigm heavily flavored
by traditional psychoanalytic thinking, with the therapist's role as
abstinent interpreter of unconscious processes. Self psychology provided a model, one that added a new dimension to my understanding of the phenomenon I was observing and loosened constraints
that I felt with the classical model. Moreover, applying the theory to
practice seemed to invigorate the groups and seemed more helpful
to the members.

My psychiatric career began with residency training at the University of Cincinnati in 1961, four years following graduation from
Vanderbilt Medical School. In the interim, I had a year internship
and a year of internal medicine residency at the University of Wisconsin. My formal training was interrupted by the draft, and I served
from July 1959 through June of 1961 as a partially trained internist
in United States Air Force. The experience freed me to reflect upon

what aspects of a medical career most appealed to me. I chose to get a fresh start and shift my specialty choice to psychiatry.

I was accepted for training at the University of Cincinnati, one of the premier dynamically oriented programs in the country. A department wide enthusiasm for group treatment had been stimulated during the late 1950's by a six-month Sabbatical visit of British psychoanalyst Michael Balint. He had engaged many of the young faculty with a group training/treatment experience, which they transported to their supervisory work in the hospital settings and in their private practice. An additional stimulus to group work was the presence on the full-time faculty of Roy Whitman, M.D., author of a series of papers formulating the Group Focal Conflict as a way of understanding the treatment process in group therapy.

Residency began with a year of inpatient work, divided between the Veterans Administration Hospital and Cincinnati General Hospital. In the early 1960's, patients often remained in the hospital for three to six month periods. Hospital stays emphasized the importance of the milieu, and the use of groups as providing an important window into patients psychic functioning.

Outpatient clinical work was the major focus of the final two years of training. Almost all senior residents co-led groups; with younger trainees serving as recorder/observers. As a group recorder, my task was to take detailed process notes during each session, formulate the process in the model of a group focal conflict and present to the supervisor. It was a rigorous assignment. I learned to think process and hear metaphors that I was having difficult discerning in dyadic work. Moreover, I found myself often times profoundly impacted by "affect contagion," which deeply impressed me of the power of group treatment. I remain particularly appreciative of the two supervisors that year, Murray Tieger, Ph.D, and Stanley Block M.D.

Following my apprenticeship, I co-led an outpatient group for my final two years of training and as a senior resident a long term group of patients at the VA hospital. From this experience, I wrote my first group paper with my co-residents, "The treatment of a homosexual woman in a mixed group," published in 1966.

Upon completing my training in 1964, I chose to continue as a faculty member of the Department of Psychiatry assigned as ward supervisor at the Veterans Administration Hospital. I was also in part-time private practice. Bill Powles, M.D., a VA faculty colleague, generously asked if I would co-lead his private outpatient group, which I continued when he departed a year later for a university position in Canada. In 1970, I had an opportunity to move to Central Clinic, the primary outpatient service of the Psychiatry Department. With that move I was appointed coordinator of the department group psychotherapy program, a position I held until my retirement and departure from Cincinnati in 2002.

My early horizons were expanded by the twice yearly regional group therapy conferences, conducted across two days. The sixties, a period of considerable social turmoil fueled by the civil rights movement and the Vietnam war, was also filled with innovation and at times seemingly dominated by the controversial t-group movement, gestalt and transactional analytic approaches. I was exposed to many of these innovations as I gradually became involved with the American Group Psychotherapy Association, Beginning in the early 1970's attending an annual meeting became a fixture on my calendar.

During my early years in Cincinnati, aspiring psychoanalysts commuted to the Chicago Psychoanalytic Institute for training. This period coincided with Heinz Kohut's developing self psychology into a coherent theoretical framework. Paul and Anna Ornstein, faculty colleagues in Cincinnati, were early leading followers and advocates of Kohut's rather revolutionary ideas of the self, the emphasis on the empathic stance and the increased attention to manifestations of narcissism and narcissistic vulnerability in the therapeutic setting. Their enthusiasm for self psychology was re-enforced by Kohut's frequent visits and lectures in the Department of Psychiatry.

I then began thinking about how the theory might apply to my work with groups. At that point I felt I still had insufficient knowledge of this knew paradigm, and I began discussions exploring applications to group therapy with Roy Whitman, Together we wrote the original two papers applying a self psychological approach to group process and therapy. Later, Roy as Department Chair, asked me to be his co-chair, which provided me with an experience in larger group and system dynamics which enriched my understanding of those structures.

In the 1970's I began participating in Tavistock group relations conferences and became acquainted with James Gustafson, from Madison Wisconsin. His work on "Unconscious Planning in Small

Groups" (Gustafson and Cooper, 1979) later to be labeled the Hypotheses of Higher Mental Functioning, like Self Psychology, was a growth theory. Our work seemed to overlap and we agreed to collaborate on the problems of treating narcissistic and borderline patients. This led to Jim and I writing about group treatment for this difficult population from a self psychological perspective.

Through my regular involvement with the American Group Psychotherapy Association annual meetings, I was exposed to the breadth of the group therapy field. Among many others, I met Scott Rutan, and we developed a life long friendship and collaboration resulting in our authorship of *Psychodynamic Group Psychotherapy*. Scott has read and thoughtfully edited every one of my manuscripts, always with a careful eye to making my sometimes convoluted language more readable.

Beginning in the 1980's with the advent of managed care, the psychotherapeutic landscape changed. The public mandate shifted to provide greater care for the relatively neglected large population of chronically mentally ill persons. The clinic had to shift therapeutic resources from the traditional population of primarily uninsured workers or homemakers with Axis I or II disorders, to individuals with persistent and severe mental illness.

I saw an opportunity to maintain and perhaps energize the group program by shifting the focus to working with persistently ill persons. I thought that application of a self psychologically informed treatment to this population might be therapeutically effective, and increase the enthusiasm for doing this work. This model presented an attractive alternative to the somewhat derided "supportive" treatment approach that had been the mainstay of groups for the chronically ill population.

I assumed responsibility for co-leading two groups as well as supervising three others. One of the groups I supervised had been videotaped from its inception. When the staff therapist left the clinic in the middle of an academic year and no therapist was available, I assumed the leadership. I recruited residents and later social or psychology graduate students to run the video camera. In exchange, I spent time after each session plus an hour each week reviewing the tapes with the student and teaching about group processes. This was not an altogether altruistic teaching exercise, since the arrangement forced me to find time to consistently review sessions. These reviews provided wonderful feedback in how I worked, and resulted in the publication of *Group Psychotherapy for Persons with Chronic Mental Illness* (1996).

In order to further deepen my perspectives on group analytic psychotherapy, in 1992 I took a three month sabbatical to the UK. There, I became more deeply acquainted with the Group Analytic theory and subsequently joined the International Association of Group Psychotherapy, participating in International Congresses across Europe, Israel, and South America.

I retired from the University of Cincinnati in 2002 and moved to the San Francisco Bay area. In this new location I have continued my active involvement in group psychotherapy through association with the Northern California Group Psychotherapy Society and as a volunteer member of the faculty at the University of California San Francisco Department of Psychiatry and at California Pacific Medical Center.

ACKNOWLEDGEMENTS

I have tried to be careful in acknowledging those individuals who have contributed to my career and my understanding of the human condition. I apologize to those I have inadvertently neglected.

Maurice Levine, former Departmental director, who created a truly broad based, intellectually stimulating dynamic department of psychiatry, played a critical element in nurturing myself and many others in a respectful appreciation of the impact of unconscious conflict on how all of us feel and think.

I was able to enlist editorial assistance of Paul and Anna Ornstein particularly when I had questions regarding theory. Of course, my wife, Esther Stone read early drafts of my manuscripts, with a particularly keen eye to redundancy and excessive detail.

Other colleagues deserve particular mention. Robert Stewart, MD, director of Central Clinic when I joined the staff in 1990, honored me with the responsibility for the group psychotherapy training program, which provided a breadth of experience that I might never otherwise have had. Edward Klein, Ph.D. who had left Yale for a professorship in the Psychology Department at Cincinnati was a close friend. Ed taught me a great deal about the continuing evolution of the Tavistock model of group relations, about adult development and gender issues. Shirley Carroll, M.S.W and Bernard Foster, MD, who had offices adjacent to mine in the clinic were available for me to blow off steam after a difficult group session or just listen as I reviewed an interesting meeting. Lou Spitz, MD and Jack Lindy, MD were always available to listen and help me listen to myself. Milt Kramer, MD had a particularly effective manner of helping me see where I was not putting my ideas together clearly. A very important collaborator and close friend, Dianne McIntosh, RN, Ph.D. was of special support as we worked to provide dynamic groups to patients with chronic mental illness. Molly Cassady, RN and Rita Johnson, RN were faithful staff clinicians who co-led groups with the residents for many years, providing service as well as a wealth of understanding of the treatment process with the chronically ill. Walter Smitson, Ph.D., the director of Central Clinic supported my work both administratively and financially.

There were very many other influential colleagues in AGPA, and I know that I can name them all, but I want to make special mention of Howard Kibel, who taught me a great deal about object relations theory, and others working with self psychological concepts including Irene Harwood, Marty Livingston, and Rosemary Segalla. At an AGPA conference in the 1980's I also met Sigmund Karterud and Thor Kristian Island who became leading exponents of a self psychological approach to groups in Norway and throughout Europe. This led to subsequent collaboration with Dr. Karterud, particularly related to the concept of the group-self. I would be remiss, if I did not mention my group of British colleagues who I consider good friends, who were available during my sabbatical in UK and have remained so. These individuals include Earl Hopper, Malcolm Pines, Dianne LeFevre, and Beau Stevenson.

Finally, and I am dedicating this book to my patients who so generously allowed me to glimpse into their personal worlds which few are privileged to hear, and to my dear and special friend Robert Kunkel, M.D., with whom I had lunch almost weekly for more than thirty years. Bob a talented individual and group clinician and administrator listened to my struggles trying to understand my groups and my work. He was always available and encouraging, but also helpfully critical when necessary. I do not believe that I could have been as productive as I was without his valuable help.

INTRODUCTION

Section I: Theory

The section on theory spans the entire period of these writings. The papers begin with the initial publication applying self psychological ideas to the theory of group process and group therapy in 1977. However greater consolidation of theory awaited several decades until I had accumulated considerable clinical experience and had written about the therapeutic process. These papers provided firmer grounding before moving to writing experience distant theory.

The final four papers in this section, all published in the new millennium, address my most recent thinking regarding central aspects of group theory, including Kohut's original formulation of the group self, and more in-depth considerations of group-as-a-whole, and dreams and group development.

The initial paper *"Contributions of the psychology of the self to group process and group therapy,"* (1977) written in collaboration with Roy Whitman, was based on the theory available at the time Kohut's first book, *The Analysis of the Self* (1971). Narcissism was still considered as a structure within the ego, with its own separate developmental line. In the therapeutic process of rupture and repair, patients would gradually gain understanding of and internalize a greater capacity to manage narcissistic injury. Narcissism would evolve but would not be extinguished in maturity. The paper discusses basic notions of empathy and selfobject transferences, with clinical examples illustrating selfobject transferences in group therapy.

The Group Self: A Neglected Aspect of Group Psychotherapy (2003). Explores Kohut's notion of the group-self as it illuminates fluctuations in affect and self-cohesion in group treatment. The group-self is conceived of as a deep going structure, a portion of the self that represents a collective project focused on achieving the goals and ideals of the group. The norms and values of the group become internalized as the group-self and, linked to fluctuations in the group process and structure, may be experienced as growth enhancing, depleting or fragmenting. Clinical examples illustrate changes within the group that impact therapist and members and are understood to represent shifts in cohesion and functioning of the group-self.

Group-as-a-Whole: A Self Psychological Perspective (2005) examines whole group concepts as a way of integrating diverse information arising from group discourse. The group may be experienced by its members in multiple ways: as an object, subject, selfobject, or as a deep-going aspect of the self, the group-self. Members' experience of the group fluctuates across a continuum of vitalizing or destructive responses.

These concepts serve as background in the exploring elements of the interpretative process. Whole group interventions may closely approximate or widely diverge from members' experiences. Group-as-a-whole interventions have the potential for helping members feel linked, understood and re-establish inner balance, or the opposite, disorganizing and disrupting the self. Clinicians should not abandon the power of whole group interventions because of fear of injuring members or disorganizing the group. Attending to the process, therapists can track the positive or negative impact of their intervention. Clinical examples from my practice or from the literature illustrate these concepts.

Dreams as Portraits of Self and Group Interaction (2006) calls attention to how dreams may represent the self, the self in relation to others, or the self in relation to the group. Perspectives of group as object, selfobject or group-self illuminate the dreamer's experiences. The therapist may help members gain understanding in fluctuations in their self states, in their need for human responsiveness or in new ways of being. An important value of the dream is its communication to the dreamer and others. The dream may communicate the dreamer's experience of the self or the experience of the group and in particular how difficulties within the group may be interfering with the treatment.

A Self Psychological Perspective on Group Development. (2009) examines the phases of group development as they emerge when the leader has consistently maintained an empathic stance and understood and responded to the evolving group processes from a self psychological perspective. Differing selfobject needs seem to emerge at different points in time. Selfobject experiences may be used at any phase, but what is emphasized is the more prominent needs of the members during the developing phases.

In the first phase, patients' wish for safety and understanding is expressed in search for an idealizing selfobject for the experience of merger. When members begin to assert themselves in the second phase, they may require mirroring selfobject experiences. In the third, working phase, members gain skills from alter ego selfobject experiences and consolidate the group ideas and aspirations in a group- self. Leader's therapeutic and countertransference responses are examined for each phase.

Section II: Clinical Applications

This section of four papers focuses on the clinical application of some of the theoretical constructs of self psychology to work with groups. The Curative Fantasy in Group Psychotherapy (1985) and Seeking Perspective on Patients' Attendance in Group Psychotherapy (1991) are not included, but will be described in sufficient detail to enable the reader to understand the essential elements in each of the two manuscripts.

A Self Psychological Perspective on Envy in Group Psychotherapy (1992) initially presented as a companion paper to Lionel Kreeger's presentation "Envy Preemption" delivered in May 1992 to the Group Analytic Society, notes how envy of group members follows from an individual wishing for or desiring the attributes of another. The concomitant emotion is experienced as disruptive to the self. The person's expressions of envy may be self restorative by removing or destroying the object and by energizing the subject. Within this framework envy can be understood along a continuum of mobilizing energy that might be used for the purposes of growth as well as destruction. Clinical examples illustrate the therapeutic efforts to understand the narcissistic injury as the precipitant for emergence and resolution of envious behaviors.

Self psychology posits a normal developmental assertiveness. Anger is understood as a response to or an effort to prevent anticipated narcissistic injury. *Frustration, Anger and the Significance of Alter-Ego Transferences in Group Psychotherapy* (1995) explores how alter-ego transferences assist the self acquire the ability to express frustration and anger. Broadly, alter-ego phenomena encompass a sense of likeness and sameness and in the deepest sense of being human. Twinship experiences which provide for the acquisition of skills, including possessing capabilities that are self-strengthening. Groups provide multiple opportunities for development of alter-ego transferences. Clinical illustrations focus on working with angry individuals in the group setting, which involves understanding alter-ego selfobject transferences, responses to disruptions, and subsequent group dynamic processes.

Self Psychology and the Higher Mental Functioning Hypotheses: Complementary Theories (1996) examines two theories which posit that individuals enter treatment to overcome developmental blocks in their relationships. According to Higher Mental Functioning Hypotheses (HMFH) patients therapeutic encounters involves tests (unconsciously) to determine if their prior pathogenic beliefs will be sustained, and if they will be injured by their treatment. A non-pathogenic response may result in removing blocks to change. According to self psychology, patients establish selfobject transferences which provide functions that are not available to the individual. These experiences have potential for becoming internalized and helping the self to continue development. Both theories note that these efforts to overcome blocks are not conscious, and may not enter awareness until a test has failed or an empathic connection disrupted. Clinical illustrations explore the treatment process from both perspectives.

The final paper in this section, *The Role of the Therapist's Affect in the Detection of Empathic Failures, Misunderstandings and Injury,*

(2001) explores the clinician's emotional responses arising from a variety of sources including their backgrounds, values, theories of therapy, interactions with patients, the group, and most broadly societal norms. This paper describes how a therapist is influenced by his affective responses as he tries to understand and then transmit that understanding to his group in the most therapeutically effective manner. The affects which accompany therapists' interventions may carry greater impact than the words themselves, and the patients responses may come as a surprise temporarily derailing the clinician's empathic connectedness.

Examples highlight the impact of emotions related to making therapeutic decisions that arise from diverse sources: those that are counter to implicit theory, those that arise from public (or semipublic) information about the clinician, that the emerge from feelings of relief when troublesome patients miss sessions, or those following major decisions in the clinician's personal life. Suggestions are put forth in dealing with the discomfort when the clinician is confronted directly with a countertransference enactment.

Section III: Severe Disorders

This section expands the application of self psychological theory to working with severe disorders of the self, including schizophrenia, bipolar illness and chronic depression. The four papers represent a shift from group treatments patients in the narcissistic and borderline spectrum to individuals with severe and persistent mental illness. The papers taken as a whole espouse the notion that the relationships established by the therapist's consistent empathic stance and understanding of patients selfobject needs has considerable therapeutic impact, and as a result patients can exhibit greater self and relational awareness.

Technique in group psychotherapy of narcissistic and borderline patients, (1982) coauthored with James Gustafson, focuses on applications of self psychology to "difficult patients" in groups. We explore the therapeutic impact of non-interpretative therapist activities, which may be seen as a precursor of more recent theorizing about the therapeutic impact attributable to a responsive empathic relationship. The therapist's technical stance is further reflected in understanding difficult patients behaviors as self-protective that had been labeled defensive/resistive. This shift represents a move to a more empathic position from one of an external observer. In this formulation of technique, the therapist strives to create an "average expectable environment" which may include responding directly to questions, accepting idealization or noting the potential for confrontations to evoke narcissistic injury.

Working with long-term groups for persons with severe and persistent mental illness, the paper *Affect and Therapeutic Process in Groups for Chronically Mentally Ill Persons* (1998) addresses the difficulty these individuals exhibit in identifying and managing emotions. The therapist as selfobject, supplies missing or incompletely formed psychic structures which help patients tolerate and speak about emotions. The therapeutic strategy of collaboratively working with members to identify emotions is central to achieve these goals. Patients' dread of injury further contributes to their caution. The clinical example illustrates some patients' capacities to engage in meaningful emotional interaction, manage strong feelings and gain insight into their contributions to the discourse.

The emphasis in Self Psychology on development of the self rather than in resolving conflict is further elaborated in *Strivings and Expectations: An Examination of Process in Groups for Persons with Chronic Mental Illness*, (2003). Building on the self psychological thesis that individuals enter therapy to cautiously explore the possibilities of changing and growing, this paper examines manifestations of these wishes in the group treatment of persons with severe and persistent mental illness. The model, adapted from M. Tolpin, proposes that therapists attend not only to repetition of old patterns, but to patients cautious, fragile efforts to try new ways of relating and managing their difficulties. Examples from groups with chronically mentally ill persons illustrate these processes.

The final paper addresses group and individual process when the therapist leaves a group. *Saying Goodbye: Exploring Attachments as a Therapist Leaves a Group of Chronically Ill Persons* (2005) reviews the literature on a particular vexing but not uncommon situation, particularly in training settings, when the therapist discontinues his leadership. In this paper I describe my experience of saying goodbye to a group of persons with chronic and persistent mental illness who I had treated for more than a dozen years. Within a general model described by Kubler-Ross of emotional sequences in coping with impending death, the situation in the group differs in that the group may not die, but continue with new leadership. This possibility requires that the therapist must not only say goodbye, but help prepare for change leadership. I illustrate the difficulties in saying goodbye through illustrations of my countertransferences, not only to the process of saying goodbye, but in anticipation of the new leaders taking over "my group."

SECTION I

THEORY

CHAPTER ONE

Contributions of the psychology of the self to group process and group therapy

Walter N. Stone and Roy M. Whitman

Recent contributions by Kohut and his co-workers to the psychology of the self (Kohut, 1966, 1968, 1970, 1971; Ornstein, 1974; Gedo and Goldberg, 1973) and the vicissitudes of narcissism (Kohut, 1972) have direct relevance to the understanding of certain aspects of relationships of group members with one another and the leader as well as group formation, (group) cohesion, and (group) fragmentation. In this paper we propose to integrate the implications of narcissistic transferences as they emerge in group process laboratories and group therapy. We do not mean to negate other developmental and interactional considerations of the individual and group but are adding narcissism as a hitherto not clearly recognized central area.

Developmental models of therapy groups patterned after Freud's initial contribution (1921) and elaborated particularly by Bion (1960), and Bennis and Shepard (1956) emphasize the "object-love" relationships with the leader and subsequent "object-love" relationships with co-members. Their understanding of group behaviour was based on the model of transference neurosis. The relationships between the members of the group and in particular with the leader were considered object directed transferences involving libidinal and aggressive drives. Understanding the nature of the relationship with the help of the structural model, it is assumed that the group leader is experienced as a separate "object" who is loved or hated, or who, by his behaviour, or indeed by his mere presence mobilizes defenses against such strong feelings. The model for this approach to group behaviour is the oedipal model in which the leader (father) is seen as a person stimulating an intense, positive, erotic or, conversely, intense negative, hostile transference. As additional implication of this model is that the group members are seen as siblings who also relate along the lines of object-love. The opportunity to engage in multiple object-love or object-hate relationships, both vertically and laterally, has been an oft-stated advantage of group therapy over individual therapy.

Along the lines of a separate (but not independent) development of narcissism, Kohut (1971) has made some extremely cogent reconstructions of early intrapsychic structure. Mental life (Gedo and Goldberg, 1973) begins with a phase of uncoordinated, separate nuclei of function from which the whole cohesive self emerges.

Though from the vantage point of an outside observer, an object relationship develops, it is hypothetically experienced by the patient as a one person system in which the "other" is experienced as a part of the self, a so-called "self-object."

The group, and in particular the group leader, may therefore, be seen as separate entities but they and he may be experienced as part of the patient's psychic structure, and indeed, a necessary part.

Prior to a stage of "object constancy," objects are not loved for their attributes but, rather, their need-fulfilling functions, hence self-objects. Kohut's observations not only permit the clarification of self-objects from libidinal objects but also are also pertinent to another crucial issue, the development of the self.

The sense of self, especially one that may become cohesive or fragmented, is related to the sense of a stable identity (Lichtenstein, 1961). This self is not equivalent to identity as a halfway term between psychology and sociology, but has an intrapsychic form related to the ego but not coexistent with it since it exists at a level of abstraction closer to actual clinical experience. We thus have a self which consolidates from individual ego nuclei (Glover, 1932) and which may coalesce but also fragment. After the formation of the superego, the tripartite model of ego, superego, and id becomes the illuminating conceptual approach, but preoedipal issues of nuclei, self and self-objects become useful conceptual tools in both individual and group psychology.

In group psychology, when this model is used, the leader and/or the group is seen as a "self-object" which maintains the cohesion of the individual by confirming the archaic grandiose self or by offering itself as an idealized vehicle for archaic fantasies of greatness. Therefore, on the level of the group-as-group, we see that each individual, and especially the leader, becomes not only a love object, but also a necessary part of the self of each individual.

Several authors have previously suggested that groups can serve both as a libidinal and a narcissistic object but have not separated these two developmental lines. In this regard, the concept of group-as-mother (Whitman and Stock, 1958) can be seen in two ways: the mother as a libidinal object and the mother prior to the separation of self and object, i.e., a narcissistic self-object (Whitman, 1973). The developing interest in this area was recently reviewed and summarized by Scheidlinger (1974), who linked the concept of the group-as-mother with the deeper emotional meanings of the group. Scheidlinger suggests that a split occurs, with positive affects directed to the group-as-a-whole and negative affects to the leader and other group members as stimulators of threatening, fearful feelings. But Scheidlinger was operating within the frame of reference of the mother as a separate object rather than an even earlier developmental framework in which there is no self-mother differentiation into separate entities.

Gibbard and Hartman (1973), in their description of Utopian fantasies, seem to be referring to a transitional phase in which "group members attempt to institute a state of affairs which is perfect or ideal in some or all respects ... The Utopian fantasy is most likely to appear when the positive and appealing aspects of the group-as-mother (the warmth, security, protectiveness, etc.) seem to be attainable and the negative aspects (the engulfment, malevolence, obliteration of boundaries, etc.) appear to be well defended against." These authors, however, have not differentiated the preoedipal mother as a separate object from Kohut's formulation in which the mother functions as a self-object and is an integral part of the individual, existing totally for his gratification.

Earlier, Slater (1966) hinted at a developmental approach by theorizing that the initial unconscious perception of the group is an undifferentiated mass from which the leader is gradually differentiated. The dependence upon the powerful leader is necessary to avoid engulfment by the more threatening undifferentiated mass. The leader's power in this phase is comforting and reassuring. Only later: "revolt becomes imminent, in order for the members to stave off their fear of being overwhelmed by their helpless dependence on the leader" [p. 190]. This is essentially an approach to the differentiation of self and object but implies what Kohut has so cogently criticized, that object-love relations are not necessarily derived from narcissistic relationships in the course of development. We recognize that the leader emerges as a separate object, or he may remain a self-object, and in that sense is not strictly differentiated from the group as a separate independent entity. Therefore, we employ Kohut's hypothesis that narcissism has it own lines of continuing development to understand both individual and group life.

Crucial to the fruitful use of the concept of narcissism and self is the concept of objects as self-objects, i.e., parts of the self whose only function is to supply missing or needed parts of the self. Both the leader and the group can be usefully conceptualized this way, and this understanding leads to a second major observation; two basic forms of transference may exist for the individual: object-narcissism or an idealizing transference ("my group or leader is the greatest") or subject-narcissism, thus keeping the original perfection of a grandiose self-concept.

We shall now give examples from groups of the function of self-object relationships as they appear in: (1) exhibitionistic, grandiose reactions; (2) twinship and merger reactions; and (3) idealizing transferences. We shall then examine these concepts as they shed light on (4) narcissistic considerations in some special character problems, and (5) implications for the therapist's behaviour.

Exhibitionistic, grandiose needs with wish for mirroring

Infantile exhibitionism and grandiosity are important parts of self-esteem development. The early forms gradually are transformed into adult ego functions related to pride and enjoyment of individual accomplishment. Developmental arrests may lead to the persistent search for someone to reflect the over-inflated and unmodulated grandiosity. In the transference the other is not experienced as a separate object but, instead, as a self-object whose function is to mirror the grandiosity. Gratification of these archaic wishes, however, may be so over-stimulating that even though such a state is ardently hoped for, the internal discomfort may become intolerable. Thus, the wished for praise of one's accomplishments or of one's "self" can lead to withdrawal in order to reduce internal tension.

A thirty-one year old single woman, Katherine, was in combined therapy (both with the group leader) and was particularly sensitive to over-stimulation of her affects. She found herself especially anxious in a group session in which the major theme was discussion of sexual feelings. In the subsequent individual session this patient revealed she had a fantasy of startling the group by announcing that she and the therapist were secretly dating. She felt a great anxiety associated with that fantasy and found herself withdrawing markedly from the group after having it. Her wish to show off, to be seen as special, was clearly demonstrated in this fantasy. Other aspects of paring with the leader and of emerging positive oedipal transferences seemed relevant but less significant than the idea of the "bombshell" that she would exhibit to the group. This patient previously presented a dream in which she was naked, standing on a balcony in front of a large symphony orchestra some hundred yards away. She had been anxious in the dream, but the manifest content indicated her wish to show off and exhibit herself before a large, admiring audience. The dating fantasy within the group thus represents some progress in that she had become more accepting of her exhibitionistic fantasies.

A second example occurred in which a 37-year-old woman, Jackie, was in simultaneous individual and group therapy (with different therapists). In her individual therapy she reported an incident in which she had become the central figure in a series of group interactions. Frequent references by the group as well as her own fantasies led to the idea that the spotlight was on her. She basked in this spotlight and enjoyed being the centre of attention in the group. She experienced a heightened feeling of self-esteem when the group, and particularly the leader, became an admiring "other" concentrating solely on her. The scrutiny and envy of other group members increased her inner excitement, which then became intolerable, and she said: "I see a dark corner of the room where I would like to go which seems comfortable and snuggle." She retreated to a corner of the room away from the group.

One possible explanation of this sequence was the patient's avoidance of the envy of others as separate competing objects. The possibility suggested by the concept of narcissism we are present is that she had to hide because of over stimulation of her grandiose exhibitionism. These possibilities highlight the two chief alternative understandings of such behaviour, but we feel that the narcissistic over stimulation was most central and that it was this, which caused her to take the defensive extreme of retiring into a dark corner.

We would like to present a third example from the literature: Glatzer (1962) describes a patient who was particularly intolerant of praise and transformed recognition into self-depreciation. She noted that a major therapeutic task was to confront the patient with his patterned response. Glatzer's interpretative emphasis was on the masochistic elements of the patient's response rather than what we would now suggest was the patient's defense against the grandiose self being over stimulated. The three possibilities for the interpretation of this phenomenon are: (1) the classical one of superego guilt linked to obvious success; (2) guilt about omnipotent fantasies being realized; and (3) shame about the mobilization of primitive exhibitionist grandiose wishes. It is our thesis that the emergence of exhibitionistic grandiose fantasies must be understood in order to respond empathically to the patient.

Twinship and merger fantasies (Subtypes of mirror transferences)

More archaic forms of the grandiose self can be seen in the twinship and merger fantasies. In the twinship fantasies the other person is experienced as an alter ego, a twin exactly like the patient. A theoretical note needs to be made in this connection. The original description of pairing phenomenon in groups by Bion (1960) describes one particular form of a two-person relationship occurring with a group. Rioch (1970) in her summary of this concept states: "The basic assumption is that when two people get together it is for sexual purposes. When this basic assumption is operative, the other group members are not bored [by the pair] … but the group, through the pair, is living in the hope of the creation of a new leader or a new thought or something which will bring about a new life, will solve the old problems and bring Utopia or heaven, or something of that sort." This model again refers to the pair being experienced as separate individuals joined together for a specific (although unconscious) purpose. Twinship, which also involves intense interaction between two people, is characterized by patients attempting to emphasize the identical nature of the other. The other person is essentially part of the self.

Merger fantasies, an even earlier developmental stage of grandiosity, arise often in the beginning phase in groups, but may be present throughout the life of the group and may only be exposed after a period of therapy. Slater's (1956) description of early group phenomenon refers to this process: "In the absence ... of clear evidence of conscious attachment and differentiations, and in the presence of an imperative inner desire for unity and belonging, the fear strikes then that perhaps [the members] may forget this fact and 'lose' themselves." In the merger transferences this state is actually wished for although greatly feared.

A twinship transference was illustrated by Norma and Wanda during a period of adjustment following the addition of several new members to a group. Wanda, a new patient, started with several casual and superficial remarks and was interrupted by Norma, who exclaimed, "She sounds exactly like me," overtly referring to the tone of Wanda's voice and her expressions. Later, as Wanda was telling the group about her shoplifting, she said, "I could do something about my shoplifting if I really want to, but I don't think I really want to." Norma, who had never shoplifted, said with exuberance and pleasure, "That's so much like me," referring to the thought of being able to control unacceptable behaviour, and later in the same meeting she shrieked, "That's me ... that's me," in response to Wanda's description of her lack of sexual satisfaction. The need to be identical was clear on all three occasions. While it is possible that such a response was simply this person's way of controlling anxiety by trying to establish mutuality, continuation of such statements should alert the therapist to the possibility of a twinship transference.

Merger fantasies or defenses against the loss of self are frequently observed and can be clues to unrecognized narcissistic problems. IN a therapy group of hospitalized patients, just prior to the end of the session, one recompensating schizophrenic patient said he wanted to curl up and go to sleep in the therapist's lap. Again there are two possible interpretations: one, an anaclitic dependent relationship with the preoedipal mother, or the second, a merger with the pre-object mother. Slater (1966) provides an additional example of fusion of the individual with the group. It was neatly expressed when a member referred to a previous attack on him by other group members with the phrase "we attacked me."

Defenses against merger and loss of self had impeded the progress of an outpatient group. Jan dealt with these problems, which she labelled as "being too influenced," by talking about her need to leave the city and try living on her own. In her real life she was a functioning schoolteacher who had lived alone many years. When confronted by the group members with her fears of "involvement," Jan complained that she didn't understand, and the following week revealed fantasies of quietly leaving and going to South America where she would have time to think and find herself. During the same meeting Pat described a situation, which she didn't know how to handle. She said that if her husband remarked that she might enjoy a forthcoming party, she felt trapped because, if she did enjoy it, the enjoyment wouldn't be hers but his. Such themes, which reverberated through the group, dealt not only with concern over influence by another but reflected the deepening sense of belonging and concomitant fear of losing the self. If the fear of merger predominates, the solution may be actual flight to avoid feelings of loss of self.

Idealizing transferences

Projection of primitive grandiosity onto others who then will be all-protecting is the basic mechanism of the idealizing transference. Marked idealization, whether it be of the leader or of the group-as-a-whole, is often observed during the course of group treatment. Particular stages of group development may mobilize these transferences, and "getting stuck" at such a nodal point may indicate narcissistic idealizing transferences. In Bennis and Shepard's (1956) classic paper on developmental sequences in groups, the first stage of dependency upon the leader may be re-examined in the light of the leader not as a separate object but, rather, as an idealized self-object. In this sequence, after rebellion against the leader, the group may enter a phase in which everyone agrees about everything and a group atmosphere of harmony temporarily exists. Such a stage when prolonged for the group or an individual suggests the possibility of the group-as-a-whole functioning as an idealized parental imago and stabilizing a state of narcissistic equilibrium between the group and its members.

A straightforward example of immediate idealization occurred in a Tavistock training group during an early phase when the group was actively hoping to elicit more responses from the leader; one participant, with superb mimicry and humour, managed to "break up" the group, including the leader. In response, one of the participants, who was familiar with the technique, became enraged because the leader had dropped out of role and therefore could no longer be an effective teach and leader of this group. The rage was a response to the de-idealization of the leader.

In a more traditional training group, which included the requirement that members make a record of each meeting, Bill harangued the leader to tell the participants how to take notes; only the leader knew how! There was no value in anything produced by others because they did not have the experience or the wisdom of the leader.

An example of defenses against the emergence of idealizing transferences can be illustrated by Joan. She characteristically related in an intuitive fashion, rather readily understanding others and thereby being quite helpful. Repeatedly she stated she had a problem of dependency upon her husband and did not want to allow those feelings to control her life anymore since she had already worked them out in her previous individual therapy. She participated actively, but little seemed to be happening to her. During a period when the group began to work on more overt sexual themes, Joan suddenly revealed her feelings about two men in the group. Both men, who were actually of high social status, were idealized as being perfect and wonderful, feelings which Joan was fearful of acknowledging and wished to disavow. The therapist, who was aware that Joan felt the same way toward him, indicated that it must be a terrible struggle for Joan to have to fend off the intense feelings of needing such relationships. For the first time in month, Joan cried. She said that she felt relieved, and in the subsequent meetings she became more animated and was able to verbalize the enormous discomfort from the internal pull she felt to attach herself in an idealizing mode. Concomitantly, she had the first sustained argument with her husband, whom she had always seen as reasonable and logical and therefore impossible to argue with. The argument represented a beginning ability to view herself as a separate person without the idealized other as necessary for her equilibrium.

An illustration of the direct expression of idealizing transferences occurred in a group of borderline patients, which had a membership increase from four to eight. Amanda, one of the new patients, dominated the first two meetings by talking about her dead sister. But at the third session, she came in calmer and gave a brief speech saying that she realized that the group, as well as the people at her church, were telling her the same thing: continue living. Several members remarked that Amanda did indeed seem better. Then one of the original patients turned to the leader and said, "Martha and I were talking and we agreed that if you could help Amanda you are a genius." The leader sloughed this off and pointed out that the group was more important than the leader in Amanda's life. The discussion then turned to talk about religion and God. One patient asked, "What makes you all feel there is a God?" Three of the four patients indicted there had to be a God because you really couldn't live unless there was a God." The leader responded by asking the group if talking about God was a safe subject. One of the new members insisted that God was important and that one needed to believe in Him all the time. Another mentioned that God was her problem.

> Unfortunately, the leader failed to appreciate the group need for "genius" and unempathically depreciated himself. A shift then occurred as the patients searched for another object, which would gratify their need to idealize, and the lengthy discussion concerning God followed. Concomitantly, the potential for disappointment and consequent disillusion was evident in the references to questions about life and death. The leader's confrontation of the group with their solution was based on a defensive and object-relations-conflict model. He neither appreciated nor accepted the narcissistic overidealization that the group found necessary.

Narcissistic considerations in some special
character problems

Conceptualization of separate developmental lines of narcissism throws light on several difficult clinical problems faced in the conduct of group psychotherapy, among them the help-rejecting complainer (HRC) and the monopolizer.

A help-rejecting complainer as defined by Berger and Rosenbaum (1967) is a patient who is driven to make demands on, as well as to manipulate and govern, others. Advice, interpretations, suggestions, etc., which are directed toward him fail to alleviate his stance. He rejects help given to him.

Berger and Rosenbaum (1967) note that these patients were subject early in life to severe deprivation and/or abandonment; some have had psychotic mothers or were raised in orphanages. We would like to add to this description what we have learned from the study of narcissistic personality disorders. The most significant element lacking in the early life of the HRC was an empathic parenting figure. Failure of appropriate mirroring and confirming responses leads to the stance: "Nobody cares enough." These patients, with their help-rejecting behaviour, end up alienating other members of the group, thereby demonstrating that no one really does care or can do enough for them. Though this pattern has been conceived of in terms of masochism, that is not a sufficient explanation of such behaviour. It should be noted that the HRC maintains an ongoing narcissistic orientation to other members of the group, which he would have to give up were his problem to be resolved.

A joke illustrates this neatly: A woman was sitting on a train moaning over and over to herself but loud enough to be hear, "Boy, am I thirsty! Boy, am I thirsty!" Finally, one of the other passengers said to her after he handed her a flask, "Here's your water, now please be quiet!" The woman drank deeply and then began to moan to herself, "Boy, was I thirsty! Boy, was I thirsty!"

Not only does the HRC maintain his relationship with the group, but he maintains a central position. He is willing to tolerate the hostility so long as he has attention and intense involvement. To have no attention is to be empty and alone, and that is intolerable. Along with the ongoing need for attention is the infantile need for revenge on the group for the infantile narcissistic hurt visited upon him when he was ignored or responded to unempathically.

In contrast to the help-rejecting complainer with his desire for revenge and ongoing merger with the group is the monopolizer. The monopolizer sets up a situation in which he acts out his infantile grandiose fantasies of being responded to by the group. He believes that his every word is important and worthy of interest by the group. So great is his need for admiration and love that he allows any sensitivity he may have for the group feelings and responses to take a back seat. The group and leader become self-objects who have no existence or functions of their own, other than to attend to and mirror the monopolizer's desire for admiration. A true understanding of such monopolizers, who have a strong core of untamed narcissistic needs, would lead to empathizing with the strength of their need for approval no matter what audience, rather than confronting them with their lack of sensitivity to other's needs.

In both the monopolizer and the HRC there are primitive exhibitionistic needs that the person is trying to satisfy and which have been overlaid by years of unsuccessful resolution. Consequently, the end result is manifested by a character pattern. The inappropriateness and compulsivity of the behaviour is a clue to the strength of the underlying infantile struggles for admiration, attention, and appreciation. The narcissistic core thus must be deal with to cause a diminution of the self-defeating behaviour. In this respect, non-depreciatory empathic recognition of the basic wishes is crucial to successful modification of these personality constellations. This leads us to principles of the therapeutic stance necessary for the resolution of such narcissistic personality constellations.

Implications for leader behaviour

Appreciation of narcissistic issues has direct relevance for leadership responses. The traditional dictum to the leader of trying to help shape the group so that the atmosphere allows safe and open expression of feelings and fantasies becomes even more meaningful from this vantage. The leader may permit appropriate development of narcissistic transferences by recognition of the wish for mirroring response and/or acceptance of idealization. The therapist is not alone in providing these responses, for the group may serve as an accepting arena for display of grandiose and exhibitionistic drives, as well as provide a sense of belonging to a wonderful (ideal) group. Fried (1973) quotes from a patient's letter after termination of the group, "I'm helped when I recall how blessed it was to share the love and kindness of my friends in the group and of you (the therapist). The memory of the intimacies we shared and the openness of our feelings helps keep me together." This letter indicates the patient's internalization of the group-as-a-whole and the leader in maintaining a cohesive feeling of self. A group atmosphere which enables regression to and expression of early developmental forms of narcissism thus serves as a therapeutic base from which patients can examine these needs.

In mirror transferences, appreciation of the individual's contribution to the functioning of the group needs attention by the therapist. For instance, excessive adherence to group-as-a-whole interpretations may leave the individual patient with the feeling of being a cog in a machine and therefore depersonalized. Historically, some of the resistance to considering group-as-a-whole phenomena may have arisen because sensitive therapists were attuned to the potential for narcissistic injury to the individual group member. We are not suggesting that central group issues be avoided because of the potential for narcissistic blows to the individual, but, rather, that the therapist be alerted to the possibility that group-as-a-whole interpretations may be experienced by a particular patient as a non-recognition of his uniqueness. Psychological withdrawal or rage reactions, at times so intense as to lead to dropping from the group, are observable following such interpretations. More precise clarification of this process with acknowledgment of the patient's wish for appreciation or recognition may have not only a soothing effect but also enable further legitimization of these needs.

Horner (1975), utilizing similar concepts of narcissistic personality, arrives at a different conclusion. She suggests that these patients' transferential needs for a self-object are so great that their presence greatly diminishes therapeutic work. We would agree that in some instances narcissistic patients may respond to the group with intensification of their needs but we have also observed considerable therapeutic growth in the group, and blanket exclusion is not warranted.

Non-judgemental appreciation of the patient's wish to be admired or to be the centre of attention has been useful in understanding the monopolizer and the help-rejecting complainer. Yalom (1970) has suggested that the monopolizer not be told to stop talking or control himself but to tell the more meaningful aspects of his life. This approach indeed does gratify the patient's need for attention but does not directly and empathically acknowledge the patient's need for such attention in order to maintain his equilibrium. In essence, the therapist should point out the wish for admiration but not directly gratify the patient. Such interventions do not lead to greater exhibitionistic demands but rather, to the patient's increased self-awareness and feelings of being understood.

Idealizing transferences often present a particular problem for therapists because they seem so unreal. Fried (1955) thinks individual sessions are necessary to prevent dropouts from the group. Traditionally, patients have been admonished to give up their unrealistic expectation of the leader and to see things more realistically. This debunking of the idealizations has left patients confused since most appreciate their unrealistic expectations but are unaware of the function they serve in their incessant seeking for an idealized self-object.

Ornstein (1974) has succinctly summarized the typical sequence of events when the analyst, as so often happens, fails to empathically recognize the patient's archaic needs: "Then episodes of failure in empathy ... will trigger specific pathognomonic symptoms of despair, a feeling of being drained of energy, and a lowering of working capacity and self-esteem. The patient will regress to archaic forms of idealization, vague, diffuse and ecstatic religiosity, and to a mystical union with God or the universe. Under certain circumstances he may even regress to an activation of the grandiose self, with a heightened self-consciousness, shame propensity and finally a hypochondriacal preoccupation with ill-defined mental and physical discomforts." This sequence was exemplified in the group in which the leader debunked his role as a genius in helping the patient over her acute depressive symptoms. It is not easy for many therapists to accept idealizing statements, particularly if they are patently out of line with their own self-concepts, but recognition of the patient's needs for such transferential self-object relationships may help counter the premature tendency to make the patient face the realistic limitations of the therapist. Sensitivity on the part of the therapists to mirror transferences and to idealizations, as well as an understanding that these transferential needs may be central in the patient's personality problems, helps dispel the common negative attitudes toward patients with narcissistic problems.

Above all, the therapist who adheres to the concept of narcissism as a separate developmental line sees narcissism as eventuating in humour, creativity, empathy and wisdom. He will not attempt to push group members away from narcissistic issues to object-love.

Summary and conclusions

In this paper we have tried to highlight a new dimension, the separate developmental line of narcissism, to the study of group and individuals in groups. Basic to this is the understanding of the early response to parents both as libidinal objects as "self-objects" which mirror and enhance the developing self. The developmental concept of narcissism and that of narcissistic transference which leads to idealization, mirroring needs, twinship, and merger sheds light on a variety of interactions taking place in group therapy. The leader, other group members, or the group-as-a-whole supply a missing part of the self rather than functioning as separate objects with whom there is conflict. This adds a further dimension to the understanding of certain troublesome group members with narcissistic pathology, particularly the help-rejecting complainer and the monopolizer.

These formulations have clear implications for the leader. The non-judgemental acceptance of the patient's needs to idealize either the leader of the group and to receive recognition and admiration provide a theoretical basis for soothing and empathic intervention. In this function the therapist is experienced as a self-object mother who exists primarily for the needs of the patient. The working through of these narcissistic problems can lead to a higher level of function, genuine therapeutic growth, and a more stable sense of self.

CHAPTER TWO

The group self: A neglected aspect of group psychotherapy

Sigmund Karterud and Walter N. Stone

Abstract: The authors explore and expand on Heinz Kohut's concept "the group self", which is related to, yet different from the concepts "intersubjective field" and "group matrix". The group self is defined as a collective project with inherent ambitions, ideals and resources. From this perspective the authors discuss group-as-a-whole phenomena, empathy, aspects of group development and the kind of discourse which is appropriate for group psychotherapy. This particular discourse should contain multiple selfobject functions as well as aspects of otherness not accounted for by the selfobject concept. Partaking in this discourse has a beneficial effect by itself which justifies a concept of "discoursive selfobject function". This selfobject function is of a partial supraindividual nature. Two clinical vignettes illustrates aspects of group self development and fear of depletion of the group self.

Key words: The group self, self psychology, group psychotherapy, group-as-a-whole, selfobject function.

In the last two decades self psychology has exerted considerable influence on group psychotherapy, particularly when applied to understanding clinical phenomena and therapeutic technique.

However, to a large extent this has been an application of dyadic self psychology theory and principles to the group situation. In this paper we will discuss a more radical position by addressing the concept of the group as a whole from a self psychological perspective. As we shall see, this turn will illuminate some dim aspects of groups, but also reveal some shortcomings in self psychological theory itself.

The group self

Kohut was not particularly favourable to group psychotherapy (Arensberg, 1998), but he was preoccupied with historical group processes. In the essay Creativeness, Charisma, Group Psychology: Reflections on the Self-Analysis of Freud (1976), he introduced the concept of "the group self". He suggested that "we posit the existence of a certain psychological configuration with regard to the group—let us call it the 'group self'—which is analogous to the self of the individual" (pp. 420–421). In the accompanying footnote, Kohut writes, "The psychoanalytic concept of the self, however—whether it refers to the self of an individual or to the self of a person as a member of a group or, as a 'group self' to the self of a stable association of people—concerns a structure which dips into the deepest reach of the psyche" (p. 420). He adds, "The basic patterns of a nuclear group self (the group's central ambitions and ideals) account not only for the continuity and the cohesion of the group but also determines its most important actions" (p. 420). Kohut did not develop these ideas theoretically any further although some of his essays, in particular "On Leadership" (Kohut, 1985), contain the group self as an implicit presupposition. Theoretically speaking, the group self is thus an underdeveloped concept. In this paper we will try to give clinical meaning to the concept.

The group-as-a-whole—as object, agent, selfobject and self

In the group psychotherapy literature the common usage of the term "group-as-a-whole" is ambiguous. Firstly it refers to the group-as-a-whole conceived as object. This usage refers to group members experiential reports and behaviour which suggest that they experience the group as an entity which resembles so-called internal objects. This usage dates back to W.R. Bion (1959) who claimed that the ultimate reason for basic assumption phenomena, was the group's resemblance (in the mind of the members) with primitive internal objects. According to this tradition one speaks of the group as an idealised ("good") mother/breast or alternatively as a persecutory or devouring ("bad") mother/breast (H. Durkin, 1964; Scheidlinger, 1974).

Secondly, one has referred to the group-as-a-whole *as agent* (or subject). This usage is displayed in group-as-a-whole interpretations, such as "the group tends to avoid ...", "the problem for the group is ...", "the group tends to rid itself of painful conflicts by ...", etc. This second usage is closer to a notion of an (agentic) group self. However, group psychotherapists have (rightly) maintained an ambivalent attitude towards the group as agent. Group-agentic interpretations are probably used rather frequently, yet the theoretical grounds for such interpretations are not satisfactory within existing paradigms since accepting the group as agent is close to investing the group with a supraindividual mind.

Thirdly, the group-as-a-whole has been conceived of as a selfobject (Stone, 1992). This refers to experiences of being strengthened by group membership in itself. Nowadays many will refer to attachment needs in order to explain this phenomenon. Later in this paper we will relate the group-as-selfobject to the supraindividual nature of group discourse.

Fourth, the group-as-a-whole can be approached from the perspective of the self, as will be outlined in the following paragraphs.

The group-as-a-whole conceived as object, agent/subject, selfobject or self refers to different aspects of experience and behaviour in groups. These concepts are more experience near than the concepts of group matrix and interpersonal field. The group matrix refers to the conscious and unconscious communicational network in the group (Foulkes & Anthony, 1957; Foulkes, 1973). It is related to established group norms and group solutions (Whitaker & Lieberman, 1964). Thus the group matrix is impregnated with an interpersonal "direction" so to speak. An intersubjective field is more abstract. It lacks a foundation in an interpersonal project, which we will elaborate in the next paragraph. It is crucial to underline that neither the concept of matrix nor the intersubjective field, catches the agentic aspect of the group-as-a-whole. *It does not make sense to attribute intentions to a matrix or to an intersubjective field.* How can we properly say that a group *wants something*, without violating ordinary language rules? In our opinion, claiming that there exist needs on a group-as-a-whole level, presupposes a concept of a group self.

The group self as project

Whatever are the reasons for people being together, they will necessarily construct meanings and purposes for their togetherness. This quality, the purpose of togetherness, is fundamental to group formation, and, we will add, a fundamental quality of the group self. With reference to J.P. Sartre's (1943) notion of a fundamental project for the individual existence/self, we will argue that this purposeness of being together is part of a larger phenomenon, of a *collective project*. People come together in order to achieve something, and the group self is the conscious and unconscious structure that embodies the project. The project contains both the rational deliberative part of group formation ("I join this group because of my interest in the subject matter") and a host of unconscious motivations (e.g., attachment needs).

The supraindividual qualities of groups are consequences of the collective nature of the project. Groups do not contain any supraindividual group mind, but a supraindividual project. The project consists of certain ambitions, ideals and resources embedded in a specific history (similar to the individual self), and the project can be carried out on all levels of sophistication. Thus one is justified to speak of a restricted and primitive versus a mature group self and a disorganised versus an organised group self. The group self is typically composed of a core member subgroup that, more than other members, profoundly identifies with the ambitions and ideals of the project (Kohut, 1985). They are the main spokespersons for the group qua project. They act on behalf of the group self. Experientially they can have difficulties in differentiating between their personal self and their part of the group self. The group project can become identical to the personal life project. An insult to the group will then be perceived as an insult to the personal self.

The concept of project resolves the problem of the agentic aspect of groups. As a collective supraindividual project, we are justified to say that the group needs and wants something and resists other things. *What* it wants and resists depends on the nature of the project and the group's interactions with the surroundings. As with the individual self, a group self is full of shortcomings and conflicts and contains an unconscious domain as well as a conscious rational part. These conscious and unconscious conflicts and shortcomings *in the perspective of the needs and the aims of the group self* justify, in our opinion, group-as-a-whole interpretations.

It follows from taking the needs and the aims of the group self seriously, that the question of the future appears as a legitimate theme also at the level of the group-as-a-whole. Aspirations and fears of the future are powerful motivational forces for group actions. Without a perspective of the future, things become meaningless. Where should the concern for the future of the group be located, if not in the group self?

The nature of the project defines the *kind of discourse* that is most appropriate for the group. There are quite different discourses (defined as communicational patterns, attitudes, belief systems, etc.) in a Hells Angels group compared to a scientific committee. The discourse concept covers much of the same terrain as matrix and intersubjective field, but takes it a bit further. The discourse also conveys a supraindividual structure. It is kin to Wittgenstein's notion of *language games*. The language game of contemporary psychotherapy is quite different from the language game of bridge. The crucial point is that the established discourse, or language game, which tradition has established within a profession, will set the stage for the events to be displayed. One is not personal author of an established discourse tradition, e.g., psychodynamic group psychotherapy. One is an actor within the rules set by the discourse and in a certain respect one can say that one is played with by the discourse (group). In our opinion, this points to a limitation in intersubjective theory, where the intersubjective field is conceived as created by the protagonists ways of organising experience according to different cognitive-affective schemata (Stolorow et al. 1987). This definition does not give sufficient space for the supraindividual forces embedded in the operative discourse tradition.

The project of (long term) psychodynamic group psychotherapy is promoting self understanding and self development **for** the members. The main task of the group therapist is to recruit members to understand and identify with the kind of discourse rules and paradigms of understanding that are most appropriate for this project. By basic discourse rules we mean typically group psychotherapy rules such as regular attendance, commitment, no outside contact, free and open communication, etc. (Rutan & Stone, 2001). By discourse paradigms of understanding we mean a paradigmatic way of attributing meaning to the current group events. Adherents to different schools of group psychotherapy may share basic discourse rules, but differ in paradigms of understanding.

In our opinion, it is crucial for *the discourse of self understanding and self development*, to pay due attention to the themes which are explicated in the self psychology tradition, such as the basic needs of the self, empathy, the significance of selfobject functions, the repetitive and selfobject transferences, empathic and self object failures, etc. During treatment members gradually learn aspects of the language of self understanding. In particular they will learn to appreciate selfobject functions from other members (and the therapist) and to identify and manage their own experiences of selfobject failures.

However, in addition to selfobject functions that members (or the therapist) perform for each other, we would like to emphasise a kind of selfobject function which has been unrecognised, and which cannot be attributed to acts of care and understanding from one person to another. We will label this selfobject function as a *discursive self-object function*. We contend that when people feel strengthened after a group session, this is partly due to participating in a kind of discourse, rich in cognitive and affective perspectives and nuances, that the individual is unable to perform for himself. This conversation, which enables the individual to understand more fully intrapsychic, interpersonal and group events, is not attributable to specific individuals. It is a *supraindividual discourse event*.

In the following we will comment upon the topics of empathy and developmental stages involved in the establishment of a discourse of self understanding and self development and thereafter discuss two clinical vignettes.

Aspects of group development

Most contemporary group psychotherapists adhere to a progressive theory of group development, i.e., a development from a state of low cohesion and immaturity to a state of maturity and cohesion.

A progressive view is analogous to the development of the individual self (from an emergent sense of self to a consolidated and competent self) as well as the development of whole nations (from despotism, slavery and injustice to liberalism and democracy). We shall not discuss the details of developmental subphases, but restrict ourselves to issues of paramount importance for the formation of a group self.

What developments and interactions are necessary for members to feel that belonging to the group will be emotionally satisfying, will help them feel that they belong to a worthwhile enterprise, that they will feel more powerful, more complete, more able to pursue their personal goals and stand-up for their ideals? In the opening phase of group formation, members are concerned about how to proceed and how the experience can feel safe and trustworthy. Myers (1996) asserts that members' initial anxiety is that others will fail to provide mirroring. Joining a group evokes feelings of relative helplessness and narcissistic imbalance. According to Myers this is countered by mobilising an idealising transference to the therapist, and by extension to the group as a whole. Members attempt to orient themselves by obtaining information from the leader on what ways to make the experience useful, which they hope will not only reduce anxiety but provide direction. Inevitably these efforts will be frustrated and fail, resulting in experiences of anxiety and disequilibrium (Stone, 1985, 1995).

In our opinion the term "idealisation" is too ambiguous to capture the essence of the *orientation phase* dynamics. What is labelled "idealisation" covers an existential terrain that extends from submission to idealisation proper. We contend that submission is the predominant mode in the orientation phase. It represents defensive self structures which are activated due to the fear of retraumatization. Idealising selfobject transferences usually occur much later. They develop slowly after the resolution of the conflict ("storming") phase (Karterud, 1999).

We believe that differentiating between submission and idealising selfobject transferences is crucial and points to a problem in contemporary self psychology. It is no longer en vogue to talk about defensive self structures. In contemporary self psychology one has moved from optimal frustration (Kohut & Seitz, 1963) to other ways of conceptualising "optimal" therapist-patient exchange, e.g., optimal responsiveness, optimal provision, optimal restraint and facilitating responsiveness (Bacal, 1985; Siegel, 1999).

Although we sympathise with these efforts, we worry that these conceptualisations blur the ingredient of frustration which is inherent in analytic relations. The phenomenon of submission pinpoints these different attitudes: Should one frustrate or provide gratification for submissive needs? In group psychotherapy a considerable element of frustration is inevitable. However, group therapists differ in their technique and the way they theorise about it. In our opinion self understanding and self development requires an oscillation between deconstruction of defensive self structures and construction of authentic self structures by reactivation and working through of archaic selfobject transferences.

Initially, the group is (rightly) perceived as therapist centred. The clinician's main task is to guide members through a phase of partial resolution of individual and collective submissiveness, to mobilise anger towards old and new authoritative figures, to activate the striving for autonomy, to facilitate a fresh series of negotiations of the basic rules and grounding discourse rules, whereby the members can properly say they "own" the group, which means that the group self is grounded in a collective project.

Since the therapist's attitude is deliberately group-oriented and interpretative, and not fundamentally individualistic-supportive, he/she will inevitably evoke experiences of selfobject failures (i.e., narcissistic injuries). Members' responses may be withdrawal or exploring connections with emotionally available others, i.e., those who can recognise and appreciate what the person emotionally needs. However, withdrawal from the therapist is seldom complete, and patients' experiences of the therapist as predictable, dependable and reliable while listening, attempting to understand and respond, provides a backdrop to which patients can return when peer relations are aversive.

It is each person's inner experience to the response of the therapist and members that lead to stabilising or enhancing the self. Under optimal circumstances trust develops and increased risk taking follows. These interactions create group norms and the slow development of a discourse that promotes self understanding and self development (Stone, 1996).

The therapist's abdication from gratifying submissive needs "forces" patients to address their fellow group members. By turning to others, individuals have a fair chance to find repositories for a wide variety of human needs, be they "defensive", "perverse" or "sympathetic". The result is covert and overt subgroups and alliances, and we are in agreement with Agazarian (1997) who emphasises that a substantial part of the dynamics is played out (at least in the earlier phases of group development) between subgroups. Subgrouping is an important source of stabilising a threatened self in group psychotherapy.

This leads us to some remarks on *the significance of the other* in group psychotherapy. Self psychology has traditionally emphasised the selfobject function of the other. We fully agree with the view that selfobject availability is the single most important ingredient in a psychotherapeutic group culture. If patients do not modify defences and permit experiences of being respected, listened to, cared for, confirmed, understood in depth, supported, finding crucial similarities in others, finding crucial aspects to idealise, etc.,— group psychotherapy will not work. To use Kohut's phrase, there would be insufficient oxygen for the group to develop or even survive. However, *selfobject experiences are necessary but not sufficient prerequisites for growth*. The others are needed for several other purposes, of which we will emphasise two: 1) The others are needed as repositories for projections. Without the other(s) there would be no possibility for enactments of the dramas of the inner world. Group psychotherapy presupposes a willingness to take on projected roles and become actors in externalised dramas. When individual members hate, despise and envy each other, they usually do not realise that they also need others in such roles. The individual will co-construct with others a wide range of transferential scenarios (Gans & Alonso, 1998). 2) The others are needed as sheer otherness. A group consisting of mere selfobjects (which can hardly be conceived) would be extremely dull and boring. The others are needed to bring in diversities and differences, other and opposing point of views, other perspectives on the world. Without this otherness, no deconstruction could be possible.

These elements are somewhat neglected in contemporary self psychological theory. The concept of "adversarial selfobjects" tries to repair this theoretical lacuna (Wolf, 1988). However, this concept is a contradiction in terms. In our opinion, selfobjects can never be "adversarial". In Kohut's theory selfobject experiences are univocally positive experiences (conscious and unconscious) that strengthens the self. The crucial point is that the self needs more than selfobject experiences. It also needs resistance, opposition and disagreement. It even needs selfobject failures. It is only through a dialogue with another than self that the self can come to know itself and develop (Karterud, 1998).

The developmental aim of psychodynamic group psychotherapy is thus to establish a group culture which has a rich potential for selfobject experiences, which contains the courage to set in motion inner dramas in the here and now and a tolerance for diversities and differences. This represents an ideal group self. This ideal group self should be considered as a *regulatory idea*. It is seldom fully realised, but the striving for it is worthwhile in itself since the striving to establish an ideal group self is the very activity through which the individual self comes to a fuller understanding of itself and proceeds with development. A group which has lost the "memoirs of the ideal group self", has lost crucial perspectives of the future. It will be locked in depression or chronically internal fightings which will lead nowhere.

Empathy

We fully agree with Kohut that empathy is the primary mode of access to the inner world of the patients (as well as the group as a whole). Empathy is the effort to understand the other "from within". The ability to engage in a sustained immersion with the other's perspective on the world is a prerequisite for psychotherapeutic work. The challenges for the group psychotherapist in this respect are enormous. One is presumed to be in empathic contact with 6–8 persons, the ongoing interactions as well as the state of the group self at each moments of time. It goes without saying that this is an impossible task. Consequently, the therapist's empathic failures are inevitable, making his/her ability to detect and address these failures all the more important (Stone, 2001).

However, what we would like to emphasise here is the relation between empathy and theory. Schematically, the very operation of empathy involves an emotional attuneness as well as a cognitive element of constructing meaning to the perceptions of the other. The cognitive element is necessarily suffused by "preunderstanding" (Gadamer, 1960). One cannot understand another without

presuppositions, and group therapists' presuppositions are replete
with theoretical constructs. Since, theoretically, group events are systemic events, the cognitive elements of the empathy operations come
to the forefront. One cannot understand a systemic event without a
preunderstanding of the structure and dynamics of the system.

Contemporary group psychotherapists explore a group event
from at least three perspectives: From the perspective of the individual intrapsychic, from interpersonal transactions, and from the
group-as-a-whole; all three perspectives contain hypotheses about
the unconscious operations at work. This complex perspectivity is a
hallmark of modernity. It was not accessible to previous generations
simply because it was unthought of. When contemporary group
psychotherapists "spontaneously" oscillate between these perspectives in their effort to understand, and by these "manoeuvres"
understand more fully, this does not imply that, as individuals, they
are more empathetic than say Hippocrates or Joseph Pratt, but that
these theoretically listening perspectives are internalised through
tradition and training. They have become a part of his/hers "natu-
ral" presuppositions. By this we mean to underline that theoretical
presuppositions are intrinsically embedded in the very operation of
empathy.

The most difficult empathic operation, in our opinion, is empathy
with the group self. This is so because the therapist is such an integral part of the group self. Initially the group self is solely a phantasy
in his own mind. He contains the ambitions to carry out a project
which he labels psychodynamic group psychotherapy. When he
materialises this phantasy to a concrete group, he will realise that
the externalisation of his internal project will take on unexpected
forms and courses. He will be caught in a drama much larger than
he ever conceived of. The two main "debates", or negotiation processes, that inevitably will evolve is 1) the "debate" between the
members about the why and how and where of the group, and 2)
the "debate" between the members and the therapist on the same
issues. The guiding principles for the therapist in these negotiation
processes are (often vague and contradictory) ideas about the ideal
group self. He wants to implement various aspects of the kind of
discourse which we have discussed above. However, he will eventually realise that the group self that emerges through the negotiations
in the group often will deviate considerably from his own ideals.

The larger group self thus contains a tension between the ideals and aspirations of the therapist (as well as those of the members) and the actual discourse that is established as a result of a large series of "negotiations". When this gap is considerable, the therapist may lose empathic contact with several elements in this dialectics. He may "forget" several of his initial ambitions and ideals and resort to supportive strategies; he may resign, "these patients are too disturbed"; he may act out his impatience and disappointment, etc. In our opinion it is crucial for group vitality that the therapist endure the pain and the grief located in the space between the ideals and the factual discourse, keep an empathic contact with both aspects and use this tension as a productive ground for thought.

Clinical illustrations

Example 1

Members of a six person outpatient group struggled to enter into meaningful dialogue. The meetings were often characterised by extended periods of silence. Two members were almost totally silent. Consistent efforts focused on understanding the meaning of this rather sterile group formation were not productive.

Eunice, a single woman, with a diagnosis of borderline personality disorder, was the most vocal member. She complained about almost all aspects of the treatment: the starkeness of the consulting room, the lack of recognition of her special sensitivities and assets, and the silences and stilted interaction in the sessions (in many respects the sessions reflected her marked social isolation and complaints that those in her work environment did not appreciate her talents or abilities). She spoke of both the great relief she felt when she left the city for a business meeting, and yet she said that she wanted the group to succeed because she needed a group to make her life meaningful

Depicting her perception of the therapist's responsibility, Eunice reported a dream in which the therapist was shutting off the group's view of the outside world by pulling the blinds over a picture window. The members' associations contrasted the relatively free chatter in the period before the start of the session to their silence when the therapist entered the room. They attributed their behaviour to his disapproval of their "social" discussion. This dream helped the therapist appreciate the personal limitations of the members.

In supervision, the therapist began to appreciate that the members appeared to need an extensive period of "social" discussion. They were not yet prepared to take the step of a psychodynamic group in exploring within group interactions the meaning of their discourse. The group self they hoped for (which was compatible with their level of self development) seemed at odds with that of their therapist. With this understanding, the clinician was able to interact with the members at the level they functioned. This "loosened" the discourse, which, over an extended period, led to their nascent capacity to self reflect and examine their relationships.

Comment: This example illustrates a countertransference that arose specifically from the clinician's notion of an ideal group self formation. He overestimated members' capacities and became impatient. Eunice's dream brought to the surface the rift between patients and therapist in regard to an ideal group self.

Example 2

A long-term outpatient group, led by one of the authors, composed of four men and three women, was focused on two somewhat overlapping issues. The primary focus was on Eve, a senior member, who had shown substantial growth and had been wondering about ending treatment. The group reacted to her plan to terminate with pleasure, recognising her achievement as she evolved from a person who barely spoke to one who would take a sentient leadership role. Several members expressed envy of her achievements. Ken expressed regret and wished that she would not leave.

In the context of Eve's processing her plan to terminate, several events impinged upon the group boundary or alluded to disrupted relationship: A patient who had precipitously terminated the group several years previously began a brief affair with a current member, and Aaron who had planned to end his loveless marriage, announced he could not deliver divorce papers and felt stuck. The members listened to descriptions of these events, which the therapist linked to Eve's departure, but they seemed unable to reflect upon their inner experience. The therapist became aware of a sense of doom—the group would not function with Eve's departure.

Near the end of the session prior to Eve's departure, as Aaron described his wife's incompetence in purchasing a new car, the discussion became highly critical of used car dealers. These were unscrupulous individuals who manipulated, lied, withheld information and took people in. Aaron acknowledged that his wife had nearly made a very bad deal, as a symptom of her behaviour. In the final minutes of the session, tension erupted as several members encouraged Aaron to patch up the marriage while others suggested he move towards divorce.

The therapist felt that he had been unable to fit this discussion into any coherent framework. Rather, he found himself unable to concentrate on the process and was preoccupied with what the group would be like after Eve departed. Only in retrospect, did he realise that the countertransference arose from his anticipation that the group self would be disrupted and instead of a lively and interactive group he was anticipating an emotionally unengaging, concrete discourse.

Comment: The session illustrates what we believe to be the impact of the unconscious fantasy that the group discourse was about to be shattered. Segalla (1996) asserts "the need to associate/affiliate with a group cannot be satisfied without some *capacity to experience the self as equal to the requirements of members*" (italics in original) (p. 264). In the therapist's mind, Eve's leadership had obscured others' capacities. The therapist feared the members could not maintain a psychodynamic group self. His ability to empathise with the members and with the disruption to the group was temporarily impaired.

These vignettes bring into focus the two threads we have been addressing in this paper: that of the theory of the group self and the role of theory in our use of empathy. The first example illustrates the precarious process of integrating (a subgroup of) silent individuals in a developing group self, while simultaneously fearing that "the owner of the group", the therapist, would resist the elements of autonomous action ("social talk") contained therein. This group is on the way from a dependent group self to a more autonomous group self. The second example concerns an upcoming loss and fear of depletion of the group self and focuses on the therapist's fantasies and resultant countertransference response.

Conclusions

Group psychotherapy is in a privileged position to explore and expand on Kohut's concept "the group self", which has been ignored by contemporary self psychology.

1. The group self is conceptually related to, but different from "inter-subjective field" and "group matrix".
2. The group self is defined as a collective project and justifies the agentic perspective that is implicit in group-as-a-whole interpretations.
3. Exploration of the concept leads to a selfobject function which has not previously been acknowledged—"a discoursive selfobject function".
4. Contemporary self psychology has neglected the significance of "the other" outside the realm of selfobject functions. An examination of the "discourse of self understanding and self development" reveals the significance of the other(s) as 1) repository of projections and 2) otherness as a necessary ingredient in a true dialogue.
5. The very operation of empathy is suffused by theoretical presuppositions.
6. Empathy with the group self is particularly difficult since it implies a reflective empathy with the discrepancies between the therapists ambitions and ideals and that of the factual group discourse.
7. The clinical vignettes highlight difficulties with the development of an autonomous group self and the emergent loss of a vital part of a group self and the members' and the therapist's responses to threats of fragmentation.

CHAPTER THREE

Group-as-a-whole: A self psychological perspective

Walter N. Stone

Abstract: As Self-psychology has evolved from exclusively dyadic treatment, it has illuminated transference configurations that are applicable to group treatment. Selfobject transferences not only are directed to individuals and to the whole group. In addition the concept of the group-self, refers to members' deeply felt inner experience of the group ideals and goals.

Individual's experience of whole group interpretations often stirs a basic ambivalence between group membership and self-expression. Self psychologically informed interventions, understanding and explaining, focus on therapists tasks of empathically understanding individuals prior to explaining (interpreting) the group-as-a-whole. Examples will illustrate transference and countertransference aspects of the treatment process.

Key words: Selfobject; group-self; empathy; interpretative understanding; interpretative explaining.

Group-as-a-whole: A self psychological perspective

Emerging from the ferment of interest in group phenomenon, Kurt Lewin (1951) conceptualized a group as a system, different from the sum of its parts. Groups were understood to have unique properties that were embedded in a hierarchy of systems and containing subsystems within their boundaries. Clinicians were thereby provided a conceptual tool with which to understand the interactions (verbal and behavioural) of a dynamic system frequently referred to as the group-as-a-whole. Systems' views encompass group dynamic perspectives, including goals, boundaries, norms, roles and values.

It soon became apparent that different meanings were attached to the group-as-a-whole concept. Helen Durkin (1981), reported findings from the General System Theory (GST) Task Force of the American Group Psychotherapy Association, noting the presence of two therapy group models: "[One was] to integrate current models [analytic/dynamic] within the overarching theoretical GST framework .... The other was to create new, more strictly GST models which were based on the isomorphic structure of living systems" (p. 14). It is my impression that the integrated approach has been dominant within the psychotherapeutic treatment milieu. Nevertheless, uniformity has not resulted. Group-as-a-whole has acquired differing meanings: it is experienced or appreciated as an object, subject, a selfobject, and as an internal group-self (Karterud & Stone 2003).

The goal of this paper is to selectively review group-as-a-whole concepts as background to understanding the contributions of self psychology to understanding the clinical applications of whole group phenomena.

The group-as-a-whole

Group-as-a-whole theories are just that, theories. They are overarching understandings of the data. They are a way of organizing observational and experiential phenomena, which can provide a comprehensive (although never complete) understanding of the phenomena. Representative of efforts to use systems perspectives in defining a group, Wells (1985) wrote:

> "In sum, the group-as-a-whole phenomenon assumes that individuals are human vessels that reflect and express the group's gestalt. Individual co-actors are bonded together, into an interdependent, symbolic, tacit, unconscious, and collusive nexus in which their interactions and shared fantasies and phantasies create and represent at once the

group-a-a-whole" (p. 114). Phantasies, in the Kleinian tradition, denote unconscious fantasies.

Similarly, Agazarian and Janoff (1997) formulate group behaviour as, "although functionally related [it] is separate and distinct from the behaviour of its members" (p. 33–34).

Groups are often referred to in a manner in which they seem to be concretized, reified and personalized. For members (and observers) groups come to be experienced as having broad personal meanings: "This group is really good. Everyone tries to understand." "This group is really harmful, as it has made a number of people leave." These generalizations, which can be deeply felt, fuse the individual with the group.

However, I believe there is an unexpressed ambivalence in such statements, because they erase the member's individuality. I see a basic ambivalence in wishing to belong (merge) to an all nurturing and caring group, and simultaneously wishing to express one's own individuality—this is who I am; I am separate. At times the goals of the group and the individual may have almost identical aims and then group-as-a-whole interventions may be readily acceptable to the members. At other times the opposite may be true, and then group-as-a-whole comments will be experienced as inaccurate or noxious. An additional element is individuals' varying capacities to manage differences, to be able to see others' point of view or perspectives, i.e., to mentalize (Fonagy et al, 2002) Achieving this developmental landmark enables individuals to regulate (sometimes intense) differences without psychological disruption.

Conceptualizing the group as a unitary entity has the potential for endowing it with human attributes and functions. Thus the literature often expresses the group-as-a-whole as an object, subject or a selfobject. Making these distinctions clarifies for the reader the particular meaning the author intended.

Groups as objects, subjects, and selfobjects

1. Group as object theories are derived from members' perceptions and thinking about the group as an entity that would respond to their needs in either a facilitating or aversive manner. Object

relations concepts, derived from the work of Sigmund Freud (1914, 1917) and Melanie Klein, are concerned with internal representations of external persons—in the process of internalization, these representation have been modified and do not represent a "true" image of the external persons or things. Bion (1960) conceived of the group as potentially a need satisfying/frustrating object. "The group meets this challenge [basic assumption mentality] by the elaboration of the characteristic culture of the group …. I include in it [culture] the structure which the group achieves at any given moment, the occupations it pursues and the organization it adopts" (p. 54). The group then may or may not meet members' needs. Similar projections and generalizations may lead members to experience the "group" as an idealized or demonized mother (H. Durkin 1964, Scheidlinger 1974).

Group focal conflict theory (Whitman and Stock, 1957; Whitaker and Lieberman, 1964) also is based on the group as an object. "Fears," which interfere with members expressing their wishes and desires, emerge in the group setting and are experienced as a property of the group. The group may also be experienced as facilitating members resolving focal conflicts.

The Higher Mental Functioning Hypothesis (HMFH) (Cooper & Gustafson, 1979; Weiss et al, 1986; Stone, 1996a) conceptualize a central group dynamic as members' efforts to test (primarily unconsciously) their environment to determine if they will be traumatized in the present as they had been in the past. The group will either pass or fail tests. Passing a test enables the individual to modify (or abandon) pathogenic beliefs developed in childhood. This hypothesis posits that, optimally, the group, as a separate object, through the manner in which it responds may repeat old traumatic patterns, leading individuals to resurrect old defenses, or the group may provide a positive response, enabling individuals to change and grow.

2. The group as subject or agent are conceptions perceiving the group as separate and capable of initiating action. This reified version of the group-as-a-whole is expressed often in such comments as "the group is resisting …" or "the group is struggling to find a way to address the problem …" Cohen and Ettin (2002), describe a group transpersonal self, i.e., members' perceptions of the group *as if* it had agency, and "is experienced as though it were an entity

that exists externally to the experiencing person and thus capable of being experienced *directly* [emphasis in the original] by others as well as oneself ..." (p. 291). These descriptions of the group express perceptions of the group as having a mind of its own, and capable of action, i.e., a subject or agent.

3. The group as selfobject concept assumes that members experience their group as capable of fulfilling functions necessary for their well being (but also capable of inflicting injury through failure or shortcomings of empathic responsiveness). *It is the function that is central to the concept, not the person who is "supplying" the function.* Distinguishing selfobject from traditional usage of the term object, Kohut (1984) conceived of others providing certain essential human functions, which he labelled selfobject. He distinguished two aspects of the selfobject concept as, "... the *general meaning* of the term selfobject as that dimension of our experience of another person that relates to this person's functions in shoring up our self and a specific meaning of the term selfobject—in this sense it should always be referred to as an *archaic* self object—that relates to the beginning stages of the development of selfobjects ...." (p. 49). Archaic selfobject functions are presumed, in the transference by the subject, not by the external observer, to be under the subject's control. This experience is not quite conscious and has qualities as if the "other" was part of the self. The process could be conceived of as being experienced as having control over one's own hand. Selfobject needs may be experienced as if such needs were provided by his/her group. The need for selfobject functions changes with maturation, but does not disappear. We all need soothing or admiring responses through our lives—narcissism does not disappear. We develop ways (again both conscious and unconscious) of reinvigorating a depleted or fragmenting self, which might include human and non-human responses (i.e., a responsive pet, or listening to a Beethoven symphony).

The group, as a selfobject, may fulfil idealizing (Harwood, 1983) and mirroring transferences (Stone & Whitman, 1977) or as providing opportunities for alterego transferences experienced as similarities or sameness (Stone, 1995). An idealizing transference carries with it an experience of being safely held. In early group developmental stages the therapist serves idealized/merger needs as a self-stabilizing antidote to the stress of beginning membership (Meyers, 1996). As the group begins to fulfil needs there often develops an idealization of the whole group. Fried (1973) quotes a letter received from a former group member: "I'm helped when I recall how blessed it was to share the lives and kindness of my friends in the group and of you (the therapist). The memories of the intimacies we shared and the openness of our feelings helps keep me together." Meyers (1996) quotes a patient, "With all the years of individual treatment that I've had, I was never able to feel or express these feelings. I feel the group understands and accepts me" (p. 223). Meyers posits that this represents an internalization of (merger with) an idealized group, and that "mutual and reciprocal idealizations facilitate group cohesion" (p. 223). A particularly poignant articulation of a patient's merger experience, serving almost a magical healing force with an idealized group was expressed by a woman, diagnosed with chronic schizophrenia. In the context of her therapist's departure, following more than a decade of treatment, she commented on her sense of serenity in the treatment setting:

> "When I come here, to the clinic here, I feel like I'm in a different world compared to where I live at and work at. And, I have these thoughts all day, others of the week when I'm not coming here, when I'm working. When I come here, I kind of like I forget all those thoughts, you know, the 'miserableness' of it ...."

Such selfobject experiences can be solitary or imagined to be shared. One characteristic of the t-group movement in the 1960's was some individuals search for their next group, in which they could at least temporarily feel "more together" (Stone, 1992). These experiences, often described in mystical terms, could be readily formulated as repairing a fragmenting, disintegrating self with a merger experience. Bacal (1985) suggests that Bionian basic assumption dependency could be seen from a self psychological perspective as a need for idealizing selfobjects.

Mirroring needs can be satisfied by therapist, members and be experienced as coming from the entire group. Optimally, patients are recognized for their achievements, which is the essence of mirroring transferences. Insufficient recognition of "risks" patients take or changes they make—failures to mirror—may lead some patients to depart the group. Such experiences are spoken about as, "the group doesn't respond," or "nobody cares"—individuals are not named; it is a group phenomenon (Stone & Stevenson, 1991). Likewise, a search for similarities, often presented in seemingly superficial social talk (What kind of work do you do? "Oh, you like fishing, too?") could be understood as a way of feeling connected, and as expressions of nascent alterego transferences. As the therapeutic process deepens, patients seem to search for relief from dysphoric experiences of shame, embarrassment and guilt, not only through catharsis, but by a hoped for experience of similarity. Characteristically these experiences become attributed to the group, not to particular individuals—the group is now the source of providing alterego needs.

Resistance to entering a group or deeply joining may be formulated as a self-protective mechanism, fearing that selfobject needs will not be met. Fantasies that mirroring or idealizing needs won't be met or that the person is so different that meeting alterego needs would be unattainable are manifestations of what Ornstein (1991) has labelled the "dread to repeat." It is not the individuals but the whole group that is the object of these anticipatory fantasies.

Therapists are also affected by their perceptions of the group functioning as a selfobject. Their mood changes may reflect their sense of personal cohesion and self esteem as they reflect upon a meeting. Urgent requests for consultation following a difficult session can be appreciated as a search for help not only in gaining a cognitive handle on what has transpired, but as the therapist's own efforts to restore a derailed and possibly fragmenting self. My own growth as a group therapist was significantly facilitated by sharing a ride home with a colleague who would empathically listen to my recounting my joys and pain following a "good" or "bad" group. My ability to work with a group composed of patients diagnosed with borderline and narcissistic personality disorders was likely made possible by knowing that following the session a colleague would have his office door open and I could "pull myself together," telling him of my experience. In essence, I was provided a situation in which I could reliably count on a colleague's availability to provide selfobject functions as I processed my group experiences, particularly when "the group" went badly.

The group-self

The concept of the group-self was introduced by Kohut (1976).

> *"The psychoanalytic concept of a self, however—whether it refers to the self of an individual or to the self of a person as a member of a group or, as a 'group self,' to the self of a stable association of people—concerns a structure which dips into the deepest reaches of the psyche."*
> (p. 420)

As noted by Karterud (1998), "The boundaries between the personal self and the group self are vague .... One is part of the other and they dip far down into each other's unconscious structures. When the group is shattered so too will the individual be" (p. 88). The group-self can be conceived of as a project, [i.e., an incomplete, continuing process] in which the individual identifies with the ideals and goals of the group (Karterud & Stone, 2003). In this respect then the group-self undergoes developmental changes, analgous to that of group development (Kieffer, 2001) and to the evolution of group cohesion. Thus the group-self is not fixed, but responsive to fluctuations in the individual's experience of the group.

An ordinary understanding of an enhanced group-self experience might be the experience of Boston Red Sox fans after "their team" won the World Series in 2004. More simply, group-self might be enhanced by feeling pride during the performance of the Star Spangled Banner. Alternatively, depletion or fragmentation of the group-self might be reflected in the experience of one's country at war. Initially people, based on agreement with the country's goals and ideals, identify with the war efforts as expressions of their group-self. However, the group-self may be shattered with various kinds of failures to live up to ideals or to achieve goals.

Cohen and Ettin (2002) attempt to separate two aspects of the group self: 1) a personal group-self—"an individual's 'version of self' or 'personal identity' as a member of a group; and 2) transpersonal group's 'self', "members' personifications of the group as an 'other' having a self with is own attributes" (p. 288). In my view, the former approximates my notion of the group-self; the latter is more closely linked to the group as a subject/agent. In treatment situations, if too broad a discrepancy (not entirely conscious) exists between what the individual experiences as his/her own assets and beliefs and those that would be "required" to develop a group-self, it is likely that the individual would either dropout from the group or never join (Segalla, 1996).

I have previously written about my countertransference response to a key group member's planned departure in which I antici- pated that my sense of the group would be significantly changed, and I would be burdened with re-invigorating the therapeutic work (Karterud and Stone, 2003). The departing woman had epito- mized the group ideals: she was open, forthright, self-reflective and empathic. Others were more limited in performing these functions. As I ruminated about what the group would be like following the woman's departure, I became aware of feeling dulled and unenthu- siastic about the group. I imagined having to work much harder, an experience I recognized and resented. My fantasies led to a deple- tion of my group-self.

In sum, these condensed explications of the various concepts of the group as subject, object, selfobject and a depiction of the group- self provide background to the question of the impact of these per- spectives on the therapist's mode of listening and intervening. These listening perspectives include not only the group-as-a-system, but appreciation of a self psychological understanding of the individual members. The therapist's task is considerable, keeping in mind mul- tiple possibilities of an intervention on a particular individual and upon the overall group functioning.

The interpretative process

Group as-whole interventions (Rutan and Stone, 2001) may be distinguished by their aim: a confrontation, that is used to draw attention to behaviours or a theme within the group ("The group is very resistant today."); as clarification which illuminate recurring processes ("When I announced my vacation the group seems to find itself focusing on experiences of loss just as it did last Christmas when we had a two week interruption") or as an interpretation. Interpretations may refer to a leader ("I think that the group is focus- ing on previous losses *because* I announced my vacation, and you are afraid of being angry with me") or the group ("I wonder if you are talking about painful losses *because* you are afraid to address feel- ings towards one another, because the group might fall apart?"). In addition, group-as-a-whole interpretations might be framed from a systems perspective, in which an individual or a subgroup is seen as carrying a function or serving a role for all the members. For instance, an interpretation might focus on a member in a divergent role that protects "the group" from expressing similar feelings towards the therapist or keeps feelings out of members' awareness. These examples of whole group interventions, illustrative of the group as subject or object, are based on conflict model of psychopathology.

The basic self psychological model of pathology is one of a deficit in self organization. Symptoms or behaviours are understood as (pathological) ways to soothe or restore a disrupted or fragmented sense of self, and not as a defense/solution in the face of conflict. The fundamental thrust of self psychologically informed treatment is an empathically informed understanding and explaining (interpretation) to stabilize the disrupted self and help restart growth in concordance with the patient's goals and ideals. These tasks are accomplished through a consistent empathic approach (Kohut, 1984).

Inevitably, members are injured or traumatized (or anticipate being injured) and in efforts to re-stabilize a disrupted sense of self, they search for (maladaptive) self stabilizing/soothing or self restorative solutions. The precipitant for such disruptive experiences might be an empathic failure on the part of the therapist or a member. However, a patient might attribute the injury to the group. An additional basis for self-stabilizing responses is a member's fears of loosing him or her self in the group (e.g., being sucked into a morass, "disappearing"). Whatever the basis for the disruption, patients' attempts to restabilize themselves emerge as symptoms, or self-soothing or self enhancing behaviours.

Therapeutic change (cure) follows a general two-step process. For some, the experience of feeling understood may be sufficient to stabilize a disrupted or fragmenting sense of self, which may be sufficient to enable the person to restart growth, and sometimes unanticipated termination (Stone, 1985). For most, an additional component, explaining (interpreting), provides a cognitive element linking disrupted states to experiences in the treatment, and/or the present, and to developmental trauma. An individual's repeated experience of being understood, having the experience in the present explained, and having the linkages made to one's past, leads to the person's internalizing the selfobject function (transmuting internalization) with an increasing capacity to more successfully manage such traumata

Self psychology emphasizes the understanding portion of the process: " [T]he analyst verbalizes to the patient that he has grasped what the patient feels; he describes the patient's inner state to the patient, thus demonstrating to him that he has been understood ...." (Kohut, 1984; p. 176–177). This seemingly basic notion is reminiscent of my experience teaching interviewing to beginning medical students. Students are instructed to "feed back" to the patient what they have heard the patient say, in order to ascertain that they (the students) have understood. Yet, traditional interpretative interventions have either ignored or obscured this step (Ornstein and Ornstein, 1985).

Feeling deeply understood helps patients, caught in a downward spiral of fragmentation or disintegration, re-stabilize. Paul and Anna Ornstein (Ornstein & Ornstein, 1996) have commented on the impact on the patient of having felt understood: "Feeling understood—as simple as this may sound—in reality has profound effect on the state of the self. Feeling understood is the adult equivalent of being held, which on the level of self-experience results in firming up or consolidating the self" (p. 94). Once they have regained their balance, patients are more capable of hearing the other and reflecting upon their inner world. Feeling understood strengthens the bond between patient and therapist. This is not a simple task; most particularly, initial understandings are seldom complete or fully accurate. The therapist's consistent effort to empathically understand serves not only to stabilize a disrupted self, but acts to deepen participants' engagement in the treatment, which enhances the experience of the group-as-a-whole.

Self psychologically informed interventions

In my experience, interventions that aim at understanding (without necessarily explaining) group wide processes can be therapeutically productive. They set the stage for members being able to more readily hear explanations (interpretations). They tend to shift a hazardous, distrustful atmosphere to one of more security and "connection". Interventions do not have to be 100% accurate, an unrealistic expectation under any circumstances, because members, who feel their therapist is making genuine efforts to understand them, tend to respond more thoughtfully. Nevertheless, some members are inevitably injured. If clinicians provide an atmosphere in which their interventions can be corrected, modified, clarified, or supplemented, the experience of injury can be elaborated and utilized to enhance the injured person's sense of self. Repetition of similar sequences provides injured members opportunities for greater self-consolidation and firmer self-structure (transmuting internalization). Moreover, members who are able to provide understanding and explaining to others gain from having the experience of being helpful (altruism), which in turn may re-enforce group ideals and strengthen the group-self.

Illustration

An intervention directed to an individual can be gently expanded to include all members, thereby addressing the group-as-a-whole, including the therapist, i.e., "possibly we are all experiencing this feeling."

> *Allen, upon entering an ongoing group, promptly announced that he had recently terminated from another group because he felt the therapist was incompetent. He said that he was uncertain about how this group would function or if it would fit his needs. There followed a rather direct confrontation by Brian who said that he didn't like the idea of someone entering without being prepared to give the group a fair trial. An angry exchange followed between the two men, and thereafter Brian, who had previously been an emotional and task leader, withdrew. Allen, subsequently, dominated the session. Cloe, a reserved member who was beginning to more actively assert herself, turned to Brian, saying that she missed his participation and the group felt different when he was quiet. I commented that it seemed important for Cloe and perhaps the group that Brian not withdraw and perhaps the group didn't seem complete if all members weren't participating.*

My intervention was intended to address Cloe and the entire group. The theoretical basis for my understanding was that the group had been disrupted both as a selfobject and as group-self by Allen's uncommitted participation and his dominating behaviour, and by

Brian's withdrawal. Cloe apparently had a selfobject transference to Brian, which could be conceptualized as either to his person or as a representative of the group-as-a-whole. The bickering, contentious atmosphere represented a disruption of the group-self. Specifically, the group no longer stood for members trying to understand one another, and without that one could not count on getting help.

My intervention was framed tentatively, "perhaps," thereby facilitating the members' potential to disagree. The form of my intervention reflected my efforts to create a collaborative atmosphere in which together we would arrive at understanding of what transpired within each member and in the group.

Subsequently, Allen revealed that he had long standing struggles with self confidence and self-assertion. Retrospectively, he understood that he had entered the group with a chip on his shoulder. His insight served as self-integration and strengthened group values as worthy of being internalized.

Illustration

Disruption of the group-self may evoke countertransference responses. A therapist's enactment may be contained in a comment, which is empathic to the group, but is judgmental of the individual. Such interventions are often justified in the clinician's mind as being helpful to the whole group, and the potential for being harmful to the individual becomes obscured. Even when the meaning enters the therapist's awareness, shame may interfere with optimal management of the process

> *Martin, a successful businessman, participated in the group by talking about experiences and emotions in his past. His associations were often relevant to the topic at hand, but he was unable to address his in-group feelings. These "behaviours" for a time, did not interfere with a progressive deepening of the group discourse. I felt that members were internalizing group values as expressed by increased self-disclosure and risk taking. This was specifically represented by Nancy and Orin who began exploring deeply experienced loving feelings towards one another*
>
> *The other members gradually gained appreciation of Martin's difficulty addressing his here-and-now emotional state. Their efforts to*

gently help him explore his in-group affects seemed ineffective, and increasingly they became frustrated and annoyed. I too was caught up in this process when, unsurprisingly, Martin began a discursion into his childhood experiences. Sensing increased tension in the room and in myself, I directly asked Martin, if he could, to speak about himself in the present. My immediate sense was that my intervention was abrupt, although I thought that I might have appeared to have spoken calmly. Martin seemed startled, and discontinued his description of the past. He said that he had some feelings in his stomach, but could not go further. The remainder of the session was quite stilted although the content was additional discussion of the attraction between Nancy and Orin

My self-regulatory enactment carried extensive meaning for the group and for myself. I was not only responding from my personal history, but out of frustration in being ineffective in changing Martin. My focus had shifted from an empathic position to a confrontational, group-protective stance. For the members I was now a failed selfobject. Although my comment clearly injured Martin, it took me a while to process what I had done. In part, my difficulty in sorting out the process was compounded by the members' apparently salient discussion of Nancy and Orin's attraction to one another. When I realized how "dead" the conversation seemed, I was able to reconstruct a reasonable understanding of the process. Moreover, I was acutely aware of feeling quite ashamed of my response, which further contributed to my difficulty in addressing my original contribution to a disrupted therapeutic process. As Wolf (1993) has noted, "The *verbal* content is only a part, and often a relatively insignificant part of the total effect of an interpretation" (p. 675).

Ornstein (2003) has illuminated some of the murky notions regarding therapeutic process. He states: "When patient and analyst meet for the purpose of a therapeutic analysis, *irrespective of whatever they talk about on the manifest level,* [emphasis in the original] simultaneously, largely outside their awareness, a second dialogue begins, dependent on the nature of what each is experiencing in relation to the other, how each reacts to this encounter and what each expects of the other" (p. 21–22). Ornstein considers what happens within each session or over periods of time what transpires is considered the *microprocess.* The larger task is maintaining an overview of what needs to be accomplished and the direction in which the treatment is headed, is labelled the *macroprocess*.

In this illustration, I had acted within the *microprocess* to protect the group functioning at the expense of the individual. This is likely inevitable with any intervention where a response intended to "protect the group" injured an individual and consequently threatened the entire group. My intervention likely made me (and the group) less an idealized selfobject. Therapists must be ever alert to the impact on the individual, a subgroup or the entire group both immediately, and to the broader treatment goals, the macro-process (Stone, 2001).

Illustrations

The following illustrations were taken from the literature. The first example, from a well established group, illustrates my evolving understanding of addressing a group-as-a-whole theme of patient empowerment, and my empathic understanding of the members need for distance and for self-control, a particularly salient dynamic in working with chronically ill patients (Stone 1998). The example illustrates my empathic efforts to maintain an internal focus on the whole group, while modifying the manner in which I address the members.

The treatment model, designed for persons with persistent and severe mental illness, is that of the flexibly bound group in which the patients determine and publicly announce their plan to attend sessions, ranging from weekly to monthly. This results in a group formation in which there is a core subgroup of regular attendees and a peripheral subgroup of intermittent participants (Stone, 1996b).

> *Six of the eight members were present (a slightly greater than usual attendance for this group). The previous week only Rita and Greg had been present, and the meeting had focused on Greg's anxiety evoked by the possibility of his mother being re-hospitalized with heart failure. The session's theme had been separation and loss.*
>
> *Rita opened the meeting by noting that it was the first time in several weeks [almost] everybody was present. She added that only she and Greg had been present the preceding week. This led to an extended discussion between Rita and Greg in which he said that his mother had*

not required hospitalization. [The process seemed to be a replay of the prior week.] I intervened: "We were talking about one side of it: what it's like for Rita and Greg to be here. What about the others? What's it like to miss." Jack explicitly said that at times he wants to get away from the group, a feeling supported by Rita. Rick says he just misses, and has no real reason. I wondered what it was about the group that people wished to get away from.

This evolved into more discussion of needing at times to distance oneself from the group. Members differentiated between not coming to a meeting because of a cancelled session related to a holiday (e.g., Christmas, July 4th) or my absence and "ordinary" meetings when they could decide to miss. Lorna spoke about needing distance from the intense feelings. Rita reflected that she had dealt with the group pressures by talking over others, and Rick noted that she (Rita) no longer did that.

For the purposes of this discussion, my focus is on the evolution of my style of addressing group-as-a-whole issues. Seldom do I use expressions, "The group is ...." or "The group is reacting ..." I have come to use expressions such as "Maybe you all are responding to ...." In many situations, I will add, "And if I do not understand, please help me understand more clearly." This addition is very much in keeping with a shift in style of intervention, particularly with an effort to increase collaboration between therapist and patient (Stone, 2003; Ornstein, 2003). In the example, I illustrate another strategy, namely, to address one subgroup (Rita and Jack) and then the other (those absent). In concert with my understanding of the patients' concerns regarding empowerment, I chose to respond to the discussion of absences not as evidence of a group wide resistance, but as members' experience. The response was uncovering members' need to distance from the intensity of the meetings and Rita, exhibiting self-observation, noted she accomplished the same thing by talking. The focus was more on what they were trying to accomplish, rather than what they were resisting.

By focusing initially on subgroups, no patient was singled out, thereby diminishing the potential for scapegoating (Agazarian, 1997). By merely inviting exploration of members' experience, rather than attributing a particular meaning, the patient's were able to express their sense of inner tension and how they self-regulated.

A second example from the literature highlights the disruption of the members' group-self.

Harwood (1998) describes a patient, Ron, a member of an established group, who concomitantly entered a second group that he deemed helpful through hugging. In his primary group Ron began to request touching and holding, and he was "perceived to be, protesting ..., the lack of touching and holding he missed early in his life" (p. 38). Ron challenged a group norm and an ideal of the group that focused on exploring rather than acting on feelings. Harwood understood Ron's need for touching as a request, to notice him, approve of him ... and a confirmation of his goodness and desirability (p. 39). The others defended the "idealized virtues" of their own group. The resulting standoff was resolved following an empathic understanding of Ron's need for touching and mirroring, (his selfobject needs) and for the others, her intervention was thought to carry a meaning of her presence. She posited that the group had felt abandoned by her silence while she was sorting out a useful intervention.

I would suggest that in addition to Harwood's formulation, the members' group-self was disrupted by Ron's provocations. More than her "unavailability," the ideal of the treatment being limited to verbal interaction was threatened, which in turn disrupted the established group-self.

Discussion

Treating patients in a group demands that the therapist take into account the influence of dynamic elements including the intrapsychic, interpersonal, group and culture present in the therapeutic environment (Hopper, 2003). Awareness of these factors does not require that such understanding be conveyed to the members. In some circumstances we can be helpful to our patients without drawing their attention to the treatment context, and, in others, we further our therapeutic aims by helping members appreciate the connection between what they are experiencing and group-as-a-whole processes that have reverberations to current and past life experiences.

Self-psychology has drawn attention to two aspects of the interpretative process—understanding and explaining. Understanding is focused on conveying to members the clinician's appreciation of patients' inner experiences. As described above, this has the potential for "holding" and reversing members' sense of disruption either of their self or their group-self. Traditional group-as-a-whole interventions often neglected or assumed that patients would feel understood, if they were provided an "accurate interpretation" of group processes. In many instances such interpretations were provided from the perspective of an external observer rather than from an empathic position. Under these conditions, vulnerable patients were unlikely to be able to utilize the intervention, having felt that they personally had not been recognized and, moreover, had been narcissistically injured.

A critique of self psychology has been that too great emphasis has been placed on "understanding" as mutative, thereby diminishing the significance of explaining [interpreting] (Siegel, 1999). I believe this to be a distortion, and that explaining is an essential component of the therapeutic process. The task has been how to assist members in gaining understanding of the influence of the context—the group or the culture—on their feelings, thoughts and behaviours. In the treatment process, patients develop multiple levels of transference to the whole group and gradually internalize the values and aspirations of their membership. In most situations this process takes place beyond the immediate awareness of the members or therapist. It may emerge only when there has been or there is a potential for a disruption in the group, either as a failure of the members experience of selfobject functions or breakdown in working towards achieving goals.

Group-as-a-whole interventions draw attention to these disruptions in ways that may be affirming or further disorganizing for the individual. Horwitz (1977) addressing problems associated with group-as-a-whole interpretations stated, "The major point regarding technique ... is *the focus upon individuals, by the group and by the therapist, before a holistic interpretation is made.*" [Emphasis in original] (p. 436). Horwitz further notes that a major "holistic approach ... tends to be too restrictive and gives the impression to the patient that his individuality is secondary to the group process" (p. 438). I am in agreement with this observation, and in the language of self psychology highlight the potential for narcissistic injury resulting from poorly timed or formulated whole group interventions. By emphasizing the place for understanding prior to explaining, I believe that the therapist sets the table for patients to utilize whole group interventions. This strategy mitigates, but does not eliminate, patients' needs to express their individuality. Members' in-depth feelings of self and group-self are enhanced if they also feel that they have been understood as individuals.

CHAPTER FOUR

Dreams as portraits of self and group interaction

Walter N. Stone and Sigmund Karterud

Abstract: Dreams presented in group psychotherapy portray different aspects of the dialectic between the group and the individual. A self psychology perspective emphasizes the interplay between the current self-state of the group-as-a-whole and the selfobject needs of the individual. With this focus in mind, the therapist should help the group to deepen its awareness and capacity to reflect upon emerging new abilities ("forward edge") which dream imagery conveys, and the needed human responsiveness that can actualize these abilities, and thus help the individual and the group to break and transform chains of repetition compulsion. We illustrate this approach with two clinical examples.

Dreams as portraits of self and group interactions

From the time of Freud's classic monograph (1953/1900), dreams have been regarded as avenues into the unconscious world of wishes, conflicts, and defences. The interpretative task, with the aid of the patient's associations, was traditionally to decode unconscious elements that the dream disguised. In contrast, self psychology has

55

focused its attention upon the dream's representation of the self and self in relation to others, others in the past and the here-and-now. As Ornstein (1987) wrote, "The dream is always about the self; that is, the dream always presents various aspects of self-experience to the dreamer's attention" (p. 101).

Atwood and Stolorow (1984) highlight the value of conceptualizing dreams as concrete symbols that "serve to actualize a *particular* [sic] organization of experience in which specific configurations of self and object … are dramatized and affirmed" (p. 103). These authors suggest that "by vividly reifying the experience of self-endangerment, the dream symbols bring the state of the self into focal awareness, with a feeling of conviction and reality that can only accompany sensory perceptions" (pp. 104–105). Further emphasizing the integrative and synthetic function of dream imagery for the self, Fosshage posits that "the superordinate function of dreams is the development, maintenance (regulation), and when necessary, restoration of psychic process … and [psychological] organization" (1997, p. 433). He emphasizes that affect regulation in sustaining or restoring a disrupted self is a primary function of dreams.

In individual psychoanalytic psychotherapy dreams are progressively colored by the transference involvement as the therapeutic process deepens. In group psychotherapy dreams become responses to the highly complex social situation of the group, of which the dreamer is a part. The clinical literature has added the concept of group dreams which it defines as dreams containing concrete or "slightly" disguised references in the manifest content to the group (Karterud, 1992). We suggest that most dreams reported in psychotherapy groups portray different aspects of the dialectic interplay between the group and the individual self.

Group dreams from self psychological perspectives

Dreams, viewed from the lens of self psychology, may express exhibitionistic/grandiose strivings or searching for selfobject affirmation (Stone & Whitman, 1977) or wishes for merger with an idealized selfobject (Stone, 1992). Dreams reported in the group may reflect a wish for a response from particular members or as a representation of the dreamer's inner experience of the group-as-a-whole (Harwood, 1998). Group dreams may also reflect resistances to engaging in the group; such resistances may represent earlier family or group experiences that were traumatic or failed to provide necessary optimal responsiveness (Bacal, 1985). Group dreams can also portray the dissolution or disintegration of the group, manifested by objects breaking apart, and these may be stimulated by actual or anticipated loss (a member terminating or an interruption of regular sessions) or by reawakening of earlier losses such as death or divorce.

Threats to the self may arise from numerous sources in the group. Violations of group norms or boundaries, such as an extra-group liaison or chronic tardiness, may be experienced consciously or only subliminally and be reflected symbolically in the dream as broken fences or crumbling walls. Affect over-stimulation, as in intense erotic attractions, primitive envy, or being idealized, can fuel dream imagery of floods or tornadoes. At a less dramatic level, narcissistic injury arising from seemingly innocuous interactions, such as receiving advice, asking a question that has just been answered or repeating a comment made by another, can be experienced as injurious (traumatic) to the self and impact upon the member's inner image of the group. Discourse of this nature, characteristic of early stages of group development, is often accompanied by the recipient's experience of unverbalized shame, which may shatter his/her trust in the group. A dream may be the patient's communication of the disruptive experience.

We have previously suggested that there are three relevant perspectives to group-as-a-whole phenomena that may be reflected in dreams: 1) the group as object such as "bad mother" symbolized, for example, as a dangerous or unavailable individual or as an empty building; 2) the group as selfobject that provides supportive functions for the self reflected, for example, by a family eating a sumptuous meal, and 3) the group-self. These perspectives are not mutually exclusive. To the contrary, they enrich each other, as we will try to demonstrate in our clinical examples.

The group-self perspective, initially described by Kohut (1976), refers to the collective, supraindividual project to which all members, at least partially, have agreed to collaborate. That is, individuals internalize, as part of self, the values, aims, hopes, ideals and goals of their groups. The project of psychotherapy groups is to enhance self understanding and self development through intimate involvement with a limited numbers of peers and a therapist. The group-self carries the ideals of free and open communication, trust in the dialogue, mutual respect and concern, a sense of fairness and being member of a supportive community (Karterud & Stone, 2003). We believe these ideals are grounded in an evolutionary concern for the self as an interwoven part of groups. These ideals, however, are continuously being undermined by withdrawal, suspiciousness, hostility, greed, envy, rivalry, hate and craving for revenge. Trying to resolve these conflicts on an individual as well as a group-self level constitutes a central theme in the therapeutic process.

Thus, as described above, injuries to the self could also be understood as damage to the group-self. The termination of a valued group member, for example, likely would carry meaning at multiple levels, including loss at the level of the group and therefore a depletion of the group-self resulting from a sense of loss of the departing person's contributions to the group's work. Exploration of self-depletion or fragmentation dreams would be incomplete without considering the possibilities of their also representing a shift in the state of the group-self.

Therapeutic considerations

From the perspective of a self psychologically informed clinician, the purpose of addressing dreams is to help members gain understanding in the fluctuations in their self states, their need of human responsiveness and emergent possibilities of new ways of being. This would include self-protective, self-restorative and self-enhancing processes. Livingston (2001) suggests that dreams presented in groups can never be fully analyzed in the classical sense. "The value of working with dreams in group is not the opportunity for completeness and an orderly working through. The value that we can see clearly is in the aliveness and deepening of group process" (p. 24). In addition to representations of the individual's self or group-self stage, dreams may metaphorically depict aspects of the treatment process. Sequences may portray aspects of member's self or perceptions of the group interactions as successive scenes.

The self psychological model of pathology is that of developmental arrest, not of inner conflict (Kohut, 1984). Patients not only repeat their developmental difficulties in order to master old conflicts, but they also attempt developmental thrusts. Tolpin (2002) has labelled these "presentations" as "trailing" and "forward" edge. She depicts the tentative nature of the forward edge with the expression, "tendril," indicating the tender, cautious nature of the developmental strivings. Both these forward elements and trailing elements, reflecting the repetition of old behavioural or emotional patterns, may be embedded in any communication, and, in particular, a dream.

Illustrating this approach, Livingston (2001) reports a dream in which a dreamer was frightened by a large roach that "was gross," which he was unable to kill. He said that even though the bug's head "started to look like a kitten's head ... I wanted to wake up to get out of there because the bug wouldn't die" (p. 21). After exploring some of the frightening, ugly and disgusting parts of the dream, another member noted the appearance of the kitten's head. This intervention shifted the discussion away from the repetitive bad, ugly aspects of the dreamer's self to the gentler, sweeter aspects of self represented— the forward edge. Following reflection on the emergence of the kitten's head, the group focused on the transformation taking place in the dreamer and identified other personal transformations. This material was followed by a woman presenting a sexual dream, experienced as shameful, in which she was able to talk about previously unexplored and frightening sectors of herself.

Identification of positive (forward edge) change could be interpreted as a flight from further examination of destructive and ugly self-percepts. However, in this example, the consequence was that another member could report a dream which brought to the fore previously unexplored and frightening sectors of her self. The sequence suggests that a forward edge focus can serve a mirroring selfobject function, strengthening the therapeutic alliance and thus facilitating the patient's or group members' exploration of deeper, trailing edge self issues. From the group-self perspective the forward edge focus strengthens the group ideal of appreciating the potential of each member.

An advantage of reporting dreams in groups is the presence and availability of peers. Members, with the interpretative assistance of the therapist, soon learn that a dream is not only a personal statement about the dreamer, but contains aspects of the group culture and discourse. In situations where the dreamer is unable to meaningfully associate to his/her own dream, members can bring their own associations to the fore. These may be either to affects, main elements, fragments, or aspects of the dream sequence portraying dynamic processes within the group. As illustrated by the above example, members may learn how to comment about the dream elements and the process as portrayed by the dream. This is a crucial ability for a well functioning analytic group-self.

Our work with dreams is not prescriptive. We believe that whatever is said is heard by everyone, and this is particularly true for the therapist's utterances. Thus an intervention or exploration of a dream focusing on the dreamer is heard and experienced by all present. Others' responses may include a sense of the therapist as an enhancing selfobject or as a destructive, disruptive force. Interpretations of the dream as reflecting group-as-a-whole processes almost certainly will not be completely accurate and could narcissistically injure one or more members. By monitoring the process after each intervention, therapists can learn a good deal about injured individuals' self stabilizing responses. Fosshage (2002) notes that selfobject responsiveness through the life cycle serves to modify prior self organization and promotes growth. He asserts that without such experiences, one would be stuck with the relational patterns formed in early childhood. Peer and therapist exploration of dreams serve as a template of selfobject responsiveness and adds to the evolving group culture, which values attachments, self reflection and the understanding of others as having their own minds and perspectives.

Stern et al. (1998) have emphasized the importance of both conscious and unconscious "relational learning" that contributes to change. Of particular significance is the "moment of meeting" which reflects authentic, deeply felt personal contact. Member-to-member or therapist-to-member experiences in working to understand a dream, not only for the dreamer but for all present, may provide such moments. These intensely experienced moments are likely to increase members' capacity to manage affects and to see and appreciate others as subjects in contrast to objects primarily used to fulfil one's needs.

Fonagy et al. (2002) highlight an additional developmental task that could be facilitated by empathic exploration of dreams. This work can help shift psychic equivalence thinking—thinking characterized by the equation of the internal with the external—to self reflective functioning—thinking that demonstrates understanding of others' internal wishes and emotions. Empathic responsiveness to the dream, either from therapist or member, may provide the moment of meeting, thereby deepening the dialogue.

In the following two illustrations we will demonstrate how the dream can be an effective communication and the work within the group can mediate between the individual and the group-as-a-whole, thereby contributing to individual development (self reflective and representational functioning) and an unblocking of an arrested group-self.

Clinical examples

"The sexual assault"

Jim's behaviour towards Irene was perceived by several of the other female group members as thinly veiled sexual invitations and in several sessions they expressed their annoyance with him. The men, and in particular Frank whose characteristic defence was distancing, resisted becoming involved. It was in this context that Frank reported a dream: *"There is a man who copulates with a woman. Thereafter it is my turn. However I discover that her genitals are poorly developed. I can't get it in. It all happened on a veranda. Then somebody knocks the door. I believe there are several men coming to rape her and I flee down the gutter. Halfway down I change my mind and climb up again. On the veranda I find several men and women sitting there and talking to each other."*

Frank's associations quickly turned to an incident when he was ten years old. His 15 year-old brother and several friends had tried to seduce, if not rape, his twelve year-old sister. She had barely escaped. He was a passive, excitedly stimulated, and an upset witness who subsequently became highly self-critical for not intervening. As he told the story Frank became increasingly angry, primarily at his brother, but also at himself for his cowardice. Jim's seductive behaviour, highlighted by the women, had reminded Frank of his brother's attempted seduction. He could not involve himself then, just as he was unable to intervene now. The group readily grasped the connection between Frank's childhood story and his anger and shame in the here-and-now.

The therapist noted that not much had been said about the last part of the dream. He suggested, "There is a crucial difference between *then* and *now*. In childhood Frank had no one to speak to about this shameful experience. But in the dream he finds 'several men and women sitting together and talking on the veranda. I wonder if this might signify the opportunity to talk with people in the group." Although Frank feared fighting with the symbolic brother and being condemned for his sexual desire in the dream he was able to change his mind and return to the "veranda." The benign presence of talking adults, absent in his childhood, now enabled him to approach anew this part of his past and acquire a new perspective on himself and his group experiences.

We think of this dream as being stimulated by a conflict in the group-self, a conflict concerning what rules of discourse should reign. These rules include a "pretend mode, "in which, as a developmental step, the parent or older child also show a child that reality may be distorted by acting upon it in playful ways" (Fonagy et al. 2002, p. 57). The pretend mode is not real in the same sense as ordinary social reality. Pretend mode discourse is necessary in analytic groups in order to establish the sense of safety necessary for members to experience and express shameful ways of thinking, feeling and behaving. The presence of the pretend mode is "marked," that is signalled in some non-verbal manner.

Jim had claimed that he had done nothing more than follow the group norm by speaking about what was in his mind. He asked, "Were sexual feelings taboo in this group?" The women responded that it was *the way he talked about sexual feelings,* that it was not reflexive, but rather abusive and exploitative. They experienced him as *enacting* his lust, and further accused him of not marking his speech and transgressing the established pretend mode of the group discourse (Austin, 1962), of displaying his raw and undigested sexual lust for the sake of gratification, not reflection.

Taking sides in this conflict is not our task as therapists. There might well have been elements of "gratification" in Jim's approach towards Irene, but these elements were surely augmented by the women. When the conflict escalated, it soon reached a level of projective identification where heated mutual accusations dominated the scene at the expense of reflective functioning. Under these circumstances, the group-self was temporarily suffused by psychic equivalence thinking. The result was loss of the ordinary, more playful discourse.

Fonagy et al. (2002) assert that playing in situations governed by mature adults facilitates the transformation of psychic equivalent thinking to representational thinking. The traumatic childhood incident which Frank recalled was an episode where the boundaries of the pretend mode of play were lost. What started as a (sexual) play, had escalated and turned into a near nightmare of non-play realities. For Frank the episode had model scene qualities in which specific transactions trigger core affect laden responses within the individual or group (Correale & Celli, 1998; Lichtenberg et al. 1992). He had established characterological defences which placed him in uninvolved positions vis-à-vis his surrounds. He became a lonely onlooker; to become more involved might threaten his capacity to contain or cope with his emotional responses. He lacked the experience of playing with dangerous ideas and feelings in the presence of a benign grownup who could monitor the boundaries. The group-self dynamics came to resemble the nightmare in his unconscious. Seemingly innocent and playful impulses could turn to threatening realities.

The therapist's interpretation at the end of this sequence served didactic purposes. By equating those sitting on the veranda with the group members, he brought into greater awareness for both Frank and the others the group selfobject function, that is the experience of being in the group as a safe, responsive venue, a prerequisite for exploring frightful fantasies. For Frank the group was a contrast to what he had missed in his childhood. By highlighting the veranda group, with its differentiated members talking to each other and exchanging ideas, the therapist focused on the dreamer's hope for a new experience, in essence the forward edge (Tolpin, 2002). The ensemble imago contained a feeling of positive surprise and a wish for belonging.

While there is an ongoing debate in the literature regarding the role of insight versus (new) relational experience (Fosshage, 2002), this clinical example seems to illuminate how a new relational experience (the selfobject function of the group) can facilitates self understanding (insight). The new self understanding, in turn, had profound effects on the further treatment course, providing new perspectives for working through of self structure's pathogenic complexes.

"The playing group"

Mary told the following dream: *"I am in a conference hall where somebody is giving a talk on a serious matter. Beside me sits Allen* (another member). *We link together and swing from side to side. We have fun, smile and laugh."* The dream quickly became linked to an important theme in Mary's life. She was a dutiful woman, deeply engaged in professional and societal issues, at the expense of other aspects of her life. An important theme for Mary had been how she could lead a more joyful life. In the dream, Allen came to represent a bridge to this goal—he would serve as a model for having fun, thereby expanding Mary's restricted sense of self, a twinship selfobject transference. The group explored these themes of self-sacrifice and wish to play for an extended period. The therapist found no reason to intervene, although he noted that the group had not commented upon the theme of rebellion, as in the turning from the serious discourse of the conference to play and fun. During the following discussion Allen was unusually active and assertive. He was obviously vitalized by his role in Mary's dream.

After a while the therapist acknowledged Allen's level of activity, which he linked to a dream Allen had told in the previous meeting. In that dream, which had been given an Oedipal interpretation, Allen owned a more impressive mobile phone than the therapist. The therapist suggested that Allen, who had been rather inhibited in the group, now seemed to be in touch with a more assertive part of himself. For Allen, activity had been associated with a dangerous rivalry with the therapist. It seemed as if that were no longer the case. Noting that in the previous dream Allen used his mobile phone to call a woman, the therapist, continuing his long interpretation, observed that it was as if Mary had understood the unconscious (but interpreted) message in Allen's dream. Her own Oedipal conflict involved a need to satisfy her father's claim for serious work on important societal issues and renounce sexual explorative play with peers. Allen, who now dared to challenge the therapist in a sexual arena, seemed to confirm for Mary some of her own suppressed sexual and joyful desires. Through this affirmation, she too could dare to rebel against the deadly serious father/therapist. In order to justify the last element in the interpretation, the therapist reminded Mary of her experience several months previously when she had attended the therapist's lecture at a professional meeting. Following this extended interpretation, the group immersed itself in further associations to the themes in these dreams.

These dreams occurred in a well functioning, long-term analytic group. They emerged from the matrix of an advanced group-self unhampered by any conflicts suffused by projective identifications. The group-self was characterized by a well established pretend mode which provided the members freedom to play with "dangerous things."

In our opinion a sophisticated group-self has integrated at least some notion of the social unconscious that members influence each other and influence the group-self through unconscious mechanisms. While the reality of the unconscious cannot be proved, but its effects can be demonstrated through the interplay between the observable here-and-now and the dream narratives. In this instance the therapist spelled out how Mary's and Allen's Oedipal conflicts intermingled, involved the therapist, were portrayed in the dreams and played out in the theatre of the group. The therapist's intervention represented an affirmation (mirroring) of forward edge work of both patients. Both were exploring the possibility of new, more assertive behaviours.

Discussion

In *The Impossible Profession*, Janet Malcolm (1981) describes the clinician's task as maintaining multiple perspectives and not prematurely foreclosing potentially productive avenues for understanding therapeutic communication. Harwood (2002) lists seven differing perspectives in which she might examine dreams. Group therapists may be severely challenged in this respect because any dream may communicate at multiple levels. Dreams, presented in group psychotherapy, are events in which the dreamer is trying to communicate to the dreamer and others in the group about the self, other, self-with-other, group processes and/or the larger environment, including the more general culture. It may refer to the past, present or future. The manifest dream imagery is no longer seen as only a representation of a disguised wish. Rather it may be viewed as a metaphor, or representation of the dreamer's current concerns. It is not the dream itself that is therapeutic, but the subsequent responses which may amplify and solidify the members' self or the group self. In our illustrations we have attempted to exemplify these notions.

In our first vignette, Frank, stimulated by the sexuality embedded in the group transactions, brought forth a dream which addressed his conflict in the present over his passivity and shame. The undisguised nature of his sexual failure and his flight only to return to a place where gentle conversation was occurring all signal perceptions of the group that potentially can serve his developmental progressive thrust. The second vignette communicates Mary's sense of having increased ability to play even in the context of "serious matters." In these examples from long-term treatment, a group setting is overtly represented in one dream a specific group member is incorporated in to the second dream, both seeming to suggest that the group was experienced as a sufficiently safe setting in which growth and change could take place.

Certainly the value of any group dream is its communication both to the dreamer and others. How and in what manner the therapist and the other members respond in order to take advantage of the opportunity is multi-determined. The thrust of this paper has been to illustrate the patients' presentation of dreams in an effort to communicate about difficulties within the group setting that have interfered with their effective use of the group. And they served as a stimulus for change in a growth enhancing direction.

CHAPTER FIVE

A self psychological perspective of group development

Walter N. Stone and Gil Spielberg

Abstract: This paper examines group development from the perspective of self psychology. Members' search for particular selfobject responsiveness varies according to the particular phase of group development. In the first phase, patients' wish for safety and understanding is managed by merging with the therapist as an idealized selfobject. In the second phase, members look for mirroring selfobject functions to their assertive/ aggressive self expression. In the third phase, members continue to have periods when idealizing and mirroring selfobject responsiveness assist them in maintaining inner balance. During this phase members continue to gain skills from alter-ego selfobject experiences.

In the final phase of a group, termination involves members' ability to manage the narcissistic pain of loss and separation. Members utilize their inner consolidation and the continuing selfobject experiences to stabilize themselves as they experience loss associated with leaving the group and the real relationships they have developed. Across phases, members gradually internalize the values and norms of the group, which become part of the groupself. The leader's therapeutic and countertransference responses are also examined for each phase.

A Self Psychological perspective of group development

Every individual faces substantial tasks in satisfactorily entering and maintaining membership in any group, including family, work, friendship or the special case of a psychotherapy group. Entry into a therapeutic group activates the person's internal interactional model learned within the family and subsequently modified in play, school, work, and social settings. In each situation, individuals consciously and unconsciously determine how much of themselves they will allow to participate in the group and how much they will hold back to preserve their own sense of individuality and autonomy. The balance struck between the two ends of this dichotomy is multi-determined and includes the goals of the setting, prior experience, and interactions in the present.

Members enter a therapy group with the objectives of learning about their inner worlds, finding more comfortable and successful ways of being with themselves, and of altering dysfunctional patterns of relating. Doing this brings to the fore anxieties, vulnerabilities and defenses (solutions) that may require examination in order to achieve treatment goals. As verbal and behavioural interactions among members and the leader proceed, the subjectivities of the members interact and some resolution is achieved (to the benefit or detriment of the individuals) that become embedded as "rules," which are labelled, in group dynamic terms, values and norms. Subsequently, as a result of further transactions, norms are subject to scrutiny and to modification. These elements of group development can be observed and studied in psychotherapeutic groups.

Theory

Group developmental schemata are abstractions and only approximate the differing membership and leadership styles present in each unique group. Yet, one or more themes can often be discerned underlying any group discussion. Theories of group development compartmentalize these themes in order to describe the complexity of the group emotional environment. Contemporary theoreticians recognize that development is not linear, but may be subject to lengthy periods of working in a particular stage, and that reversals and return to earlier stages are frequent, in order to deal with particular stresses of the more advanced stage, or once more address incompletely examined issues.

Models of development arose predominantly, but not exclusively, in the context of groups organized for educational purposes (Bennis and Shepard, 1956) Early models, based on the available ego psychological and object relations theory, identified four major developmental phases labelled forming, storming, performing, and ending (Tuckman, 1965). These labels describe and categorize changes in members' behaviours and emotions across time from the vantage point of an observing other. In keeping with a self-psychological emphasis on the centrality of the self, our intent in this article is to re-examine developmental phases from a perspective that focuses on inner experiences of the members and group leader. This perspective differs from models based on object relations or ego psychological theory, which derive themes from the position of an external observer.

Self psychology, evolved within a dyadic setting from the pioneering work of Heinz Kohut (1977, 1984). In this substantial paradigm shift, the self's development and pursuit of its goals and ideals became the centre of analytic interest. Kohut conceived of the self as developing within a matrix of soothing, calming and affirming responses. These experiences, labelled selfobject experiences, were to maintain the self's internal integrity and promote growth. At the earliest stages of development, the selfobject was felt to be under the infant's control, while the other was not recognized as a separate person. Kohut initially formulated three types of selfobject experience: idealizing, mirroring and twinship. When an environment is able to provide sufficient selfobject responsiveness, the self, to a greater degree, is gradually able to assume these functions independently. Yet it is accepted that throughout life selfobject needs are present.

Consolidation of the developing self is reflected in a shift in the nature of selfobject experiences. As noted above, beginning in infancy selfobjects are experienced as under control of the self, as if they were body parts. Gradually, with maturation of the self, the selfobject is experienced as a subject with thoughts and feelings of its own. This development implies a sufficiently maturing self so that need for immediate selfobject response is unnecessary for the self's every wish or need in order to forestall major internal disruption. In addition, the self has learned to use non-human self-objects to serve necessary stabilizing functions. Examples of such selfobject experiences might include playing with pets, enjoying a concert, or reading an enjoyable book.

Inevitably, the child experiences failures or mis-attunements in needed selfobject response, which produce anxiety and experiences of fragmentation of the self. Repeated selfobject failures evoke powerful feelings of despair, hopelessness, loneliness and reactive rage. These emotions lead to personality malformations as adaptations protecting the self and managing affects. Such individuals are, at the least, wary of efforts to become intimately engaged, in part for fear that their selfobject needs will not be met, and in part because they fear their inner experience of unmanageable affects. Newman (2007) states: "Often, it is the absolute dread of re-experiencing the painful feelings of aloneness, the recognition of the failure of the selfobject—and above all, the frightening rage that accompanies such awareness—that keeps in place pathological ways of relating to the self or to others" (p. 1539). As we will discuss below, this perspective has important implications for therapeutic intervention.

Although Kohut was not inclined to apply his theory to group treatment (Strozier, 2001), he formulated a concept of the self that included a deeply embedded groupself (Kohut, 1976). The groupself is considered to be a portion of the self, which represents a consolidation of family, environmental, and cultural goals, and ideals that are compatible with those of the individual. It refers to an attachment to the group, and not to an individual (i.e., mother). As part of the self, the groupself requires selfobject experiences, i.e., belonging to a family in which parents are seen as successful, or to a country that is honoured and esteemed. If these experiences are aversive, the groupself (and therefore the self) may become anxious. In a therapeutic setting, if the group becomes disrupted by such factors as a departure of an important member, a newcomer, or an unmanageable conflict, the groupself may experience anxiety and fragmentation. The groupself also includes the "rules" of discourse. For example, a new member previously treated in a non-dynamic therapeutic modality has to internalize norms such as talking about one's own feelings, not attacking others, or attending regularly on time. How people talk to one another in a group differs from how they might speak at a political meeting (Karterud and Stone, 2003).

The groupself is distinguished from the group-as-a-whole primarily based on the perspective of the observer (therapist). The group-as-a-whole is the experience of the outside observer who is positing that something central to group functioning is shared by the majority of the membership. The groupself is an organized internal experience derived from the experience of the group serving as a selfobject. It is an internal portion of the self having to do with stabilization and repair of the self. Thus the group-as-a-whole might be sharing a similar fantasy, defensive style and affective experience. The therapist intervenes with a comment that addresses the collective without regard to the internal felt experience of the participants. The groupself, which may represent group-wide emotions, is addressed from an empathic position.

In the therapeutic process, the self is exposed to experiences that illuminate (narcissistic) vulnerabilities. An injured self responds with processes, which can be understood from the patient's perspective by a clinician's consistent empathic stance. The interpretive process begins with the therapist articulating that understanding. Kohut (1977) emphasized the essential nature of a two-phase interpretative process: "first the analysand must realize that he has been understood; only then, as a second step, will the analyst demonstrate to the analysand the specific dynamic and genetic factors that explain the psychological content he had first empathically grasped" (p. 88). The individual, who has felt deeply understood by the therapist "comes to believe that his most profound emotional states and needs can be understood in depth. This in turn, encourages the patient to develop and expand his own capacity for self-reflection and at the same time to persist in articulating even more vulnerable and sequestered regions of his subjective life" (Stolorow, Brandchaft & Atwood, pp. 10–11).

The individual's broad self experience, with its variety of selfobject needs, will be examined in the context of our understanding of group development. As part of this development, the group norms and values are conceptualized as becoming internalized as part of the individual's groupself. Thus, as Brownbridge (2003) has noted, the self is in the group and group is in the self.

Developmental phases

For those engaging in any group enterprise, two overarching elements are present. From a participant's perspective, the elements can be framed as questions: Can I achieve my goals? Will attention be paid to my emotional needs? From these questions, an additional query emerges: What portions of my self must I forgo to belong to this group?

In psychotherapy the tasks of achieving emotional growth rest upon a foundation of patients' concerns for emotional safety. Self psychology addresses these concerns through a therapist's consistent efforts to understand the processes and dynamics from an empathic perspective. For the clinician, and by extension for the members, empathy includes "greater freedom to respond with deeply reverberating understanding and resonant emotionality, and the generally calmer and friendlier atmosphere of self psychological treatment ... ." (Kohut, 1984, p. 82). In the context of an empathic and responsive milieu, members are more willing to take risks, thereby exposing deeper aspects of the self for understanding and modification.

Lichtenberg (2005) formulates the therapist's stance as tuning into the subjectivities of the participants as fully as possible. This enables the clinician to maintain an empathic position and "a spirit of inquiry." "A sprit of inquiry is the therapist's gyroscope, helping to re-right the therapeutic endeavour when the immediacy of exploration is lost in the heat of struggles over a patient's pressure for provisionary [i.e., answers to questions, gratification] responses" (p. xii).

Patients need to experience the therapist and others as both old and new objects (Greenberg, 1986). Opportunities to work through old experiences of trauma or failed responsiveness must be balanced with opportunities to experience the others as new objects, which will be available to provide different growth-promoting experiences. Members who have developed a deep-seated sense of hopelessness and helplessness require opportunities to learn that their previously unexpressed rage will not be destructive either to themselves or to others. The therapist, with the aid of the group, must be capable of containing strong emotions and find ways of enabling their expression. The new experience is that of the clinician who can identify tendrils of forward movement and growth (Tolpin, 2002). The old experience is the transferential and/or the co-constructed interactions that evoked earlier selfobject failures. Greenberg (1986) has succinctly stated, "If the analyst cannot be experienced as a new object, analysis never gets under way; if he cannot be experienced as an old one, it never ends (p. 98). In groups therapist and members alike can provide these experiences.

Group developmental stages will now be discussed from the self psychological perspective of members' and leader's tasks. We artificially separate leader and members for heuristic purposes, recognizing that they are intimately involved and influence one another. This discussion is designed to supplement and enlarge previous conceptualizations of developmental processes.

First stage: Forming

The members: Individuals entering a psychotherapy group face the daunting and anxiety-laden tasks of revealing themselves and connecting to strangers. In the face of these tasks, they hope to be seen in the best possible light and to be appreciated, if not openly admired, for their positive attributes, indeed for the grandiose aspects of their self (Meyers, 1996). Such hopes may include being recognized as the most open, self-revealing person, even if the revelations seem to expose negative aspects of the self.

A fundamental anxiety of all members is that others will see only faults without recognizing positive attributes. This anxiety is fuelled by the common fantasy that the others are untrained and insensitive and will not mirror their strengths and abilities. Newcomers fear being traumatized and experiencing disruption or fragmentation of their sense of self. No amount of preparation will totally quell newcomers' anxieties, although the relationship with the therapist may provide some sense of safety (Harwood, 1983; Rutan and Stone, 2001).

In the initial phase of a group, members attempt to manage their (potentially disruptive) anxiety through merging with the therapist. Their hope is that if the clinician can be experienced as all-powerful and all-knowing (idealized), they will feel safe. These processes represent a regression to archaic selfobject needs, and generally take place outside of conscious awareness. The leader is not seen as an individual but only as a function to manage the member's anxiety.

If the leader does not seem available to idealize, members may search for other idealizable selfobjects, which can stabilize a threatened self. In early phases of austerely led training groups and in some therapeutic groups, participants may associate to religious experiences, which Slater (1966) labelled "deification as an antidote to deprivation." These references can be understood as the group's search for an idealizable selfobject in the face of feelings of powerlessness and helplessness when the group leader is too remote or unavailable to serve as an idealizable selfobject. This process could be understood as firming a disrupted portion of the self, the groupself.

Idealization and/or surrender are not the only avenues for members to manage the inner disruption provoked by joining a group. Some individuals search for commonalities with others, hoping that having similar attributes or characteristics will enable them to feel more connected and less alone. These processes may be understood as search for twinship selfobject experiences. Seemingly banal inquiries such as, "Are you married?" "What kind of work do you do?" "Where do you live?" may be expressions of such a search for soothing selfobjects (Kiefer, 2001; Weinstein, 1987). These commonalities, can serve as an antidote to feelings of aloneness and powerlessness, and expand as a pathway to feeling that the group-as-a-whole can provide useful selfobject experiences (Segalla, 1996).

In this initial phase, members begin to experience the group-as-a-whole as important to them. This represents the early manifestation of a portion of the groupself derived from the treatment experience. The group may then be experienced as a facilitating or disruptive presence—that is, in the mind of a member, it may or may not be available to fulfill selfobject needs. The groupself, based on one's perception of the group functioning, is responsive to shame, guilt, pride and pleasure.

The therapist: The primary task of the therapist is to help create a functional group where members may feel understood, respected, and safe. Therapists define the initial group structure, including boundaries between the group and the outside world, among the members, and with the leader. Without structure there can be no safety. Therapists also work to define the group norms, which define how the treatment will proceed. Therapists demonstrate (model) their capacity to reflect upon the discourse and convey (verbally and nonverbally) their efforts to understand. Understanding is based on empathy, as the clinician temporarily places him/herself in the shoes of the other. These behaviours demonstrate how leaders function in a consistent, reliable fashion that furthers members' sense of safety and is one component in being idealized.

There are limitations to what therapists can achieve. Empathizing with the entire group is a daunting task, and often not possible. Clinicians recognize the potential for every intervention to be heard through the filter of each member's personal psychology, and thus to have either a negative (de-idealizing) or positive impact. Therapists may diminish but not eliminate group disruption (narcissistic injury) by strengthening bonds among members and with the leader before making whole group interventions (Horwitz, 1977), but the potential remains for members to hear a whole group intervention as unempathic.

Self psychologically-informed clinicians maintain a dual focus on members' efforts to change and grow and on their tendency to repeat old familiar patterns. Leading edge transferences represent patients' efforts to restart growth by eliciting phase-appropriate empathic responses from the therapist or group members that will lead to new experiences. Trailing edge transferences are the patient's expectancies that the trauma will be repeated (Stone, 2003, Tolpin, 2002). If the therapist conveys understanding that patients are trying to make changes, members may experience being safer and more deeply understood, and they may be more willing and able to explore old traumas. Without a sense of safety, patients may feel interpretations of unconscious material as shaming or guilt evoking and disruptive.

A brief example might be a member's noting that one person invariably sits next to the therapist. Such comments are often experienced as critical of the individual or exposing a shameful "dependency." The therapist might illuminate this situation by wondering if sitting next to him/her helps the person feel safer, perhaps in order to take more risks. Such an intervention focused on positive change may be heard throughout the group as an alternative understanding, rather than the more stereotyped dependency formulation. The intervention, in essence, may reverberate through the group-as-a-whole. Other interpretations of the same behaviour, based on a careful reading of the individual's history, might be that the individual sitting next to the therapist is trying to address old feelings of not being a favourite child. This intervention might be accurate but is likely to stir competitive feelings in others, to be addressed as they emerge in the process.

Alternatively, the therapist may choose not to respond to the initial comment regarding where the member was sitting. The unfolding process may turn to issues of shame, embarrassment, responses of withdrawal and safety. A therapist might convey his/her understanding that the members may have tuned in to the experience of (narcissistic) injury and subsequent emotions of the member. Such an intervention conveys the therapist's attention to the process, helps the person feel understood, and adds to the experience of members that their emotional responses are carefully monitored. It does not preclude members' expressions of hurt or anger

Particular countertransferences in this opening phase tend to arise from the clinician's discomfort with being idealized. Most dynamically-trained clinicians become accustomed to helping patients struggle with frustrations imposed by the non-directive therapeutic frame. However, clinicians may be unfamiliar with the pressure they feel when they are the object of idealization. Debunking patients' expressions of the therapist as all-knowing or all-powerful can be traumatic for the group. A less common countertransferential response arises from misunderstanding members' efforts to find commonalities, seeing this effort as concerned with superficialities instead of as a way for members to orient and stabilize themselves.

Second stage: Storming

The storming phase is not characteristic of all groups, just as not every teenager experiences adolescent turmoil and defiance. Rather the label represents an abstraction derived from many groups and describes members' and therapists' experiences when members feel they have been ignored, misunderstood, depreciated or narcissistically harmed in a context of increasing group cohesion and functioning. Yet this phase provides important self experiences, as members learn that their anger, rage and rebellion can be accepted and understood without retaliation.

The members: The storming phase is described as the members' responses to what they experience as restrictive and controlling group norms and values and to unresolved sibling rivalry remaining from the first phase. Transferences develop toward peers and the leader. A general tenor of trying to understand and create safety in the first phase may inadvertently lead to restrictive group norms that are experienced as stringent, immovable, and hurtful. In one respect, the initial process sets the stage for the possibility of members, who are frightened of the destructiveness of their anger to self or others, to begin experimenting with expressing these rageful emotions. Members must overcome these fears, which can be reinforced by group dynamic processes of contagion, which amplify emotions. In response they may search for whatever might be available to prevent fragmentation or to re-stabilize a disrupted self. At times the feelings may focus on a single individual who serves as the voice for the group (a group role). In such circumstances, the person feels emotions are amplified beyond anything previously experienced, to the detriment of the self.

The dynamics of the protest may emerge from deeply embedded self deficits arising from failures of appropriate mirroring or idealizing experiences in early childhood. In childhood the infant or toddler's self assertion may be responded to with criticism, derision or simply ignored, creating a self that is unable to sustain pleasure in assertive activity. The older child's efforts to enjoy experiences of school or play with others may be seen by the parents as violations of family norms, and therefore deprecated. In these individuals the joy and pleasure, which accompanies such assertion, is short-lived and replaced by a loss of vitality and a sense of dullness (Stolorow, 1984). Self-deficits acquired in childhood may not appear until adolescence and be seen dynamically as typical of teen-age years.

In this stage, members' self-assertion is mixed with fears of rejection and condemnation. Some more traumatized persons fear the consequences to themselves of their rage. Overcoming inner restrictions and hopelessness for many individuals may reverse these emotions and create a more confident self-assertive self. The therapist's capacity to serve a holding containing function and validation and affirmation of anger or assertiveness is a central element in the change process. More active mirroring selfobject responses may be liberating. Interventions that try to understand or explain the anger can interfere with its expression, being experienced as out of touch with the person's need to rage in a safe environment. For persons whose characteristic response is anger, a therapist's understanding of the self-protective function of this affect may help the member to restore an inner balance and establish improved emotional containment. This may help the member to be more effective in achieving goals and aspirations. As Ornstein & Ornstein (1993) noted, when the impediments to personal goals are removed, narcissistic rage disappears.

Persistent rage may signal previously unnoticed narcissistic vulnerability. Not all persistent rage is attributable to selfobject failure. It may be a member's defensive strategy to protect against engagement and fears that he/she will be traumatized again.

In the storming stage members learn from others how to address conflict, be empathic, or listen carefully—abilities possessed by peers or therapist (twinship selfobjects). Some members are cautious; their protest is not loud or sharply critical, but, at times, barely perceptible, which represents a cautious new behaviour and a more cohesive self. These responses have been described as tendrils, a delicate sprouting, by Tolpin (2002). Sensitive members can mirror the emerging assertiveness. Successfully learning self-assertive skills is self-affirming. Moreover, members who provide the learning for others enhance their own sense of self by being genuinely helpful, a particular aspect of therapy groups that is not so present in dyadic treatment. Indeed, for members who develop a stable sense of self, there is some pleasure in being a selfobject for another.

As members internalize their group experiences, particularly affirming and stabilizing responses, they become more effective in expressing themselves and managing conflict. Group membership is experienced as valuable, and the self and groupself are enhanced.

The potential for negative outcome in this stage is also present. In a group filled with protest or anger, members may experience a depletion or fragmentation of the groupself portion of the self. The group is no longer experienced as a vehicle, which is concordant with the individual's deeply, felt ideals and values. As a result some members may choose to terminate their treatment.

The therapist: In this phase, therapists often feel battered and self-doubting about the value or success of the group enterprise. At times the entire project may feel on the verge of disintegration. Only a rare clinician is not beset with discouragement or fantasies of retaliation.

The clinician weathers some of the emotional storms by recognizing that anger and rebellion are members' self-stabilizing efforts and potential growth responses. Attempts to soothe members rather than to understand and explain the process may temporarily reduce the turmoil, but such interventions do not enable patients to learn of their self vulnerability and self-calming responses, nor do they allow patients who have been frightened by their own rage to test the limits of their inner tolerance. Soothing interventions may also be in the service of calming a distraught clinician.

Therapists' knowledge of group dynamics adds to their ability to effectively intervene in the face of rebellion. By explaining the rebellion as a group phenomenon and not an individual process, one or more individuals will not be seen as disruptive, but as potentially voicing a group-wide concern. The non-judgmental quality of the therapist's remarks allows members to become self-reflective and aware of previously unrecognized or disavowed aspects of themselves. Scapegoating can be understood and explained, to the potential benefit of all.

Clinical example: Three months into the life of a private practice outpatient psychotherapy group, Gloria arrived fifteen minutes late. This was the third time in recent weeks that she had been tardy. Several members irritably inquired about the reasons for her behaviour. Gloria provided a "reality" reason: she had experienced a car problem. This explanation was not fully accepted, and inquiries were made about the reasons for her prior lateness. Gloria became anxious and testily said that the meeting could go on when she wasn't present. Her reply further irritated the others and increased tension within the room.

The therapist struggled to gain perspective about the situation. He was aware that he, too, was annoyed with Gloria, and he decided that further reflection was in order. He silently thought: What was happening inside Gloria? Was she rebelling against the group norms? Was she frightened of developing intimacy? Was she enacting some sadomasochistic drama? Could others' responses reflect Gloria's ordinary relational experience? Were others extruding her in order to avoid feelings she was possibly expressing?

As the therapist was quietly processing these thoughts, a member suddenly wondered if Gloria was becoming a scapegoat. This only served to increase tension as Gloria angrily admonished the others for criticizing her. The therapist inquired what feelings the members might be extruding if Gloria was indeed a scapegoat; was she expressing some resentment or rebellion that they too might wish to express. This intervention seemed to serve a mirroring selfobject experience for Gloria—the therapist had implicitly accepted her behaviour as a legitimate expression of feelings. The members felt freer to describe their own frustrations, including previously unexpressed fantasies of "taking off for a session" or quitting the group. They talked about their fears of being ostracized or of retaliation if they directly expressed dissatisfaction or anger. They, too, had felt understood by the therapist's intervention. Subsequently, Gloria was prompt in her attendance. She also began to express dissatisfactions verbally, which we understood as an indicator of a more cohesive self, and not merely compliance.

Comment: This example illustrates commonplace expressions of acting on dissatisfaction or frustration with the group norms and/ or process. The therapist's observation implied that scapegoats are more than people bearing the blame for others; they also carry important group feelings. The intervention directly reflected the effort to understand everyone's experience. Gloria experienced the intervention as conveying that she was doing something positive for the group, an experience of a mirroring selfobject. For the others, the notion that they were acting to scapegoat Gloria could possibly be shaming. The therapist, by inquiring about the nature of the feelings rather than criticizing members, served an idealizing function. If such formulations are accurate, they highlight the complexity of empathizing with a group. A single intervention may be experienced as serving different selfobject functions for the members. The example also highlights the members' contribution to the therapist's ability to make a useful intervention.

Third stage: Performing

The members: If the work has progressed satisfactorily, in the third stage of long-term dynamic groups, members have to a considerable degree internalized the values, ideals, and working methods of the group and can apply them within the group and within their daily lives. Members' inner images of the group and of other members function as positive and enhancing selfobjects. Repeated experiences of being understood and of having their conscious and unconscious processes explained (interpreted) gradually strengthens members' capacity to manage narcissistic injury. At this point, members have greater access to, and are more willing to identify, emotional responses in themselves and in others. They can reflect upon their feelings and can more openly express both tender and assertive emotions. They have become more fully cognizant of the power of unconscious forces and that errors or mishaps may not be due to chance. They can more successfully empathize with others and with themselves. When they have been narcissistically injured, there is usually lessened intensity of their typical responses and the duration of the reaction is shortened. With a greater sense of self and increased flexibility, members can try out unfamiliar roles (such as divergent leader) with a degree of confidence that their efforts will be appreciated and explored if their efforts are mismanaged.

In the outside world, when the inevitable frustrations occur, members learn to recognize their own self-stabilizing, self-soothing behaviours. Their "pathological" responses become muted and of briefer duration (Rubovits-Seitz, 2001). They find new self-stabilizing, self-restorative ways of soothing themselves, using both human and nonhuman selfobjects (e.g., listening to music, engaging in pleasurable activities). They may be able to pursue their goals more effectively and live within their ideals more comfortably.

This expansion of the self includes the groupself. Group values such as self-reflection, self-assertion, openness, and exploring processes of injury and repair, have been internalized in major ways, so that it is almost impossible to determine where a boundary exists between the self and the portion labelled groupself. With these additional attributes, the overall functioning of the self is enhanced.

Clinical example: Sheila, a single woman in her mid-40s, had been a member of a heterogeneous therapy group for almost three years. She had been referred to the group following several trials of brief psychotherapy and more extended medical (antidepressant) treatment for depression.

Sheila was initially reluctant to enter the group, believing that she had spent considerable time in psychotherapy over the years and knew her "issues" very well. This was true, as Sheila was able to recite, without undue anxiety, the tensions of growing up in the shadows of a brilliant brother and an abusive father. This knowledge had not lessened Sheila's depression. Much of Sheila's relationship history was marked by avoidance of intense emotional situations. She feared her own aggression (it might become uncontrollable) and the responses it might evoke.

In the group, Sheila at first maintained primarily affable contact with others and kept her distance from the leader. As her capacity for selfobject connectedness increased, Sheila took small steps toward more authentic contact with others by expressing moments of both warmth and minor annoyance. The members seemed quite accepting of both emotions. Sheila, likely feeling more accepted and safer, brought examples of her painting to the group. The members were surprised and pleased with her sharing this aspect of her self, disconfirming Sheila's expected disinterest or critique. She reported that much to her surprise she had not found herself ruminating about the responses. More typically, she would wonder, "Are they just being nice? Do they really mean what they say?" She found herself enjoying the members' responses in a new and invigorating way.

As Sheila felt more confident, she angrily confronted the leader with his announcement that a new member would be joining the group, even threatening to quit the group She was not going to be a passive, disempowered victim of an insensitive parent.

During the week between groups, Sheila was able to reflect on the unexpected intensity of her feelings and feel pleased that she had grown to the point where she could express herself rather than nurse a grudge. Sheila felt calmed by the voices of the group members and the knowledge that any relationship disruption within the group was temporary and not permanently damaging. She found herself utilizing her painting for self soothing and was able to look forward to attending the next session without a sense of internal fragmentation and panic. The next session began quickly with members referring to Sheila's uninhibited expression of anger at the leader. The group expressed appreciation for Sheila's expression of what other members felt but did not say. As members noted her growth, Sheila was able to share with the group their role in her increasing capacity to risk more authentic communication, soothe herself, and stave off the familiar anxiety. In turn, members felt a sense of accomplishment in themselves and the group. Completing this process, Sheila was open to hearing that some of the members had been frightened by her aggression and had the fantasy that they wished she would leave rather than carry on as she had. Sheila was able to listen, understand the others experience and not "defend" herself. Rather she was rather proud of what she had said as well as her subsequent reflection on the process. She was able to add several previously undisclosed incidents in which she had been severely punished as a child for being angry.

Sheila's behaviours impacted upon the group process to the benefit of all. As suggested above, her ability to express anger in response to the prospect of a new group member coming in and, as she saw it, intruding and upsetting the supportive functioning of the group, provided opportunities for members to address and understand their own narcissistic injuries and self-restorative responses.

Sheila's experiences helped other members to appreciate their own emotional growth: their improved ability to manage differences, their expanded self-reflection to episodes in the group and in their extra-group life; their ability to express admiration at another's growth; their diminished self-criticism and greater self-empathy when they mismanaged or misunderstood others. These achievements became embedded in the group process as part of the norms and values, and as part of the groupself. The group was truly in the self.

The therapist: In the performing phase, therapists experience a broad spectrum of feelings. Prominent are pleasure and pride in helping to create a group atmosphere in which members can achieve and demonstrate personal growth. They hear them tell of more successful and satisfying human relationships and more effective pursuit of their personal goals. Within the meetings, clinicians observe patients assuming expanded leadership roles, being empathic with one another and themselves, and being creatively helpful to one another. Therapists can see the growth in members' self-reflective capacity. Another pleasure is in therapists' feeling that they have learned something new about themselves. No dynamic treatment is successful without the therapist becoming significantly emotionally engaged. Something new is bound to emerge for all parties in such an encounter.

Clinicians also experience times of confusion and uncertainty. Lichtenberg (2005) comments, "Dealing with the powerful affects generated by human desire is, and has to be, 'messy' at times .... They [clinicians] must appreciate retaining an open mind, the influence of context, the high probability of error, and the unpredictability of many human responses." (p. xii). They may be unsure at which level to make an intervention—that of the group, the individual, and the present or past, either within or outside the group. Therapists worry that they might be abandoning their leadership role and feel less important if members are making helpful interpretations or connecting empathically with one another. The setting is ripe for countertransference enactments, which may be demonstrated through increased competitiveness with members' emerging leadership capacities or through withdrawal, as if punishing the group for making them feel less important. Therapists come to recognize these responses as attempts to stabilize their inner equilibrium and learn to monitor their responses in the service of understanding the treatment process.

Fourth stage: Ending

The members: Individuals whose treatments are deemed as successful are marked by a substantial strengthening of the self, one that no longer quickly complies or surrenders, that can reflect upon experiences and examine inner states and work to fulfil its goals and ambitions. Although possibly vulnerable to narcissistic injuries that may have emerged and been central to the therapeutic process, these individuals respond with greater resilience, less intense emotions and briefer disruptions. They have the capacity to search and utilize selfobjects throughout their life cycle.

Individuals who successfully complete their treatment have to say goodbye to colleagues, the therapist, and to their experience of the group-as-a-whole. Successful patients can justifiably feel pride in their accomplishments. They can be painfully aware that although they have learned a great deal and are better able to manage themselves and their relationships, they will still have to face the inevitable stresses and misfortunes of life. Members learn that in the future there will be circumstances when they will need soothing selfobject experiences.

Saying farewells are often bittersweet experiences. The entire group is impacted by a member's announced departure. Previously unexpressed emotions may come to the fore and provide another opportunity to learn of self vulnerabilities and to strengthen the self. The departing person may experience others' and their own sadness, envy, anger or intense affection. These emotions may be felt as disruptive but also provide an additional opportunity for strengthening the self. The departing person may mourn the loss of the selfobject function of the group. For those who remain, the groupself may be depleted. They may experience the group as deadened and not functioning as before the loss. In such groups, members may become familiar with their characteristic responses to loss. They will experience loss, not only of the individual, but also the selfobject provisions that person may have supplied. The members' groupself may be depleted.

Not all departures are result of successful treatment. Abrupt departures, particularly of seasoned members, can be fragmenting to a self vulnerable to loss. Individuals who leave abruptly may be doing so as a self protective, self-stabilizing behaviour. A termination maybe foreshortened by a self that is vulnerable to the emotions of saying goodbye, and managed by making an active decision to hastily leave. The therapist may be left with the task of explaining the process to the remaining members, which can serve as a soothing selfobject function for their distress at being abandoned.

The therapist: Therapists also have the important task of saying goodbye and of continuing treatment with those who remain. When the individual has had a successful treatment, the therapist can feel pride in helping the person develop a self that is able, under ordinary circumstances and with the aid of appropriate selfobjects to pursue its goals and ideals (Kohut, 1984). Any successful therapy carries personal meaning for therapists, as does any meaningful relationship. Therapists need to appreciate that they narcissistically invest themselves into their work. Ending that endeavour with an individual patient is a very real loss, which is painful to the self. Therapists may appreciate that they, too, have changed on the basis of their encounters with the departing member. This realization may add to the sense of therapist's satisfaction with the treatment.

In this emotionally charged period, clinicians may find themselves having participated in countertransference enactments. Many treatments are considered successful by the patient but do not meet the hopes or expectations of the clinician. In these circumstances, the clinician may not be able to engage wholeheartedly in the member's departure. The therapist may inadvertently join the inevitable resistance to saying goodbye or misunderstand symptoms that emerge as patients reprise their difficulties by enacting their countertransference both before and after the person's departure. Enactments are also linked to the therapist's personal loss of a successful member and to the real loss of a portion of the group.

Difficulties in addressing and sorting out these losses may be compounded by the therapist's self vulnerabilities. Slight variations in managing the treatment frame can be clues to some of the therapist's less obvious responses. Presence of new somatic feelings or increases in prior sensations can be additional clues to the therapist's affective response to the losses. Consultation may be useful under these circumstances; the therapist, like a patient, is a vulnerable person who can profit from assistance from an empathic and thoughtful colleague.

Concluding thoughts

As noted in the beginning of this paper, a self psychologically informed clinician takes a fundamental position of empathy as a mode of inquiry with each patient. This presents an inherent difficulty: How can a therapist be empathic with an entire group of differing subjectivities without causing some to feel misunderstood? As with any such effort, we believe that the clinician needs to maintain an openness to his misunderstanding and misattunement. An ability to hear and appreciate patients who feel misunderstood helps create an environment of safety and a place where members can expose what they feel as less desirable or unacceptable aspects of their self.

The patient entering a group also is concerned with being listened to, understood and responded to. Patients enter with their habitual defenses, and, most importantly, subtle efforts to determine the extent of safety and the availability of necessary selfobject responses. The task is ongoing, non-linear, with forward and regressive phases.

As individuals work together, their ways of relating evolve, we suggest, in relation to an appropriate selfobject milieu. These phases have been traditionally described as group developmental phases. We have emphasized members' more prominent selfobject experiences as they become more fully engaged in the developmental phases. Concomitantly, we have noted the internalization of the group interactions as aspects of the groupself, which can deeply influence the overall sense of self. Across all group developmental levels, members acquire or strengthen portions of self that enable them to listen to others and to themselves. They have selfobject experiences with the others and with the image of the group as a whole that serve to consolidate and firm a self that can reflect upon itself and also experience and understand others as separate persons with their own needs, strengths and vulnerabilities. They can become empathic with themselves and with others.

No single theory can fully explain the observed phenomena. Self psychology emerged from a dyadic setting and has been extensively explored as applied to work with groups. We believe it enriches our understanding of group dynamics and development. We await future research that can add to our understanding of the complex relationship between the individual and the group.

SECTION II

CLINICAL APPLICATIONS

CHAPTER SIX

A self psychological perspective of envy in group psychotherapy

Walter N. Stone

It is indeed a privilege to be asked to contribute to the examination of envy, which has received so little attention in the expanding exploration of the psychology of the self. Following receipt of the invitation to respond to Lionel Kreeger's presentation of envy preemption, I enquired if I might have a draft of his manuscript, which he promptly forwarded. I read it rather quickly, and proceeded with my research and my clinical explorations. I was aided in my study by the responses of my patients, colleagues and friends following the announcement of my forthcoming sabbatical leave that included three months in England.

In these circumstances, I recalled a paper by Manny Schwartz (1972), which I initially read with some dismay. He described a training group in which he would pick a theme, and then he would interpret all material along that single dynamic. I remember one theme that he chose was incest. Of course, soon all the students began reporting manifestation of incest occurring in their therapy groups. This process obviously ran the risk of seeing a theme where it did not belong. Discussion of the implications of this model is beyond the goal of this paper, but like the students, I saw envy where I had not seen it before, and my patients began to wonder what I had been studying. In the midst of this exploration, I received a second version of Dr. Kreeger's manuscript. My response was delight and amusement. We were similar; we had common experiences and thought (I too had found myself thinking of the Groucho Marx joke as a defense against being envied). We had addressed similar writing tasks, and I felt an identification with him. My preparatory anxiety diminished—was I experiencing an alter-ego transference.

This preamble is by way of introducing my focus of exploring envy in groups from the perspective of self psychology.

Theory

Groups provide a compelling laboratory for patients to explore a multitude of affective experiences (Stone, 1990). The stimuli of interpersonal transactions with peers, authorities and the group-as-a-whole evoke a wide range of feelings. The belief that transferences, with their attendant affects, would be diminished with a shift from dyadic to group treatment has been inaccurate (Ethan, 1978). Indeed, passionate feelings are evoked. Within the regressive context of analytically conducted groups, patients regress, undergo affect de-differentiation with an attendant inability to articulate specific feelings, or they experience emerge of somatic symptoms (Krystal, 1974). Affect contagion, which is signalled by periods of manic excitement or scapegoating, has never been adequately theoretically explained but may be a manifestation of the biologically based reciprocal responsivity between mother and infant (Stern, 1985). The network of interactions in groups provides multiple opportunities to experience, identify and gradually tolerate a wide range of feelings, which may lead to their eventual integration.

In view of such a fertile field, surprisingly, there is a paucity of in-depth references to envy in the group psychotherapy literature. It is mentioned only briefly in group therapy texts. Anger, rage, shame and exhibitionism and other intense affects have been more thoroughly explored, but the relative absence of envy is difficult to explain.

Difficulties in differentiating between envy and jealousy may be a partial explanation. Envy is defined as a two-person transaction. It is evoked when one individual desires what another possesses. In contrast, jealousy involves three people and refers to feelings that one person possesses something or someone that has been taken or is in danger of being taken away by the third person. Overlap across these two affective states is not uncommon. For instance, a man may envy attributes of the rival who takes his girlfriend, and simultaneously be jealous of the love that his rival receives.

Roy Whitman, who collaborated with Dorothy Stock in formulating the notion of the group focal conflict (Whitman and Stock, 1958), more recently working with Ellen Bloch (Whitman and Bloch, 1990) has usefully categorized envy within the biopsychosocial model. The biological level of envy includes physical attributes such as the male envy of the breast of or the ability to bear children; the psychological level includes envy of cognitive and reasoning processes or emotional awareness and flexibility; and the social level includes envy of material possessions such as a Mercedes or a luxury apartment in Manhattan.[1] Wishing or desiring attributes or possessions at any of these levels potentially diminishes one's own self-evaluation and disrupts inner equilibrium. The reaction to such an emotional position might well be to destroy that which one covets, thereby removing the stimulus and restoring an inner balance.

An additional element contributing to the clinical neglect of envy may be part of the heritage of the seminal work of Klein (1957). Her theoretical position is that envy is a fundamental drive derivative, that by its very nature contains oral-sadistic and anal-sadistic expressions of destructive impulses (Klein, 1957). Her emphasis on the destructive component of envy bypasses other affects that are part of the complexity of the envious feelings.

The perspective of self psychology posits that envy, rather than arising from instinctual drives, follows from a narcissistic injury, diminished self-esteem, and disruption of the stability of the self. The manifestations of destructiveness are the self's efforts to be rid of the noxious envied object and simultaneously achieve a sense of self-efficacy. Thus envy might be best understood as a variant of narcissistic rage, which is a response of an injured or fragmenting self. Joseph Epstein, editor of the literary magazine, *The American Scholar*, in his essay "A Few Kind Words for Envy" offers the following definition.

... envy I say is desiring what someone else has, a desire usually heightened by the knowledge that one is unlikely to attain it. My home made definition leaves out the dark elements of spite, hostility, ill will and begrudging that most definitions usually include (Epstein, 1991, p. 86).

Webster's *New Collegiate Dictionary* similarly describes envious feeling:

> ... it may imply an urgent, even malicious desire to see him [the envied individual] dispossessed or no more than a mild innocuous coveting.

Examined from this perspective envy may be experienced along a continuum based on the underlying capacity of the self to manage and contain narcissistic injury. Envy implies a gap between what one has and what one desires. In such circumstances, there is the potential for diminished self-esteem on the part of the envier.

Self psychology

Kohut (1971, 1977, 1984) has made fundamental contributions to our understanding of narcissism and the developing self. His psychology of the self removed narcissism from its morally tinged trappings and as a manifestation of immaturity that was to be eliminated in an adult, to an attribute of the self that would be present throughout life and would undergo developmental processes with increasing personal maturity. Central to Kohut's thesis is the self as a supraordinate psychological organizing structure which is conceived of as the "center of initiative and a recipient of impressions" (Kohut, 1977, p. 99).[2] The self develops along a pathway from immature to mature structures, with increasing capacity to manage the everyday narcissistic injuries without feelings of excessive dysphoria or fragmentation.

The self matures with the aid of a self-object, which is conceived of not as a separate individual, but as a function that will provide the soothing necessary to prevent overwhelming anxiety and psychic disintegration. The archaic experiences of the self-object are as if it is part of the self, that is a body part. The self-object is then subject to the control of the self. Development follows from the inevitable empathic failures, which if not too severe or protracted enables the growing person gradually to internalize the self-object functions and being to experience the self-object as having a separate, independent existence. Stolorow et al. (1987) have suggested that self-object functions are primarily concerned with affect regulation.

Kohut (1971) initially described two archaic self-objects: the mirroring self-object and the idealizable self-object. The former, as seen in the mirror transference, was equivalent to the phase-appropriate needs for response to archaic grandiose and exhibitionistic self-states. These would mature into the capacity to pursue one's goals and ambitions. The latter, as seen in the idealizing transference, was the experience of merging with a calm, omnipotent self-object. These needs would mature into the capacity for empathy, creativeness, humour and wisdom. As his theorizing progressed, Kohut (1977) conceived of these two self-object needs as two ends of the bipolar self. Subsequently, Kohut (1984) added a third developmental line, that of the alter-ego and twinship self-objects, which was intermediate between the two others. Kohut described that alter-ego experience as

> ... a sense of security, a sense of belonging that cannot be explained in terms of a mirroring response or a merger with ideals. Instead these feelings derive from confirmation of the feeling that one is a human being among other human beings (Kohut, 1984, p. 200).

This experience has an obvious reference to groups, and although presented in another paradigm, it has many descriptive similarities to Abse's (1983) exploration of a phylogenetic transference to the primal horde. More succinctly, the self-object is understood as the self's need for sameness. Thus my reference to the pleasure and reassurance I felt when reading Dr. Kreeger's manuscript.

Envy is a response to an anxious and fragmenting self. It arises from the self's inability to control the self-object. Signals of an overburdened self are the presence of restitutive response in the form of neurotic symptoms or character traits. These include destructiveness in all of its overt and covert forms, or any of the multitude of responses that are aimed at restoring the self's equilibrium. Kohut (1972), in a seminal essay on narcissistic rage, elucidated Captain Ahab's persistent, all-absorbing pursuit of Moby Dick as chronic narcissistic rage. It would not be far-fetched to recast Ahab's all-consuming search as a consequence of envy.

Ahab may represent the destructive end of a response continuum. The other end would be a much more benign manifestation. For instance, it does not require a finely tuned ear to enjoy a Luciano Pavarotti concert. Initial envy of such talent, in the well-integrated self, may be "metabolized" into admiration and gratitude.

The stability of self-cohesion may dictate the intensity of the response to narcissistic injury. Envious feelings are ubiquitous, they do not disappear with maturity, but may be stimulated by larger societal forces. Unfortunately, one of the excesses of envy is greed, "an impetuous and insatiable craving, exceeding what the subject needs and what the object is able and willing to give" (Klein, 1957, p. 181). Johnson (1991) documents these excesses in his book *Sleepwalking Through History*, which describes America in the 1980s, during the presidency of Ronald Reagan. Greed and the acquisition of money and power suffused the culture, leading to the savings and loan crises, insider trading, corruption in mergers and acquisitions and officials taking temporary positions with the federal government and then, following their termination from governmental services, using their connections for personal gain. In the turmoil of the stock market crash beginning 19 October 1987, and continuing the following day, Johnson wrote:

> How close the New York Stock Exchange, and with it the world's financial system, came to extinction then was never appreciated by the general public. For obvious reasons, neither was it ever fully addressed publicly by U.S. business leaders and political policy makers (Johnson, 1991, p. 380).

Johnson was referring to the contagion of fear and the conspiracy of silence, but underneath, and left unmentioned, was acquisitiveness and envy of "those who had." Epstein (1991, p. 92) succinctly summarizes the human condition "and where there is desire envy lurks."

In the following section, I explore envy as it emerges in small groups with the emphasis on understanding the therapeutic processes from a self psychological perspective.

The therapeutic process

Working within the self psychology paradigm shifts the treatment focus. Therapeutic change is no longer conceived of as a result of taming instinctual drives or as healing of splits in internal object relations. Instead, the self psychologically informed therapist understands the patient's psychopathology as the best solution for that individual whose need for a responsive, empathic self-object environment has been flawed and has inhibited growth. From this perspective, patients enter into treatment with a curative fantasy that, if realized, will enable them to restart growth of a distorted self (Stone, 1985). Ornstein (1992) states

> "In the therapeutic relationship, patients hope that the main-
> tenance of the contact with the therapist will not require the
> same compromises to their self that were required in the
> original relationship."

Some individuals manifest their self-object needs quite promptly as they enter a group. Others will have erected defenses against being narcissistically retraumatized, and only through continuing empathic responsivity will they gradually expose their archaic needs. These transferences may occur silently, out of awareness of both patient and therapist. The commonly observed disappearance of somatic symptoms in patients shortly after entering into treatment is most likely a manifestation of increased self-cohesion following the silent establishment of an alter-ego transference with the group.

Inevitably, failures of self-object functions will occur, followed by a patient's efforts to regain his or her balance, or as experienced by a person with a more fragile fragmenting self, to regain cohesion. Repeated experiences of empathic failure, narcissistic injury and response followed by the therapist's empathic understanding and explaining (interpreting) provide opportunities for the self to assume some of the soothing, stabilizing functions previously provided by the self-object. This process has been labelled transmuting internalization.

Clinical illustrations

Patients enter groups not only to solve their problems but also to have their skills, talents and aspirations affirmed. Moreover, they wish to share of themselves, feel like they are not so alone and that they are part of the human condition. These wishes represent self-object developmental needs that seem fundamental to the human condition. For some, group membership highlights their vulnerability to feelings of alienation or difference that may be so great that they insist on entering a group in which members are at least superficially similar. This wish for an alter-ego experience has contributed to the development of homogenous groups. In the United States there is almost a landslide movement to enter groups for victims or sexual abuse, adult children of alcoholics, men's and women's groups. Alcoholic s Anonymous is the classic example of such an organization. No one is ever cured; one is always recovering. This structure initially diminishes differences, and the potential for unmetabolizable envy[3] (Wahba, 1991).

The situation in heterogeneous groups is more fraught with the possibility of narcissistic injury and lowered self-esteem. New members make immediate comparisons with others, and for those with a fragile self-structure, the comparisons can be disorganizing. A newcomer to a group may immediately notice others' dress, hairstyles, their use of language or their apparent comfort in interacting. They may observe the therapist being attacked, a possibility that seems so unlikely for a constricted person. These observations may all touch upon one's self-evaluation. Patients embark upon group treatment hoping to alter their alienation from others and reconnect with their inner world. These individuals may be particularly envious of others' ease in managing their affects. The "confrontation" of their deficits upon joining may lower self-esteem, further distancing the envier from the envied. Thus the group and its members become less available to serve as necessary self-objects.

We are all familiar with defenses against such feelings—a silent withdrawal or an exhibitionistic monologue, which has built-in risks for rejection. As Kreeger (this issue, pp. 391–408) observes, aspects of the presentation may contain envy preemption in which suffering and misery are presented. This may take place when the new patient perceives him- or herself to have a higher social status such as physician, minister or public official. These manifestations of envy and defenses do not necessarily imply a major deficit in self-regulation. Rather, they may be ordinary experiences of self-disregulation and reactive envy that are managed by each individual with prior characteristic responses.

Just as newly admitted persons have anxieties about exhibiting potentially envied aspects of themselves, so do the older members. A subgroup of patients, diagnosed in the borderline and narcissistic spectrum, colluded not to reveal their occupations to a newcomer. The therapist was unable to sort out aspects of the subsequent interactions until one of the members shamefully "confessed" to the

secrete agreement. The subgroup members' self-esteem was sufficiently shaky that they could not tolerate their own envy or, conversely, being the object of an envious attack. The transferential
nature of these fantasies was clear, since the only advance information they had received about the new member was that of gender.
The empathic response within the group to the newcomer may
depend upon the state of group organization and cohesion. A group
suffused with envy directed at a recently departed member will be
much less empathic with the anxieties of the newcomer, and members may displace their envious destructiveness on the new object.
For the vulnerable individual, these experiences may be a repetition
of prior developmental failures and sufficiently toxic to disorganize
the self. The patient is then left with little "choice" other than to resort
to prior successful restitutive strategies, that may include an abrupt
termination. Fortunately, such circumstances are not common, and
established patients' memories of their own initial group experiences
enable the continuing members to respond with understanding. the
group then functions as an accepting alter-ego self-object.

Envy needs to be explored even when other self-object transferences have been identified. Weinstein (1991) describes an adult
group of six members that found a way of managing their envy.
One member complained that she knew of other groups that were
more activity oriented, and where members would share things
they enjoyed. Those people came to know each other more completely, and she envied them. The members soon hit upon the idea
of a hobby night in which they would share their talents. As the
plan evolved, time for discussion was allowed and a date was set for
members to bring examples of their work to the meeting. The therapist responded to this as "a piece of important transferential material; let's understand the needs that this represent" (Weinstein, 1991,
p. 223). The night arrived and two of the three members who were
to present failed to appear. The therapist's understanding that the
hobbies represented a split-off part of the self that had been insuffi-
ciently mirrored seemed accurate, but incomplete. Envy as a source
of anxiety was not mentioned. Could fears of envious destructiveness (which differs from competitiveness) have been the basis for
the absence?

The vignette raises another salient possibility. Because many of the
patients' talents had not been mirrored as children, was it possible that
the parents' empathic failures were a consequence of their envy of the

children's budding talents? Weinstein describes in detail one woman whose talents were piano playing and dancing. The former was strongly endorsed by her parents and the latter depreciated and discouraged. Her dancing, which she had exhibited on video, was described as sensuous and sexual. Possibly the patient had experienced her parents' behaviour accurately, or her response may have been part of a guilty response to her own oedipal fantasies, but envy might be a significant affect from the first perspective and envy preemption from the second. Previously we wrote about the anxiety of over-stimulation to the self as one becomes the centre of attention (Stone and Whitman, 1977). The notion now seems incomplete and anxiety over becoming the object of envy also contributes to "hiding one's light under a bushel."

Recent contributions to the place of shame in the developing self have minimally touched upon the connections between that affect and envy. Morrison (1990) suggests that envy may conceal shame. He observed:

> ... one major impediment to the treatment of shame is the fact that shame characteristically leads to concealment, *hiding* of the "real" or imagined failures and inferiority feelings which generate it.

Shame then appears as another self-response to a differential between what one is and what one might wish to be, often reawakened in comparison with others. Morrison describes a man, Derek, suffering with low self-esteem, who was raised by his promiscuous mother and his loving aunt. During latency, Derek had witnessed his mother being sexually intimate with a number of men. His efforts at mastery of his feelings included voyeurism. Derek's overt problem related to his marriage and to women in authority. In the group, he initially externalized all his difficulties, but slowly developed what Morrison labelled as an idealizing transference to the group-as-a-whole and a twinship transference to another man. Derek, in the context of discussing his marital problems, tearfully told of his experiences observing his mother, and sobbed as he told of his beloved aunt's death. He was very ashamed of feeling like an "abandoned boy." In response, a woman told how her mother continuously humiliated her because of her obesity and disparagingly compared her with her brother. She was very ashamed of being overweight. In both instances shame was emphasized, but envy most likely lurked behind the shame. For Derek the likely experience was envy and jealousy of other children with intact families, since the unconscious often believes that it is a personal attribute that causes misfortune. The woman, similarly, but more consciously, suffered from the same dysphoric affects in relation to her brother. Epstein (1991, p. 83) quotes Herman Melville:

> Well though many an arraigned mortal has in hopes of mitigated penalty pleaded guilty to horrible actions, did ever anybody seriously confess to envy? Something there is in it [is] universally felt to be more shameful than even felonious crime.

Similarly, the confession of shameful experiences can serve to both hide and expose envy.

Illustrative of the many faces of envy were my groups' responses to my announced sabbatical leave, and my three-month absence from Cincinnati. I prepared myself for major affective turmoil, anticipating responses to feelings of abandonment and loss and envy of my opportunity and power. A gamut of reactions followed my announcement, made five months in advance of my departure. The patients responded with shock and disbelief, with threats to terminate, confusion as to the dates and duration of my absence, depreciation of the therapy and of myself. One man hoped that I would learn something, because certainly I had not been of any help during his period of group membership. Only twenty minutes earlier he had been praising the treatment. The shift, precipitated by a member's questioning whether or not I would supply a replacement therapist, signalled the affective liability and emotional contagion so common in the contest of narcissistic injury. Of course, he was speaking for one part of the group.

The request for an alternative therapist, that spontaneously arose from the members of both my groups, was to be one of their major preoccupations, arising to a crescendo in the final two months before I was to depart. They wished to experience a different leader who would be better than I. Perhaps a woman would be more responsive. They could grow more with someone else. The continued depreciation of me, of course, stirred my anxiety—if I supplied a locum, would they return or would they elect to remain with the substitute? I began to doubt my effectiveness. However, their ambivalence was very powerful, and there were voices wishing to try the three months on their own. They could use the time for fun things that the evening session prevented. They might see how much they had gained and might not return. Of course this stimulated my anxiety. However, they too were haunted by the discussion, as concerns were raised that my absence meant the end of the group. These fantasies only served to highlight my power and their powerlessness, which further stimulated envy. It was not until the final month could both groups make a firm request for a replacement.

The ambivalence these patients experienced was not worked though during this stressful period. Boris (1986) suggests that ambivalence is based on envy.

> I can imagine an infant, I sometimes feel it necessary to say, held by two ample breasts—yet starving out of pain of losing either by choosing one (p. 45).

The use of such metaphors with their powerful confrontive message in the context of emotional liability, is frequently experienced as injurious. For patients to integrate such an interpretation, particularly when it is introduced by the therapist, requires that they have a reasonably stable sense of self.

In the context of the emotional upheaval, on a number of occasions I lost my balance and was unable to maintain an empathic position and instead, countertransferentially, responded from the position of the external observer. Soon after I announced the forthcoming sabbatical, a member, with apparent naivety, asked if I had chosen to take the leave or if the University had requested that I take it. I retorted: "Of course I chose." A woman promptly commented, "That was arrogant!" Not having heard the affect in my response, I asked her to repeat what I had said, which she did accurately. Her tone and the words were clear, and I apologized. This interaction was a signal of the considerable progress this woman had achieved. Her reaction was direct and prompt to my unintended narcissistic injury. She did not rage or resort to other responses, but spoke directly through a self that had maintained its cohesiveness. If there had not been such a direct response, I would imagine that various reactions to my empathic failure would have followed. Then an apology would have been insufficient. Instead an optimal response would have included a description of each individual's feelings of injury and their efforts to regain their balance. The intervention would have been presented as tentative, and the members would have been invited to modify or correct what had not been accurately understood. A collaboratively worded interpretation strengthens the therapeutic dialogue.

Therapist envy

Not surprisingly, therapists suffer envy of their patients. An example from a supervisory experience may elucidate the complex interplay of exhibitionistic and envious responses.

> Dr M, the supervisee, said he was troubled by what had happened in his group, but he was unable to identify what was upsetting. He described the particular meeting, which focused on the successful termination of Mr A from the group. The evening of Mr. A's final meeting, the other members brought gifts which the felt represented Mr. A's positive characteristics and strengths. The gifts seemed to be a genuine expression of their fondness and admiration of the departing member. As Dr M movingly described a pen and ink sketch of Mr A drawn by another member, I wondered if there had been any expression of envy within the group. I had in mind envy of Mr A and his achievements and of the artist, whose talents had been so graphically described. In response, Dr M told me about his own guitar concerts which had received some notoriety in the local press. Dr M said, with some shame, that he had wondered if he should mention his performances in the group because he thought members might have been aware of them from the newspapers. He went on in some detail to describe the nature of his music. Dr M continued that he had been preoccupied with his own musical performances during the session and had lost contact with the group. These unarticulated affects contributed to his subsequent failure to explore the darker side of members' feelings about the departure of Mr A or any envy of one another's gifts.

I will add one more personal note to this vignette. As I listened to Dr M describe his music, I became aware of his wish for recognition of his work from me and also my own envy of his talents. I commented that he clearly was pleased with the response to his concerts, but I did not share my own envy.

The preceding vignette illustrates patients' capacity for related-ness, so much a part of any group experience. Patients' unselfcon-scious display of their ability for emotional relatedness serves as a source of therapist envy. How often do we admire or envy mem-bers' capacity to find "just the right words", to make contact, break an impasse or calm an overwrought individual. As Friedman (1998) has observed: "The therapist's undeliberate search for an interactive response plays a special role in psychotherapy." (p. 107) The diffi-culty in making such contact is particularly problematic for therapists working with the chronic mentally ill (Stone, 1991). When others are able to achieve emotionally meaningful contact, and the therapist has not experienced that success, the result may be envy. Serious counter-transference blocks occur when therapists are unable to manage their competitive and narcissistic affects in the face of members' empathic skills. Hearst and Sharpe (1991) remark that talented candidates for group-analytic training will display their therapeutic insights, observing: "This also gives the conductor the opportunity to contain his or her envy of the talent and expertise a trainee has" (Hearst and Sharpe, 1991, pp. 151–152). Failure to contain the envy, further dis-torting the therapy, is likely to increase distance between members and therapist, thereby potentially increasing envy.

Not uncommonly, beginning group therapists, feeling alone and isolated as they struggle to consolidate their professional identity, will be surprised, envious and jealous of the depth of support and affective attunement taking place in the group. These experiences are not limited to neophytes, as the vicissitudes of our practice and our inevitable incomplete understandings, with their associated uncertainties and self-questioning, become burdensome.

Whitman and Bloch (1990) suggest another source of therapist's envy as the quality of treatment the members are receiving. Recog-nition of the therapist's own analyst's misunderstandings or later advances in theory may enable the therapist to provide a more effec-tive treatment than he or she received. Envy of the patient's treat-ment may result.

Countertransferencial responses are particularly likely to emerge at termination. Envy of departing members by those remaining is usually disguised, but may be present over both the success the indi-viduals have achieved or merely because they are leaving (Rutan and Stone, 1984). Departing members, in a properly managed termination, will usually experience a period of regression, with reappearance of symptoms. Moreover, all patients leave with some unfinished work, and we can only hope to prepare them to know themselves sufficiently to handle most stresses. Envious members may use these inevitable dynamisms to try to demonstrate that the individual is not ready to leave. A therapist whose narcissistic aspirations would be punctured with a less than totally cured patient is vulnerable to having his or her feelings reinforced by the other members' envy. As a consequence, the therapist would be poorly positioned to assist in the termination process.

Conclusion

The advent of self psychology has added a dimension to our understanding of group-dynamic processes. This psychology emphasizes the hopes and aspirations of the members, and focuses on their vulnerabilities to utilizing their skills, achieving their goals and fulfilling their ideals. It bridges the intrapsychic and the interpersonal worlds. The responses of the members are not merely displacements from the past onto the present, but are reactions to their hope for a new experience that will help alter the ability to soothe themselves and maintain their sense of self. In such an environment, others' abilities and talents are an ever-present reminder of what one might desire. The potential for envy, with all of its manifestations, defenses and opportunities for growth, is increased. Envy will not go away. Only with achievement of a firmly anchored self can these affects be contained and integrated. Indeed, the self will gain further strength from experiences of envy which have been empathically understood.

Finally, with this emphasis on a single aspect of human interaction, hopefully I have not recreated the experiences of Schwartz's trainees, leaving you with the impression envy is omnipresent. As we try to explore these difficult feelings, inevitably misunderstandings and narcissistic injury will occur. The study of the vicissitudes of the self and its restitutive efforts following injury may enable us, as clinicians, to use such experiences for the patients' and group's benefit.

Notes

1. These categories may be clinically useful when transferences in the group are explored. They categorize specific attributes that are

actually present or are projected into the group members, but initially were experienced in relation to either the family of origin or with peers or those in authority.

2. This double usage of the self has created conceptual confusion. Stolorow et al. (1987, pp. 18–19) suggest that this difficulty could be minimized by restricting the "concept of the self to describe organizations of experience and use the term person ... to refer to the existential agent who initiates action".

3. Obviously this statement is a generalization that will melt away if groups are conducted on an analytic model and in depth work is encouraged. Then the exposure of differences inevitably leads to manifestations of envy.

CHAPTER SEVEN

Frustration, anger, and the significance of alter-ego transferences in group psychotherapy

Walter N. Stone

For most clinicians, the topic of the angry patient evokes associations to troublesome borderline and narcissistic individuals. There are patients who are not reliably capable of distancing themselves from their immediate therapeutic experience in order to cognitively contemplate their interactions. They are individuals who respond to treatment as a real life experience, without an "as if" quality.

Malcolm Pines, in a 1975 paper addressing the impact of the angry person on the group and on the therapist wrote:

Diagnostically most of these individuals fall into the "borderline" category; they are extraordinarily self-involved, sensitive, dissatisfied and angry. Their impact on the group may be intense and not always constructive, since they attempt to destroy, monopolize, and to provoke counter-aggression from other members. Moreover, they engage in struggle with the group leader which can be disturbing to the latter to say the least (p. 102).

Discussion of the angry patient, however, entails an understanding of the clinician's perspective on the genesis of anger affects in the therapeutic process. The psychology of the self, with its emphasis on the universal need for self-objects, has brought into sharper focus the affective responses to narcissistic injury. In this contribution, I will focus on the relevance of alter-ego and twinship transferences in understanding experiences of frustration and anger as they emerge in group psychotherapy. A clinical vignette will illustrate some of the selfobject transferences emerging in the relationships among the group members and with the therapist.

The psychology of the self

In what Ornstein and Kay (1990) called a paradigm shift, Kohut (1977) revised his earlier formulations that had place the self within traditional drive psychology and posited the presence of a superordinate organizing structure: the bipolar self. Kohut (1977) considered the self "as a unit, cohesive in space and enduring in time, which is a center of initiative and recipient of impressions (p. 99) that is present at birth, but is "not knowable in its essence" (p. 311). The archaic self develops and consolidates in an environment of phase appropriate responsive selfobjects. Although the mature self is less vulnerable to dysphoric states or feelings of fragmentation in response to narcissistic injury, the need for selfobjects continues though all states of the life cycle.

In his initial contributions, Kohut (1971, 1977) emphasized two developmental lines: those of the grandiose self (mirroring selfobject needs) and ideal self (idealizing self-object needs) Archaic self states of grandiosity and idealization mature into self-assertive goals and ambitions and into values and ideals.

In 1984 Kohut elucidated a third developmental line, that of the alter-ego (twinship) relations and transferences. He did not differentiate between the two terms. Kohut placed alter-ego requirements as the individual's "need to experience the presence of essential alikeness" and like mirroring and idealizing needs, as "present from the moment of birth to the moment of death" (p. 194).

Alter-ego phenomena include the sense of being human, a kinship (Basch, 1992). They are experiences of sameness or likeness to others that link individuals to a human group (Detrick, 1985, 1986). Twinship phenomena are experiences that provide for the acquisition of skill. Illustrative of these latter needs are the little boy imitating his father shaving, or the little girl imitating her mother in activities such as cooking or sewing. The individual's inner experience of possessing capabilities, including cognitive and empathic capacities similar to others is self-strengthening. These are not surface phenomena but depth experiences of feeling of belonging to the human condition, of being in the presence of someone who is sufficiently similar to understand (Kohut, 1984). These phenomena include aspects of oneself that are disavowed or hidden (Brothers, 1993).

Developmentally alter-ego needs may present from infancy and underlie mirroring and idealizing relationships (Basch, 1992, pp. 115–116). These needs appear to emerge more fully in the Oedipal (Martinez, 1993) and latency developmental stages. Feelings of alienation, of being different, or having ideas that seem strange and bizarre may occur at all stages, however, and experiences of "sameness" can restore inner balance.

Ascertaining the precise meaning of a selfobject transference is illustrated in Kohut's (1984) exploration of the meaning of touch. When a distressed person is touched (or held) by another the calming and comforting response to the gesture is universally understood, but the inner meaning of such an action may be that of merger with a mirroring or idealized selfobject, or the meaning may be that of belonging to a common human experience, "a sense of sameness with the object" (Bacal, 1992, p. 61). Through empathic emersion in the recipient's internal experience, a clinician can being to collaboratively ferret the specific meaning of such acts.

Narcissistic rage

The psychology of the self does not posit a fundamental aggressive drive that requires taming and socialization. Rather, the experience of frustration or disappointment in expectations of phase-appropriate responsivity from selfobjects leads to disruption of the stability of the self, which may vary from experiences of mild dysphoria to that of psychic disintegration. Among the multitude of restorative response are expressions of narcissistic rage that may be considered on a continuum, scanning the spectrum from irritability, anger, rage to hostile destructiveness (Ornstein & Ornstein, 1993).

Anger responses create distance, perhaps in anticipation of injury; they are a response to being hurt and contain a message, "stop hurting me"; they serve as a self-organizing affect, because for brief periods, angry expression may create a sense of power and control over others, which counteracts underlying emptiness or vulnerability; or they simply may serve to destroy the object, as in malignant envy (Krystal, 1975; Wahba, 1991).

Stimuli evoke an angry response may appear inconsequential to the external observer, and as a consequence the angry response may be deemed inappropriate. Among the stimuli evoking injury are comparisons patients make with one another. Thus, attributes of another, such as psychological mindedness or empathic capacities, may be the bases for negative comparisons, lowered self-esteem, and reactive anger and envy (Stone, 1992b). These affects often evoke secondary feelings of shame, or if they are acted on they evoke fears of destroying the other or of retaliation. In order for individuals to maintain their inner equilibrium, these feelings may be inhibited, displaced, or transformed, sometimes into idealization. An empathic stance enables the clinician to temporarily join with the patient in understanding the basis for the anger. Understanding does not signify agreement.

The therapeutic process

Patients enter psychotherapy with a wish for a suitably responsive selfobject that will enable them to solidify an unbalanced or weakened self. They are fearful that they will be traumatized in the present as they had in their family or in prior life situations (Stone and Gustafson, (1982). A. Ornstein (1990) describes patients' wishes in the treatment encounter in the following fashion: "In the therapeutic relationship, patients hope that the maintenance of the contact with the therapist will not require the same compromises to their self that were required in the original relationship" (p. 22); Through their underlying search for connectedness, patients hope thereby to restart growth (Ornstein, 1974).

In the treatment process, patients' fears, as expressed through character defenses and resistances, are empathically explored. As therapists attempt to understand patients' inner world, inevitably there will be misunderstanding and error, causing narcissistic injury. The therapists' recognition of the meaning of patients' response to such injuries provide opportunities for growth. Through optimally timed empathic communication, clinicians can convey the sequence of narcissistic injury and restitutive response that enables patients to feel understood and to gain a non-judgemental understanding of their responses. Gradually, patients may acquire an increased capacity for self-understanding and for self-soothing.

In group psychotherapy, our vision must be expanded beyond the dyad to include an awareness of the treatment context that includes the therapist, other members, and the group culture and norms. Just as some cultures accept and/or tolerate disturbed and disturbing behaviour, so some therapy groups are more accepting of disturbed "difficult" individuals. Other groups may not be as flexible or tolerant. Variation in group cultures may be looked on as expressions of group development, which emerges as members are able to manage inevitable narcissistic injury in emotionally charged interactions.

Considerable attention has been paid to the need for mirroring selfobject and for idealizing selfobject experiences in groups (Stone, 1992a). Manifestations of alter-ego and twinship relations and transferences have received less attention. Nevertheless, manifestations of these needs are commonplace. In early group development, newcomers search for similarities as a ticket to membership. Transactions that may seem banal to the external observer may have important meaning for patients entering into a group. Where do you work? Where did you go to school? Oh, you grew up in that neighbourhood? These questions are a search for similarity and familiarity. Many of the change processes are imbedded in members imitating or identifying with one another in how they think about problems or how they respond to emotionally lade interactions.

Deficits in interpersonal skill underlie a variety of patients' symptomatic presentations and their entry into a group provides them an arena in which to learn from others. The development of skills and talents is not limited to concrete achievements. The sense of pride and accomplishment is patent when a member can make genuine contact with another in the course of their work together. Being of value to another, and using one's skills is a self-strengthening experience that is not reported in dyadic treatment, but takes place in front of an audience in group psychotherapy. Detrick (1985) suggests that "the experience of *sameness* [emphasis in the original] gives us an empathically based definition of a group and its boundary" (p. 255).

An alter-ego transference differs from formation of a trusting relationship. Trust is the emotion activated in the search for a reliable selfobject and implies that the person feels sufficient self-esteem and cohesion plus an expectation that he/she will not be traumatized in the new relationship. An alter-ego transference is seen as a developmental process in which the experience of having a fundamental likeness with others leads to a strengthening of the self. When frustration or disappointment in alter-ego transferences occurs, the overt response may be loss of trust and rage.

The clinical experience

Angry individuals representing a subgroup of difficult patients, present themselves for treatment in many different ways. Their problems may be expressed as an inability to sustain relationships, in part because they or the "other" in the relationship become angry. Often difficult individuals enter treatment at the behest of someone who is disturbed by their behaviour. Not infrequently such persons present with vague or neurotic complaints and only during the therapeutic process do difficult behaviours emerge that signal a self-deficit (Waldinger, 1993).

Group psychotherapy provides an arena in which reverberating responses to failed selfobject transferences result in disturbed and disturbing interactions. Therapists often wonder why patients can not be empathic with one another, when "obviously" someone has been injured. Exploration of the interactions may reveal that members' hidden vulnerabilities have been stimulated leading to retaliation and self-restorative responses. The therapeutic task is particularly problematic when a difficult patient has "invited" angry responses. Under these circumstances, members' counteraggression is viewed as reasonable, rather than as a response to an injury. This process is made more complex, because emotional contagion may magnify affects and engulf the clinician. Therapists have difficulty maintaining their empathic stance in the face of such affective stimulation.

The clinician's primary task, even in the face of the multiple forces reverberating in the treatment setting, is to gain an empathic understanding of the sequence of injury and self repair from the several differing perspectives of the individuals and the group-as-a-whole. Through the process of understanding and explaining (interpretation) the treatment environment becomes safer, and members, feeling more connected via an alter-ego experience, are more willing to risk exposing hidden aspects of themselves. Gaining insight into both the present and the developmental sources of the self-vulnerability adds another component to self-stability. The processes eventuate in members achieving greater self-cohesion and less internal disruption following narcissistic injury.

Clinical illustrations

A Clinical vignette will elucidate problems encountered in working with patients who entered group treatment to learn more about how their relationships were affected because they either expressed anger too openly or inhibited anger too habitually. The example will emphasize an alter-ego transference in understanding the unfolding dynamic processes. The group of eight with both men and women meets weekly for 90 minutes. New patients are added when openings occur. Thumbnail sketches of three men and one woman will provide the flavour of these members' disturbances.

Andrew, a married historian in mid-life, had moved from one university to another, generally at the behest of his department head. He described himself as an angry man with few friends. Andrew grew up fearing his mother's wrath but simultaneously trying to please her. He ultimately entered a career of her choice. He seldom felt that he succeeded in soothing her, and he struggled between wishing to reject his entire family and longing for their warm acceptance. Although brilliant, Andrew was an extremely difficult person with whom to get along. He would easily become angry and be unable to contain himself, often ending up in heated arguments with colleagues. On one occasion while in an enraged state, he stormed out of a colleague's office, striking the edge of a door and knocking himself out. The resultant concussion disabled him for several months. When he would not live up to his ideals, Andrew would purposely injure himself; at times in an agitated state, this would take place in front of students.

In the group, Andrew exhibited considerable tension nonverbally by rocking or drumming. On numerous occasions, he would respond irritably to members or to the therapist's effort to understand him when he was in the midst of a seemingly rambling self-referential discourse loosely related to the group topic. He would have brief angry outbursts and then dismiss them as a reflection of tension at work, where his position seemed perpetually under review. He would frequently arrive late to meetings, stating that he had an important task he wished to finish at the university, and he would be too tired to return to his office following the session.

Ben, a 32-year-old single son of a deceased alcoholic father, is a confirmed peacemaker. He is a regular attender of groups for adult children of alcoholics (ACOA) and labels himself a people pleaser. He states that his goal is to have everyone like him. His depth experience is that he is different.

Ben assiduously avoids addressing angry feelings toward peers within the group, but on occasion they "slip out." He can be critical of the therapist, who he says is paid to accept that. Ben partially contains his anger by making a mantra of his self-help group's expression "I'm a people pleaser." Although Ben does not appear to be emotionally involved with the group, during a holiday period, he successfully organized the group to meet at a restaurant during the time of the scheduled session.

Charles, a 40-year-old never married executive, reports major events without affect. He was referred for treatment by his girlfriend, who was frustrated by his lack of emotionality. The second son of a self-absorbed, demanding mother, he was very compliant, whereas his older brother was rebellious. Charles had many obsessional traits, he is a dispassionate observer of personal events. He knowingly will report on the break-up of a relationship with a woman or a failure to be promoted in a bland, unemotional fashion. His awareness of these characteristics evokes feelings of alienation and of self-defect.

Cynthia, a divorcee in mid-life, was not present at the meeting to be described. She had entered the group wishing to learn about how own contributions to her recent demotion, which she said had been the result of her difficulties getting along with customers and co-workers. She saw herself as a victim and different from others in some unspecified way. In describing her job, Cynthia would become progressively enraged and see only others shortcomings and no justification for her humiliating demotion. Members' experienced frustration by her self-righteous obsessive recounting of work incidents and her anger if she was interrupted, or if others did not fully appreciate how much she had been mistreated.

The context for the session was Andrew's turmoil at work prior to the beginning of a school year. He recently had been asked to teach more elementary courses, which he felt as a blow to his self-esteem. He also experienced it as a threat to his future income in relation to promotion, merit increases, and tenure. He had raged during the prior session, verbalizing fantasies of smashing the departmental chairman's head.

In the meeting under review, Andrew entered a few moments late, and immediately testily inquired if Cynthia, one of the two absent members, would ever return. He was informed that she had called to say that she was ill and would not attend the session. Andrew recalled that Cynthia had been absent the previous week because her company president had expected her at a business dinner. The therapist observed that Andrew seemed angry when he asked about Cynthia. He replied that he was angry all day, and that his irritation was not directed at Cynthia. He continued that this is how he gets into trouble. If something upsets him, he becomes angry with everyone. He went on to describe himself, again, as an angry man.

Ben, enacting his role as people pleaser, wondered if Andrew was angry with him, because he believed that his questions of Andrew the previous week had been upsetting. With some effort, Ben cautiously acknowledged that his questions contained a barb because he had been annoyed with Andrew. Several members observed that Ben rarely acknowledged such feelings. They praised him for expressing his annoyance. Despite these kudos, Ben insisted that he did not wish to upset anyone, and he merely wanted to be liked. Andrew seemed to take all of this in, and assured Ben that he had not been offended.

The therapist then wondered if there was a similarity between Ben and Andrew in that they both were concerned about appearing too angry, and that showing their anger directly toward others within the group would result in feeling displeased with themselves. Returning to the manner in which Andrew had entered the meeting, he went on to suggest that perhaps there was something in Cynthia's absence that had angered Andrew, but he was fearful of alienating others if he became specific in his critique. The therapist asked Andrew to tell him if this was accurate, and if not to make corrections. Andrew replied that he missed Cynthia; they had many similarities, including Cynthia's difficulty with her anger, but he said there was more to it. They seemed to communicate in a manner he could not describe, but there was a kinship between them. Andrew continued that he was aware that he did not feel that way about the other missing woman, a senior executive who had little difficulty asserting herself.

During exploration of Andrew's differential response to the absent members, Charles inquired if Andrew was upset with him for recently having come late (Charles had explained previously that he would be late because he was filling in for a vacationing colleague). Andrew said he hadn't even noticed his lateness. Charles dismissed Andrew's comment, but following several members' questions Charles blandly acknowledged feeling hurt by Andrew's "blowing him off." In turn, Andrew seemed unable to understand that what he had said could have been injurious.

As the session continued, a woman addressed a prior experience in which Ben had complained to Andrew about unbuttoning his shirt and exposing his chest. Andrew responded that he had complied with Ben's request because it was reasonable, but he resented it. He was aware that he would ruminate about their interaction, ready to pounce on Ben at any opportunity. He continued that he had struggled for much of his life with the feelings that "I want what I want when I want it." Several others then acknowledged similar feelings.

The meeting ended with a discussion of a session in which Ben had come dressed in a costume in preparation to going to a party. The subsequent dialogue encouraged Ben to try to loosen up as he had on that evening. Ben responded that he wished he had not worn the costume and would not do it again. Andrew was smiling broadly during this segment of the meeting, and remarked that he was feeling more relaxed and comfortable, which seemed unique for him. He could not say what had happened that produced this emotional well being.

Commentary

This session illustrates some relationships among alter-ego and twin-ship transferences and anger and assertiveness. Andrew, who had suffered a significant "demotion" and narcissistic injury to which he had responded with characteristic anger, appeared to experience Cynthia's absence as a similar injury. His partially muted anger both conveyed his feelings and preserved some contact with the other members. The more general disruption of group connectedness was signalled by Ben's question, in which he feared his own anger had been exposed. Although Ben was encouraged to express himself more forthrightly, he demurred.

Through linking Ben and Andrew and then interpreting Andrew's specific fears, the therapist began a process of restabilising members, which enabled Andrew to articulate more precisely his alter-ego needs in relation to Cynthia. Embedded in Andrew's interactions were feelings of shame that he required the relationship with Cynthia. Andrew's initial response is illustrative of Kohut's (1971) description of a "vertical split" in the psychic structure, in which a persons with a self-disorder experiences particular affects, but disavows their meaning. The feelings are conscious, but are not spoken until there is a sense of being understood and establishing a selfobject connection. Andrew's response that he did not miss the other woman may have arisen from disavowal of envy of her self-assertive abilities.

Charles efforts to link to Andrew, most likely containing a wish for mirroring, were rejected out of hand. This led to a sequence of injury and enactment of Charles' characteristic bland acceptance, at the expense of a distortion of his self. Presumably, Charles maintained his sense of belonging to the group (alter ego relationship) with his response.

The members' efforts to modify a subgroup response of withdrawal (Ben, then Charles) served to encourage Andrew to articulate his archaic self needs ("I want what I want ..."). The discussion appeared to open a path for Andrew to feel that he belonged as others joined him (an alter-ego transference to the group-as-a-whole).

The final segment suggests that this increase in members' experience of the group as self-accepting led to expansion in which play, the form of the Halloween costume, could be explored. Koseff (1990) suggests "play is an essential precondition for true psychotherapeutic change in the group" (pp. 89–90). Perhaps it was the potential for play that had evoked the sense of comfort in Andrew.

Discussion

The dynamics of Andrew's change could be formulated in models other than that of self psychology. No single available theory enables us to account for all of the nuances and meanings embedded in the complex interactions taking place in an active and interactive therapy group. Clinicians need to have a substantial fund of knowledge of group development and group dynamics, such as developmental stages, boundaries, norms, culture, scapegoating, and emotional contagion. Self psychological theory assists in understandings aspects of the treatment that have not been illuminated satisfactorily with other theories.

Most group theory of change emphasizes the importance of the group recreating a microcosm of an individual's interpersonal and intrapsychic world. The potential for change is mobilized by patients' increasing awareness of the meaning of the here-and-now interaction in their disturbed life relationships (Gabbard, 1982; Yalom, 1985). Resistances to engaging in in-group interactions are a result of prior dysphoric or traumatic experiences and subsequent personality configurations that minimize the potential for further injury and still provide for some gratification.

A self psychological perspective focuses on each person's experience of the interactions among the members, their relationship with the therapist, their connection to the group-as-a-whole, and the effects of these experiences on the self. In the latency period, acquisition of a chum signals a process in which a child is concerned with a same sex friend's well-being, without concern for what he/she will get in return (Sullivan, 1953). Compromises are made enabling others to achieve their aims or to fulfil their own ambitions. The recipient is not expected to make a pay back. Patients seeking alter-ego transferences have not achieved this developmental level. Others are experienced primarily as fulfilling missing functions. If the selfobject fails, the injured person may react angrily or at a deeper level with hate and destructive wishes. Andrew's early experiences were punctuated by erratic outbursts from his depressive mother, who clearly wished for Andrew to fulfil some of her own frustrated ambitions. As a concentration camp survivor, she would frequently tell Andrew that he was incapable of knowing her experiences, and he would never have survived in a camp. He felt he was an emotional failure. Andrew compensated by focusing on intellectual pursuits that were aided by his intrinsic abilities. He felt appreciated only for his academic achievements. Thus in the group, when his intellectual ramblings were interrupted and not appreciated, he would become angry. Andrew had a glimmer of understanding that he would become tangential, but his need for mirroring in the sector of his intellectual achievements outweighed his "social sensitivity."

I believe, however, that in addition to needs for mirroring his grandiosity, the sector of Andrew's need for alter-ego selfobjects became activated in the group. Another of Andrew's developmental deficits involved his feeling that he was separated from the human condition because he could not make emotional contact with others. He had developed an alter-ego transference to Cynthia, and her absence and presumed termination had functioned as a narcissistic injury. I would speculate that the emergence of an alter-ego transference reflects a regression to a level that did not reach the depths of Andrew's self disturbance. Rather, as Kohut (1984) wrote, "the pivotal selfobject transference that ultimately established itself will frequently be organized around the *less* (emphasis in original) traumatic aspect of the self-object milieu of childhood, or as we can often put it, around the less traumatic of the two selfobject parents" (p. 206). Additional sectors of the self remain vulnerable, but they may be compensated by his experience of belonging, of not feeling different. The eventual outcome of the treatment is not possible to predict, but appreciation of the alter-ego relationship increased Andrew's engagement in the therapeutic dialogue and provided a temporary strengthening of the self.

The three men in this illustration suffered with a chronic sense of being different and from the lack of feeling connected. In part this arose from their difficulty in identifying affects and in part believing that anger was unmanageable, for themselves and for others. They longed for an experience of belonging and feeling like others. Ornstein and Ornstein (1993) state, "self psychology, in fact, assumes a primary need for feeling connected" (p. 108). Ben's obsessive expression, "I am a people pleaser," was his way of maintaining contact rather than merely serve as a resistance. Organizing an extra-group meeting supports that contention. For both Ben and Charles, their observations that others could more freely express themselves was likely to increase a sense of shame and be experienced as a narcissistic injury. Kohut (1984) observes, "A deficit in the realm of our mental functions, however, is experienced as a loss of self ... . They [analysands] are enraged about the sudden exposure of their lack of competence in their own mind" (p. 3838).

Clinicians working with self-disturbed and angry patients have an arduous task of maintaining their therapeutic balance. They are buffeted with feelings of not counting or existing merely to fulfil a function. Self-disturbed patients abuse others in order to maintain their own equilibrium. It is far from simple for clinicians to keep their balance in the presence of such "insensitivity." Andrew most likely displaced his anger from Cynthia to Charles. Therapists' temporarily identify with the members (which is a pathway to empathy), and they experience the injury of the traumatized other. Stepping back from this shared injury may be difficult in the context of emotional contagion that frequently suffuses a group in the presence of denigrating interactions (Stone, 1990). Therapists empathic capacities are sorely tested in such situation.

Recognition of the significance of alter-ego transferences and the process of injury and repair (in the illustration of Andrew via displaced retaliation) may enable clinicians to more accurately understand the inner states of the members in relation to the group. Transactions that may be seen as resistance, more importantly may be the individual's communication of his/her wish for a human connection.

In the realm of alter-ego relationships, patients will test to determine if there are similarities, and if they can feel that the group will become a safe place where they may expose their vulnerabilities. The feeing of similarity with one person and then with larger subgroups may be a pathway some pursue in joining a group. Detrick (1986) proposes that "the motivational core of the group is the experience of sameness among the group members as a function of the group process as it is directed by the ambition or ideals of the leader" (p. 301). He further states "that the process of change in group psychotherapy, is the acquisition of skills via transmuting internalization in the context of optimal gratification" (p. 302). These evocative theoretical ideas require further exploration. They represent a reformulation of some fundamental ways of thinking about work in groups that is beyond the scope of this article.

Summary

When working with narcissistically vulnerable and angry patients in group psychotherapy one must take into account the entire treatment context. Interaction takes place among the identified patient, the other members, the therapist, and the image of the group-as-a-whole. In members' counter-reactions to the difficult person, group-destructive forces frequently are stimulated. The offending individual may flee, or the group may reach an impasse in which little growth occurs.

In this communication, I have focused on alter-ego relationships and transferences as a way of understanding aspects of group formation and destruction. Angry patients may have intense wishes to be like others and to feel part of the human condition. They suffer from feeling alone. Disruption of an alter-ego relationship may result in rage. A self-psychological perspective in concert with knowledge of group dynamics enables the clinician to formulate ways of intervening in problematic group interactions. The therapist's capacity to attend to the vulnerabilities of the self of all persons involved in the group is often severely tested, particularly under circumstances of emotional contagion. Elucidation of twinship and alter-ego transferences may help stabilize difficult patients and enable them to restart their psychological growth.

CHAPTER EIGHT

Self Psychology and the Higher Mental Functioning hypothesis: Complementary theories

Walter N. Stone

Abstract: Self Psychology and the Higher Mental Functioning hypothesis emphasize positive aspects of patients' efforts to stabilize defective (unstable) functioning and begin growth. The theories overlap and their application increases clinical awareness of transactions with the treatment setting. Clinical examples are presented from psychotherapy groups that illustrate applications, advantages and problems of the two theoretical approaches.

Key words: Empathy, injury, Higher Mental Functioning Hypothesis, Self Psychology, testing.

The theoretical basis informing clinical work has slowly evolved to place increasing emphasis upon the contributions of the therapist to the treatment process. Formulations that focused on understanding and interpreting transferences, as arising primarily from the patient, have been modified to examine with greater specificity the impact of the therapist in the treatment encounter.

In this communication, I discuss two major modifications of traditional psychodynamic theory that have influenced clinical practice and have substantial relevance to group psychotherapy: the Higher Mental Functioning Hypothesis (HMFH) (Weiss and Sampson et al., 1986; Weiss, 1993) and Self Psychology (Kohut, 1971, 1977, 1984). The HMFH is an object relations theory according to which, in the therapeutic encounter, patients actively attempt (albeit primarily unconsciously) to alter pathogenic beliefs. In this theory patients have plans, which they "test" in order to determine if beliefs that primarily arose in childhood will be sustained or refuted in the contemporary interaction with the therapist. If the test is passed, the patient no longer finds it necessary to retain archaic beliefs and modifies previously imposed self-preservative behaviours. Similarly, Self Psychology proposes that patients search for a therapeutic experience that will provide a remedy for a previously deficient selfobject experience, thereby enabling the individual to stabilize up to that point an unstable defective Self and restart growth. An archaic selfobject is not experienced by the disordered patient as a separate person but as part of the self, which serves to fulfil, and incompletely developed structure.

Both theories stress the individuals' attempts to search through an "interpersonal" experience and change. Patients work to overcome their fears that they will be re-traumatized in the treatment situation as they have been in the past. The process of disconfirming earlier available selfobjects fill developmental deficits and stabilize the self, which experiences greater cohesion and may resume pursuit of its goals and ideals.

In this report, I selectively review the theory of change as proposed by the two theoretical approaches in dyadic and group psychotherapy. Clinical examples from psychotherapy groups illustrate applications of these theories.

Clinical theory

The HMF hypothesis, as proposed by Weiss and Sampson et al. (1986) posits that:

> ... a person is able unconsciously to exert some control over his behaviour, that he regulates it unconsciously in accordance with thoughts, beliefs, and assessments of current reality, and that he

attempts, by his regulation of behaviour to avoid putting himself in dangerous situations (p. 5).

In therapeutic encounters, patients undertake tests (unconsciously) as part of a plan to determine if they will be injured by their therapists. Through the plan, the patient attempts to determine if pathogenic beliefs, acquired in childhood, should be sustained. Testing may be expressed in different forms, but primary modes are transferring and turning passive into active. In the former, the test is assumed to be a repetition of childhood experiences; the hope is that the therapist will not traumatize the patient as had occurred in the past. In turning passive into active, the patient has identified with the parent and tests to determine if there are alternative ways of response to the ones previously adopted. Patient behaviours in the form of testing are often disturbing and confusing to the clinician (Weiss, 1993).

Some patients' pathogenic beliefs are possible to discern by careful diagnosis; others unfold in the treatment process. Clinicians often fail to understand the nature of the testing until the test has been passed or failed. Passing the test (pro plan) will result in the patient's capacity to pursue goals, which were previously blocked. Tests may be passed without conscious awareness on the clinician's part. Interpretation may be used to help the patient feel safe, see him- or herself more sympathetically, or become more conscious of pathogenic beliefs and goals. The patient then tends to work to overcome his or her character restrictions (Weiss, 1993).

In group psychotherapy members are concerned with establishing an atmosphere of safety by ascertaining if the therapist and members respond aversively to their behaviours, as had been their experience in prior social relationships (Gustafson and Cooper, 1978). Patients in groups in which therapists emphasize group process develop

> ... a particular kind of unconscious collaboration in which individuals' planning dovetails so as to dramatize a special theme in the here and now vis-à-vis the therapist (Cooper and Gustafson, 1979, p. 971).

In further elaboration of applications of HMFH, Gustafson and Cooper (1981) explore the formation of subgroups, which exhibit plans that require contradictory responses from the therapist. In these complex situations the therapist is likely to intervene in a manner that is "anti-developmental" to some members (the subgroup). Those whose tests fail may revert to "minimal forms of cooperation." By implication, individuals in the failed-test subgroup will once again proceed with plans to assess the degree of safety in the situation and to disconfirm pathogenic beliefs.

The Psychology of the Self articulates a theory of change based on the thwarted need to grow (Ornstein, 1974). In the therapeutic encounter the self-disordered patients seek to establish a selfobject transference that will provide the necessary stability to a damaged and developmentally arrested self. Patients establish mirroring, idealizing or alter-ego transferences after overcoming resistances arising from fears that they will be re-traumatized in their treatment.

Inevitably, empathic failures occur, leading to rupture in the transference. Patients respond with anxiety that may manifest as mild dysphoria or as fragmentation states. Symptoms (anger, withdrawal, enactments and so on) are understood as the self's restitutive response.

Therapists work to contact patients' inner experience empathically, to understand and then translate the sequence of injury and of restitutive response (interpretation). This sequence enables patients to feel understood and potentially to regain their inner equilibrium. With repeated variations on the sequence of injury, repair and therapeutic understanding, patients may gradually achieve greater sense of inner stability and become less vulnerable to disruption of emotions following narcissistic injury. In the therapeutic situation, patients may experience a greater sense of well-being when they have been empathically understood, and they may spontaneously attempt new behaviours or take risks. This process has experiential similarity to validation of plans as formulated in the HMFH.

In group psychotherapy, clinicians are faced with the formidable task of empathizing with each person in his or her individual interactions and with each person's experience of the group-as-a-whole. Indeed, it is seldom possible to appreciate simultaneously all the members' inner worlds. Group-as-a-whole interpretations inevitably only approximate members' experiences in the here-and-now and as a result such interpretations may injure one or more members. Depending upon the vulnerability and the self-stabilizing responses of the "approximately" understood individuals, the therapist can address the process of injury and repair.

In emotionally interactive groups, patients frequently injure one another. Following narcissistic wounds, patient behaviours including retaliation, rage, withdrawal, somatization or depreciation of treatment, create opportunities for clinicians to assess members' capacities to self-soothe or to empathize with one another. Transactions of patients empathically in tune and serving selfobject needs of one another are a particular advantage of group treatment and coincide with the widely recognized therapeutic factor of altruistic behaviour (Yalom, 1985).

The difficulty that patients and therapists alike experience in providing stabilizing selfobject functions should not be underestimated. Emotional contagion is a powerful dynamic, and members and therapists can become enmeshed in intense feeling states and provoke injury through projection and scapegoating defenses that are often difficult to address (Scheidlinger, 1982). Among the therapist's tasks are: to understand the formation of transferences, become familiar with members' characteristic defenses against engagement and their response to narcissistic injury (arising particularly but not exclusively from in-group interactions) and provide empathic interpretations in a manner intended to enhance patient-therapist collaboration and help repair the disordered self.

Considerable overlap exists between the two theories. They may be understood as complementary, each illuminate different aspects of the unfolding processes in group psychotherapy. Both emphasize the difficulty in addressing conflicts among subgroups and problems associated with empathizing with all members. Since differences among members' needs to test or for empathic responses are built into the very fabric of groups, their therapeutic management becomes of paramount significance. The following clinical examples illustrate the application of HMFH and self psychological perspectives on the treatment process.

First example

Mike, a graduate student with an extensive history of social isolation, came from a well-to-do family in which the dinner table was described as World War III. The parents would engage in strident arguing, while Mike and his sisters cowered, hoping the meal would end quickly. Eventually the parents divorced, and although he lived in another city, Mike struggled to free himself of his archaic emotional ties to his parents. Mike's first serious romantic involvement ended when his girlfriend was tragically killed in a car accident several year previously. Mike had incompletely mourned her loss and his continuing emotional bond with her (similar to the one with his family for which he had received extensive treatment during childhood and adolescence) had restricted efforts to pursue new relationships.

Mike struggled emotionally to join the group. He discussed his family at length and would respond to others' stories with associations to his parents or sister, often obscuring the original in-group stimulus. Members' comments about their relationships would stimulate Mike to retell incidents with his deceased girlfriend. He seemed very limited in his capacity to respond directly to interaction with the group.

In a meeting following a visit home, Mike monopolized a lengthy portion of the session in describing how Easter dinner had been dominated by his tyrannical grandmother, despite his sister's and his own efforts to terminate the meal. Mike introduced his lengthy commentary by observing that he and his sisters had "gotten along exceptionally well," which was mutually very satisfying. One member noted that he was "talking around the edges" and asked if Mike could say what he was feeling. Others asked clarifying questions, which remained unanswered, and as a result they soon began to exhibit considerable uneasiness, with fidgeting and facial grimacing.

The therapist then wondered if Mike was illustrating for the group what it was like to be a member of his family, and that he was trying to convey his experience by acting like his grandmother (turning passive into active).

In the subsequent discussion Mike seemed confused, and commented that he did not understand what was being said. He continued to tell disorganized stories about his grandmother's peculiar behaviour. The members, however, understood their own experience and associated to strife and arguing within their own families which had made them uncomfortable. They acknowledged that they turned Mike off during his rambling and had feared becoming too angry with him.

At the beginning of the following session Mike announced that he was stopping treatment. He felt that he no longer belonged in the group and added that members talked as if they were on another planet. Despite others' encouragement to remain, Mike, although wavering, persisted in planning to leave. One woman, restating the previous week's interpretation suggest that Mike, by talking so much and not listening, had been behaving like his grandmother, to which Mike replied that his father had sometimes said the same thing.

The therapist alerted to the presence of a narcissistic injury by Mike's plan to terminate, then commented that Mike was saying that he was unable to remain in a group where he would not be understood or could not understand others. He suggested that the Mike had been injured by the therapist's comments, since it seemed that Mike was trying to explain himself by telling about his family experiences, hoping that he would be understood. He continued that by focusing on the painful meal the interpretation had made Mike feel as though he was in his family, rather than recognizing the positive aspects of Mike's trip home. Mike responded that no one had seen that he had made meaningful contact with his sisters, which he experienced as a significant accomplishment. A woman then said she now appreciated Mike's difficulty in separating from his abusive family, as she was struggling with a similar problem herself. In this role, she paired with Mike and possibly served as a group spokesperson. Mike then retracted his decision to leave.

Several weeks later, Mike, feeling more secure but still anxious, revealed his shame-laden adolescent incestuous contact with his sisters and stepmother. This revelation signalled his further integration into membership.

This example illustrates the therapist's tasks of accurately recognizing and interpreting a patient's plan, which may include several tests. Transferring and turning passive into active may coexist (Weiss, 1993). The prominent negative affects (annoyance, anger, boredom and resignation) aroused by Mike in the therapist and the members suggests a passive-to-active test (Weiss, 1993: 105). The therapist's initial response failed the test and was empathically out of tune with Mike. The interpretation appeared to re-enact Mike's noxious family experience (the interpretation was experienced as a criticism), and as a consequence he threatened to terminate. The plan may also be formulated as a transference enactment. Mike cautiously communicated his pleasure in forming alliances with his sisters (likely a twinship transference in which similar skills in managing family stress were exchanged) and he was likely hoping that these accomplishments would be mirrored by the therapist and fellow members. He also may have been searching for an idealizing transference in which he would merge with the idealized therapist and/or group. The therapist's initial comment was empathically out of tune and failed the tests. The therapist's second interpretation illuminates an aspect of the process of recovery from injury. The interpretation specifically recognized how the therapist had injured Mike (the positive accomplishment of strengthening his ties to his sisters had not been mirrored) and clarified Mike's wish to terminate as an understandable response to being misunderstood. The interpretation set in motion a process whereby the positive aspects of Mike's visit were enacted as a woman member paired with him.

A more complete formulation of Mike's plan could be framed like the sequence he described at home: "If I can establish a positive alliance (transference) with my siblings, then I can move on to address separating from my chaotic, abusive parents and resume pursuit of adult romantic relationships."

The initial interpretation of turning passive into active, however, was salient to the other members, since it was empathic with their position. They came to understand a different perspective on Mike's behaviour, which may have increased their ability to empathize with him. Thus, as in many group-as-a-whole interventions, a subgroup (in this instance, primarily Mike) was injured while others felt understood. The members' shift in emotional position, in turn, diminished emotions impacting upon the therapist who could then recognize the source of Mike's injury and interpret the process.

Second example

> In a group composed of seriously mentally ill patients, Bruce, a schizophrenic, had missed a series of three meetings following a discussion of another patient's efforts to date. In prior sessions Bruce had often seemed grandiose (if not delusional) in talking about his adolescent successes with women, marriage(s) and children. During several years of group treatment he had not indicated that he had talked socially with a woman, nor had he

ever provided any names of children that would enable members to believe that they existed.

Upon returning to the group Bruce said that he had recently developed headaches. The therapist attempted to engage him in an exploration of any emotional precipitant for these symptoms. This was met with a statement that there were no stresses, and doctors had prescribed Tylenol, which had not helped. Carl, a dependent man, said that he too had headaches, and only received medicine. Carl added that no doctor asked if he was under stress.

Bruce's associations then shifted from pains in his head to those in his knee. He described a knee injury that had occurred many years previously, when his leg had been placed in a cast. He enquired, "Why did the doctors do that?" The therapist replied that it seemed that this was a good idea to prevent further injury and the cast would allow the knee to heal. With that Bruce seemed satisfied and became silent. The members then proceeded to explore their in-group relationships at a level that had not previously taken place. Jim asked Joan if he had upset her the preceding week when they were leaving the clinic after the meeting. Jim said he had suddenly walked away from Joan when he had entered the parking lot. The subsequent discussion elaborated feelings among the four members about saying goodbye to one another and reached a personal depth seldom achieved in this group.

Bruce had suffered a narcissistic injury (shame) as he compared himself to another patient who was exploring the possibility of dating (Stone, 1992). His response had been to distance himself from the group. Upon his return, Bruce had tested his relationship with the therapist by engaging in a discussion of a medical problem, which is a frequent mode for chronically ill patients to determine their therapist's acceptance. The therapist's attempt to explore emotional bases for headaches did not pass Bruce's test. Another member paired emotionally with Bruce, but simultaneously distanced himself by communicating that he had not been asked if there were stresses associated with his headaches. Bruce then offered a clearer communication about what he needed in his association to his injured knee. The metaphor was understood and the empathic intervention using

Bruce's imagery (the physician was trying to be helpful) appeared to be stabilizing to an unbalanced, shamed Self. The therapist's efforts seemed to have broader impacts and may have stimulated an idealizing transference where others could temporarily consolidate fragmenting Selfs, and then proceed in a rare exploration of intimate relationships among the members.

Thus a test was passed as the clinician strengthened an idealizing transference. In this instance it was passed without translating the communication into the here-and-now of the group.

Third example

Carol had made considerable progress during her several years of group treatment. She had entered therapy because of sacrificing herself and her needs for those of others. In Carol's view he mother had been primarily interested in her siblings, and Carol had turned to her father for approval and recognition. She recounted many instances in which approval was achieved only by complying with her father's wishes, which often involved spending an entire weekend in pursuit of his avocation. In treatment, Carol had gradually become more self- assertive in pursuing her own goals. She had been able to utilize her considerable talents to reach an upper management position in her firm, and she had established a loving relationship that led to marriage.

The process of termination from her group, however, was particularly difficult. After hinting for several months that she was considering stopping, Carol announced in the middle of a session that the following week would be her final meeting. The group was startled. The therapist suggested that Carol give herself sufficient time to say goodbye and not stop abruptly. He suggested remaining for a number (unspecified) weeks to say goodbye. She agreed with the suggestion.

In the succeeding meetings Carol began by talking about missing others, but she gradually assumed the role of assistant therapist, a role in which she was of considerable help to others. The topic of her leaving was intermittently addressed, and Carol would tentatively mention a stopping date. However, as each date approached, she changed her mind saying she was in a void. During one session, she furiously denounced the therapist for keeping her in the group for his own purposes because she was helpful to others. The members were startled and argued to little avail that this did not seem to be what the therapist had said or how he had behaved.

The following week Carol again made a series of clarifying and interpretative comments to others. The process included a heated discussion of a member's masochistic behaviour vis-à-vis his wife and supervisor. In this context, the therapist suggested that Carol, in the process of saying goodbye, was trying to be remembers in a most positive light, by behaving in a helpful manner as she had earlier in her life. He felt she was prepared to leave but finding it difficult to say goodbye. She was surprised at this interpretation and said that she was uncertain what she had been doing. As the other members talked about their own propensities to sacrifice themselves, Carol announced that she would be terminating after three more sessions.

Regression in the process of termination is well described in the group literature (Kauff, 1977; Rutan and Stone, 1993). Carol initially wished to foreshorten the goodbye process to essentially one meeting. Did her initial announcement represent a test in which she way trying to say that she was unimportant and she would not be missed? Was it an enactment of how she had previously managed separations? There were prior data that she would quickly replace an absent object in the face of loss, and only later realize that she had not addressed feelings of loss. A salient possibility was that the announcement represented a test to determine if the therapist would respect her own wishes to separate or use Carol for his own needs, which would represent an enactment of her weekend experiences with father. The tests were not initially fully understood, in part because they contained contradictory elements. The therapist passed one test by inviting her to remain. However, the invitation was anti-plan in that it was interpreted as an expression of the therapist's needs. In response, Carol repeated old patterns of being the therapist's (father's) helper. Carol's rage at the therapist for using her alerted him to the meaning of the assistant-therapist behaviour, and the repetitious pattern and meaning of the behaviour could be interpreted. The therapist reinforced his interpretation by expression his opinion that she was prepared to terminate. This freed Carol to make the decision to set a date to terminate without foreshortening her final goodbye.

From the perspective of the psychology of the Self, the termination process represented a mirroring transference in which Carol hoped that the therapist and group would appreciate the growth she had made and the decision to terminate. The more archaic transference elements, stimulated by the prospect of a separation, were evidence in the precipitous nature of Carol's announcement. The therapist's recommendation to stay was experienced as a replay of he father's behaviour, to which Carol resurrect old solutions. Her overall, albeit incomplete, improvement was signalled by her freedom to rage which alerted the therapist to the situation.

The confluence of a mirroring transference and a plan to terminate are illustrated in this example. Comprehending Carol's behaviour from the two perspectives broadened understanding of the clinical picture and assisted in her achieving a more meaningful termination.

Discussion

One goal of theory is to organize clinical data into a manageable framework that will both serve to understand the patient and act as a guideline on how to be helpful. The clinical theories of Higher Mental Functioning and Self Psychology posit that patients are actively seeking ways to resolve their internal problems and proceed in their development. The theories do not emphasize the resolution of conflict; rather they focus on patients' efforts to overcome developmental arrests. In this process, patients use the therapist (and others) in a manner that will promote growth and change.

The theory underlying the two clinical perspectives differs with regard to their view of the growth-promoting "object." In the paradigm of Self Psychology, the selfobject is experienced as an extension of the Self and not a separate person. The selfobject is necessary to fulfil developmental needs, and accurate assessment of those needs may enable the clinician to respond in concert with the patient's plan based on a broader theory. The HMF hypothesis focuses on the clinical experience and is not articulated as a more complete theory. The role of the object in not conceptualized in a developmental framework, but as a person who is to pass the test and/or teach the patient new ways of handling old conflicts. Guidelines for assessing successful fulfilment of a plan rest on the patient's response to the clinician's intervention. The examples are illustrative of an anti-plan response and/or an empathic failure, which was followed by an alternative plan and/or a self-stabilizing response that alerted the clinician to a more therapeutically useful intervention. In Example 1, Mike wished to be mirrored for his accomplishment with his sisters as well as having others understand his painful dinner table experience. The therapist's initial choice of response could be understood as an interpretative act (countertransference) to diminish his own discomfort in the role of an archaic selfobject. The threat to quit alerted the therapist to his having inflicted a narcissistic injury. In Example 2, Bruce had suffered a blow to his self-esteem as he compared himself to another during discussion of romantic relationships. Bruce's absence signalled his injury, and his restitutive response (primarily directed to the therapist as an initial point of re-entry) was the presentation of somatic symptoms. He wished for an idealized-merger selfobject. Bruce found a way to give the therapist a second chance when he failed the first test. In Example 3, Carol responded to separation anxiety by planning to flee therapy, and then determine more carefully if the selfobject (therapist) would mirror her therapeutic achievements (her talents) and not hold on to her for his own needs. Carol's inability to terminate and then her rage alerted the therapist to the meaning of this behaviour.

From the perspective of Self Psychology and the HMF hypothesis, the clinical process in the three examples signaled that initially a test had not been passed or an empathic failure had taken place. By carefully observing the confluence of a patient's (or group) response to failed test and/or narcissistic injury, the therapist can learn about efforts at finding new solution or erecting Self-protective barriers (defense mechanism) and find a more accurate response that would be in concert with the patient's plan.

Clinical theory of psychotherapy continues to expand to place greater emphasis on patients' strengths and positive contributions to their capacity to change and grow. Takahashi (1994), working within object relations theory, described successfully altering resistant/destructive transactions of a difficult patient by focusing on the positive contribution that the patient was making to the group process. He opines that "the very behaviour which the patient ostensibly uses to disrupt the group has an equally important function of uniting the group." By commenting on the positive aspects of the behaviour the therapist has simultaneously mirrored the patient's strengths and passed a test. The patient then experiences an increase in feelings of self-worth (Self-cohesion) and is able to traverse a therapeutic impasse. If this is a representative example, then some object relations theorists may be moving in a direction, similar to what has been described, by focusing on positive rather than defensive aspects of patients' behaviours.

The focus of this communication has been to illustrate the clinical utility of combining the Psychotherapy of the Self and the HMFH in working with psychotherapy groups. Both models provide clinicians with theoretical underpinning in following treatment processes and emphasize what patients are attempting to accomplish to overcome their personality constrictions or their developmental arrests. Attention to patients' interactive response, to therapist's or members' transactions, will provide information demonstrating their wish to overcome barriers to growth. By utilizing both formulations, clinicians can broaden their perspectives in their clinical work.

CHAPTER NINE

The role of the therapist's affect in the detection of empathic failures, misunderstandings and injury

Walter N. Stone

Abstract: Therapists cannot be expected to always understand their patients or the process of their group. Using evolving self psychology and theories of Intersubjectivity, this manuscript explores the affective responses of therapists as a valuable indication that such misunderstanding is occurring. Clinical vignettes will illustrate three specific reasons for therapist misunderstanding: over-adherence to theory, boundary crossing, and inexperience. Additional examples will illustrate how countertransference can disrupt treatment when the group therapist conveys material or affects outside his or her awareness.

Key words: Group psychotherapy, countertransference, therapist's affect; errors; misunderstanding; empathic failures.

Therapists often do not appreciate the potential for their interventions to adversely affect the therapeutic process. They fail to recognize that a well-meaning interpretation, observation, or question may be experienced by the patient as unempathic and hurtful. If a patient rejects an intervention, is it because the comment was experienced as ill timed, or touched an area of vulnerability requiring protection, or was it simply inaccurate? These certainly are knotty problems.

As therapists, we face the dual problem of accurately assessing what is happening for our patients and groups *and* of determining how best to use that information to help. We have to determine (1) if we have *understood* our patients and (2) if we have *responded* to our patients. These are separate questions representing problems in understanding and responding respectively. We may be accurate in our understanding, and then intervene in a fashion that disrupts the treatment. Attention to both aspects—understanding and responding—may enable us to determine more precisely the nature and the basis of the problem.

My central thesis is that clinicians should monitor their affective experiences to increase awareness of the possibility that an inadvertent therapeutic derailment has occurred. I am in agreement with Shapiro (1995) who reminds us to attend to the degree, quality, and direction of affect impacting upon clinician and patient alike.

The theory of therapy

Dynamic theories of psychotherapy have undergone considerable change in the past two decades. The focus has shifted from the therapist as an object of projection for the past experiences (a one-person psychology), to that of an interactive field in which each person significantly influences the other (a two-person psychology). According to Stolorow (1995), "The central metaphor of the new psychoanalytic paradigm is the larger relational system or field in which psychological phenomena crystallize and in which experience is continually and *mutually* (italics added) shaped" (p. 393). These interactive processes can be viewed as windows of varying clarity into the participant's internal psychic organization. Mindful that the ultimate focus is the patient, Schwaber (1995) asserts: "It is the delineation of the patient's experience of these interactions, with its concomitant resistant expressions, its defensive, fanciful, conscious and unconscious determinants that defines the analytic terrain— however different the perspective held by the analyst or by another observer and *however difficult it may be to grant that our perspective is only that, our own*" (emphasis in the original; p. 558).

Heeding this caveat, psychotherapy remains a setting in which we can use knowledge of *our own* internal functioning, manner of interacting, triggers to affective stimuli, and defensive responses for the purpose of understanding the patient. This shift has helped re-focus clinicians' need to do more than listen to the patient; they need to listen to their own "voice," which includes not only the words that are spoken but the tone and affect with which they are said. Wolf (1993) has stated, "The *verbal* content is only a part, and often a relatively insignificant part of the total effect of an interpretation" (p. 675). The potential for a therapist to unknowingly communicate his or her affects is considerable, and it is understandable, as well as expectable, that patients will perceive their clinician's emotions as the central message. Under these circumstances, the emotional message may or may not be concordant with the verbal content, and in the latter circumstance a disruption in the ongoing relational process may occur.

For group therapists this focus on the therapeutic process, particularly as articulated in self psychology, serves as a crucial refinement in the still incomplete task of integrating group and individual perspectives. The lengthy tradition of applying general system theory to groups has attuned therapist to the impact of the recursive influence of the intrapsychic, interpersonal, subgroup, group-as-a-whole, and the external environment (Durkin, 1981). Self psychology, with its pivotal concepts of empathy, self, selfobject and narcissistic injury, provides a more detailed framework in which group clinicians can organize their thinking about the treatment process (Stone, 1992). In this paradigm, therapists are more than transference objects. They are significantly influenced by, and in turn influence, patients' associations and responses (Harwood, 1998).

The three foci, the experience of the self, of the self in relation to others, and of the larger treatment and social systems, have become the clinician's foundation for listening and understanding. Inevitably our limitations lead to misunderstandings of patients' experiences. A therapist's level of experience or the intensity and breadth of his or her countertransference are not the sole sources of these limitations. They may arise from patients who provide insufficient data, or from our incomplete theory of group or individual dynamics, or from the therapeutic process.

The role of theory

Whether they articulate them or not, therapists often use implicit theories of efficacy that differ significantly from their public ones (Michels, 1999). Clinicians can not do their work effectively without having a notion of how they intend to be helpful. Interventions, or even decisions to remain silent, are made with a direction, if not a specific goal in mind (Kennard, 1993). A precise pre-determined response is *not* expected. Rather clinicians use their personal theories and hope that the patient will respond in what is deemed to be a therapeutically useful manner.

Clinicians recognize that no single theory adequately explains all of their therapeutic encounters, and several different perspectives may be employed in understanding a clinical transaction (Pine, 1985). Rubovits-Seitz (1998) contends that multiple perspectives are needed to "justify" (determine the effectiveness) of our interventions. Increasing flexibility, however, has not diminished the need for the clinician to remain alert to the possibility that an intervention might be experienced negatively, as disruptive or disorganizing. "Negative responses are not limited to patients' conscious verbalizations, they include associations and non-verbal behaviours. At stake here is not what the therapist intended, but what the patient experienced." As Bacal (1995) asserts, "the patient's theory about himself or herself will usually be the final arbiter of what is psychologically valid for him or for her, and offers some safeguard against the rigidification of theory and the mistreatment of the patient" (p. 354).

Theory, however can be limiting. It may prevent us from hearing or observing information that does not readily fit within our framework. Moreover, we may act in particular ways that are compatible with how therapists of our particular theoretical persuasion behave, or direct our questions or interpretations in the directions that will confirm our theory (Friedman, 1988). This sort of activity may serve to help the clinician contain anxieties about not understanding or not knowing, and may serve to maintain therapist self esteem, but it can also be constricting and limiting. Michels (1999) likens theory to a transitional object, and adds, "Old theories, like old teddy bears, are not less beloved because they are torn or perhaps a little smelly" (p. 197).

Therapist affect

An important element in Kohut's development of the psychology of the self was his recognition of his own affective state in conducting analysis with individuals who he later diagnosed as having narcissistic personality disorder. His experience and affect was not of an interacting participant in the analytic process, but rather, as Kohut (1971) conceptualized the exchange, that of a function—fulfilling certain developmental needs for the analysand. From these experiences he formulated the concept of the selfobject.

A clinician's emotional responses to the patient may be thought of as arising from the therapist, the relationship between therapist and patient, or from the patient (Rutan & Stone, 1993). Affective reactions evoked in the therapist by the patient can be further described as parallel or reciprocal. Parallel responses are those that are concordant with those expressed by the patient; reciprocal responses are those induced by the patient such as annoyance or irritation in response to a particular behaviour. A focus of considerable theoretical and clinical interest as a source of information about patients has been that of emotions induced in the clinician by projective identification, which involves both intrapsychic and interpersonal components (Horwtiz, 1983; Goldstein, 1991).

Group clinicians have long been attuned to additional sources for their emotional responses. Events external to the treatment setting powerfully influence therapist and patient alike. Greater attention is being paid to the impact of social and cultural values, both conscious and unconscious, upon all present in the therapeutic encounter. These forces may not be perceived, acknowledged or seen as problematic (Hopper, 1996). Groups in inpatient settings are often strongly influenced by tensions and pressures in the unit or hospital setting (Kibel, 1985). In mental health clinics managed care and government regulations require alterations in confidentiality and time consuming paperwork for patient and therapist alike. Illustrative of this latter situation is a state mental health board requirement that every 90 days therapists must collaborate with their patients to review and outline specific steps to achieve treatment goals. Patient and clinician must jointly sign these documents. Rarely are these interactions examined in the clinical setting: they are somehow relegated to status of non-event. This is, in effect, a denial.

Role of the therapist's affect

The group psychotherapy setting introduces additional pressures that have a powerful impact upon clinicians. The pressure to conform and not buck the affect or "ideas" that are at the forefront of a meeting represent one such experience. The impact of emotional contagion also sweeps the therapist along, and clinical judgement may be suspended. Yalom (1966) described such responses in neophyte clinicians, who found themselves swept along by group-wide emotions. He illustrated this process by describing a beginning therapist who was so deeply influenced by the thrust of an excited group that he encouraged "one of his young male married patients to act out sexually by cruising some bars for a quick pickup" (p. 52). In these situations, when reviewed in supervision, their own intense feelings evoked in the group often startle clinicians. Experience is not a preventative from intense feelings evoked in the group, and clinicians will find themselves amused, laughing, pleased, tearful annoyed, angry or envious at various times during the course of a group treatment. Indeed it would be the unfeeling therapist who was non-responsive to the flow of affect, and such a clinician would be unable to avail him or herself to essential data generated by the members.

The clinical examples will illustrate the function of therapists' affect in the detection of derailments and misunderstandings. The initial two brief examples will focus on the role of clinical theory and events in a clinician's life in interaction with group events that evoked the therapist affects, and signalled that something was amiss. The third example will focus on a therapist's affect of surprise following a sudden shift in group topics. The feeling of surprise provided a segue into helping the therapist understand how he had been out of tune with the group. Finally, I will describe two clinical situations in which the clinician had an awareness of his affects and was unable to contain the feelings, which led to interventions that were traumatic to an individual and the group. In the context of the latter two illustrations, I will make some suggestions about how to address these countertransference enactments and empathic failures.

Illustrations

As suggested above, one impediment to recognizing our own impact upon the treatment process is our tendency to behave in ways that confirm our theory. A brief example will illustrate the point.

Example 1

An experienced therapist leading her group of four women and two men was puzzled by what to do when one of the men terminated. The remaining man began to talk about stopping and needing an all male group. Although the therapist did not wish for him to stop, she had no foreseeable replacement for the departed man, and she worried about the impact of having only one man left in the group. In this circumstance, the therapist was tending toward agreeing with his stopping, but she was uncomfortable with her position. She heard the women in the group attempting to empathize with the man, link the singleton experience to his dynamic issues, and encourage him to remain in the group. The therapist was able to identify some of her discomfort in relation to group dynamic theory that suggested that a singleton would be a potential target for stereotyping and scapegoating. She was loath to expose him to those processes. Thus her subjective world was influenced by adherence to theory, which altered her capacity to listen to members' efforts to work in the changed treatment situation. The therapist's countertransference concern about harming the patient had interfered temporarily with her appreciation of his strengths and the members' interest in continuing their work together.

Example 2

Sometimes events in the personal life of the therapist can lead to errors. A clinician whose spouse had recently unexpectedly died, a fact, which was known to the group, left the meeting to answer a phone call which she knew to be from her child. Feeling uncomfortable about this action, she informed the group that she knew it was her daughter who was calling. She was uncomfortable with having left and having revealed the reason as she perceived it as a deviation from acceptable standards. When reviewing the session in a consultation, she spontaneously "heard" the members' metaphorical responses to her husband's death and its impact on both her and the members. She was able to appreciate that answering the call was necessary under the circumstances, but her feelings about having "acted" had dampened her ability to listen for what she knew to be the continuing responses to her husband's death.

In these illustrations, the therapists' capacity to be introspective and to remain in empathic attunement with the complex interactions taking place in the group was impaired: in the first instance by adherence to theory, and in the second by feelings stirred by accommodations from her typical practices in response to the major tragedy in her life. However, both clinicians were sufficiently experienced and in tune with their affective states to know that something was amiss. Such awareness is a crucial initial step in self-supervision.

Another potential source of error arises when therapists become engrossed with the content of patients' associations, and thereby fail to hear the communication embedded in the ongoing treatment process.

Example 3

A group led by an inexperienced male psychiatric resident had been struggling with containing an aggressive, monopolizing woman. During one session when the three women members were absent and only the men were present, the topics under discussion included discomfort in large family gatherings, a positive interchange with a male relative, rejection by a woman relative and difficulties in dating. The therapist remained silent. Much to his surprise, in the latter part of the meeting the focus abruptly shifted to discussion of various somatic symptoms. He quickly became engaged as an expert in medical problems.

In the supervisory discussion the therapist indicated that he was pleased that members were actively talking with one another. However, he was puzzled by the change of topic to medical issues. I suggested that the change could be understood as the members attempt to verbally engage him, a project that succeeded. Recognizing this, the resident commented how relieved he had felt to not have the burden of trying to find ways of containing the monopolizing woman. He was then able to consider some of the meanings of the patients' stories in the earlier portion of the session and to appreciate that his silence contained conscious and unconscious self protective responses—he did not want to disturb a peaceful meeting. His point of entry to these new perspectives was his puzzlement.

An important task for supervisors is assisting clinicians in becoming curious about their subjective experiences as a signal alerting them to the potential for having lost contact with the group process. In the illustrations, these clinicians experienced a variety of feelings—including relief, pleasure and surprise. The consultations focused on helping the therapists become curious about their feelings, not only to help them understand the patients, as in the model of projective identification, but as a signal that they had misunderstood the individuals or the group. However, even when the therapist is aware of feeling uneasy or anxious, he or she may not be able to contain the affects.

Example 4

An example occurred several years ago as I was preparing to take a sabbatical and informed my groups that I would be interrupting treatment for several months. I was imagining all sorts of negative responses to my announcement. Patients would be suffused with rage over abandonment or from envy. Members would quit even before I left, they would request a substitute therapist whom they would like better, or the group would simply fall apart, and I would be left with only fragments when I returned. I understood this fantasy as my own, and I used it to the best of my ability to prepare myself. Nevertheless, I was ill prepared for the initial response to announcing I was taking a sabbatical and would be out of the country for three months. A member asked if I had chosen to take the sabbatical or was I asked to take it? Not hearing the affect in the question, I responded quite concretely, that, "Of course I made the choice." She replied, "That was arrogant." I was confused and off balance. I hoped that I could gain perspective by having her repeat what I had said. As she started to repeat my words, I became acutely aware of her slightly sarcastic tone as a reflection of my similar feeling. I responded that she was right, and I was sorry for my response. The members were then able to go on and process their multi-level responses to my forthcoming absence.

Being confronted directly with an error may bewilder or disorganize the clinician. This is particularly so when the error is not recognized as such. The therapist's narcissistic injury (in this example the obvious implication of being "fired"), often experienced as anxiety or shame, is usually apparent to all. Under these circumstances, asking the member to repeat what she had heard provides the therapist with the time and space to regain his or her balance. I believe that the clinician should give overt recognition to the error, and should simultaneously make an effort to continue helping members explore their inner responses to all aspects of the interactions. This process often brings to the surface many differing transferences, and if members have not been too injured, the ensuing discussion can be of considerable therapeutic benefit.

The following example illustrates the value of maintaining an awareness of one's affective state, beyond the words, when making an intervention. In this is illustration I failed to appreciate my paraverbal influence on group decision making.

Example 5

This long-term outpatient group had been somewhat destabilized in the preceding months by terminations and additions of new members. More was to come. As I looked at my calendar, I realized due to a combination of holidays, vacations and other responsibilities affecting the specific meeting day, that I would soon be into a three month period when I would be unable to meet with the group six times, which amounted to almost 50% of the scheduled sessions. I addressed this problem with the group and suggested two possible responses: first, to meet on the same day and accept the interruptions, or second, to move the meeting to an alternate day, which would mean that only two sessions need be cancelled. Emotionally, I was aware that I would much prefer the latter solution, but I had thought I presented the options neutrally. Within less than ten minutes, a very short time period, the members unanimously agreed to change the meeting day for the following three months. I was uneasy about the rapidity with which this major decision had been reached, particularly in the view of the unsettled nature of the group formation. At the time, I did not consider if my preference had been conveyed nonverbally.

In the ensuing discussion there were several references to conflict avoidance and ambivalence about change. Ms A referred to her resolve to avoid repetition of a recent distressing experience of intense conflict in her family. I suggested that this was a metaphor for the ready acceptance of the change in the meeting day. Ms A responded that she uses humour to deal with the family.

In the final session before the change, Ms A, countering a group norm of providing details for any absences, said she would not be present the following week because of a pre-existing appointment. Another member, a passive compliant person, added that he too would be away because he had business meetings in New York on that day. His specificity re-enforced Ms A's rebellious spokesperson role. Mr B continued, self-critically recounting his girl friend's breaking off their relationship and his failure to ask her for specific reasons. Ironically, Ms A, was the person who asked him about the details of their relationship. In this context, I commented that the discussion might also have something to do with how the presentation of the forthcoming absences differed in detail. I had hoped that pointing out the differences might lead to more direct expression of the anger with me for the disruption. Mr B said he would be uncomfortable hearing that comment if he was in Ms A's shoes. She responded that it didn't bother her. The responses were not encouraging, effectively suppressing further discussion for the time being.

The week Ms A returned, the session began with a member describing his ambivalence about proceeding with his divorce. Mr B spoke of his preoccupation with his former girl friend, and his persistence in trying to get her to tell why she had broken up with him. I heard both "stories" as possible allusions to Ms. A's absence the preceding week. Ms A irritably remarked, "How many ways can she tell you no!" At this Mr B asked Ms A where she had been the preceding week. Ms A, almost shouting, responded, **"It's none of your business!"**

I was startled by the intensity of her response. Not surprisingly, major conflict ensued. Mr B became critical of Ms A, and the more he pushed to have her reveal the reason for her absence, the more she reiterated that she would not tell. Mr B adamantly held to the position that he had a right to express his feelings, no matter what. Clearly, Mr B served as the group spokesperson for the injury and anger stimulated by Ms A's disdainful response. I was not immune to this process and although I "understood" the dynamics of Ms A's stance, I still felt angry with her. My efforts to explore with the group the meaning of these exchanges were not successful. Of little avail was my intervention that Ms A seemed to be an object of displaced anger because I also had not presented the detailed reasons for my request to change the meeting day, and yet my behaviour was never questioned.

Several months later, Ms A re-evoked the continuing incompletely resolved tension when she announced her intentions to miss a meeting and provided a specific reason for her planned absence. At the same time, she adamantly refused to provide a reason for her prior absence. The group was suffused with a growing sense of distrust and a lack of safety. There were several direct angry complaints that I was not doing my job to fix it. The anger faded, only to be followed by associations to conflict avoidance.

I wondered if the theme of avoidance was also taking place within the group. The moment I said what I did, I recognized that although the words may have sounded neutral, I was inviting the group to attack Ms A for being withholding. An extended silence was broken when Ms A said that her psychiatrist had recently prescribed medications because she had become increasingly anxious following a tumultuous family gathering. I head this as almost a direct reference to the group process and a please, "leave me along— I'm fragile." A pause followed, and Ms A told of a miserably failed episode in which she tried to reconcile differences with her mother and a sibling. Others echoes her frustration in their own families.

I then chose to directly address my role in this sequence. I said that my comment had been experienced by Ms A as critical, and that she had tried to tell us about her experience by referring to a similar situation in her family. I addressed each person's family conflict, bringing them back into the room, and then repeated that my comment had been particularly hurtful to Ms A.

One member then very gently asked Ms A what her reaction to my intervention had been. Initially Ms A said she didn't know, but later she spoke of others being disrespectful of me. I heard this as her way of indicating that I had been partially successful in helping her regain her balance. The others took up the family metaphor and began a process that continued for a matter of months in which they were able to own and explore more directly their fears of intense affects and their tendency to keep secrets.

This example illustrates the therapist's difficulty keeping track of his own affects and how they are contained or communicated. Certainly, my intervention questioning avoidance was a confrontation, arising from my countertransference. Nevertheless, I was able to hear the metaphorical meaning of Ms A's associations to medication change. As Livingston (1999) has noted regarding vulnerable moments, Ms A. was signalling her vulnerability in the moment of the meeting. Fortunately, I was able to hear it at the time, regain my balance, and address the error with salutary results. Only much later did I become aware that I had not been neutral in my presentation of the initial options, thereby creating a scenario that fostered either compliance or rebellion. I can only speculate that if I had been attuned to my contribution to the ongoing process, I might have been able to directly speak about it. Perhaps members, under the condition of greater specificity on my part, would have been more able to examine some additional aspects of their behaviour.

The more obvious countertransference enactment I promptly understood as well as the implications it had for the group. Having this awareness enabled me to develop reasonable hypothesis about the meaning of the ensuing associations. I believe that my acknowledging my awareness of how all present may have experienced my intervention to Ms A served to restabilize the group, making it a more reliable selfobject (holding environment) thereby enabling members to more productively examine the meaning for each of them of this complex episode.

Discussion and summary

In the classical model of psychotherapy, the therapist's empathic failures, mistakes and misunderstandings were basically categorized as those of faulty technique or due to countertransference. In this one-person model, in which under optimal circumstances the therapist was "neutral," the patient's attribution of feelings or motives to the therapist was primarily understood as transference. Countertransference was considered to be unconscious, and the problem of detecting when one was experiencing countertransference was problematic. Therapists used their dreams, parapraxes or boundary alterations as potential paths to recognizing countertransference enactments. Affects in the therapist were generally felt to be signals of an incomplete analysis. As a consequence, an entire generation of clinicians struggled to overcome inhibitions to using their emotional responses and fantasies to aid in understanding the treatment.

Modern approaches to the conduct of psychotherapy have begun greater integration of therapists' contributions to the therapeutic process, as particularly emphasized by the models of self psychology, Intersubjectivity, and relational therapies (Goldberg, 1998). These approaches suggest that clinicians utilize their affects in the service of understanding the therapeutic environment. Blum (1992) states: "The patient is always attempting to elicit particular affective responses from the analyst and reacting to the analyst's affective style and response" (p. 279). This perspective, although freeing clinicians to utilize their emotional responses, maintains the focus on understanding patients' communications with relative neglect of using them to inform the clinician of his or her misunderstanding or error.

In the conduct of group therapy, clinicians' affects will be aroused from multiple sources. Group theory is incomplete, and as such clinicians must suffer not knowing or not understanding. The impact of external events crosses boundaries and enters into the transactions. Emotions arising from group-as-a-whole pressures and contagion powerfully impact upon therapists. In addition affects from patients' particular pathological conditions are readily communicated directly or indirectly through others. In example number five, Ms A's emotional position was re-enforced by the member who provided a detailed explanation of his absence—one of the processes intrinsic to projective identification (Goldstein, 1991) and scapegoating.

Therapists must consider that their feelings may be a response to a feedback loop that can be stimulated by responses to their own interventions or their nonverbal communications. This approach recognizes the mutuality of influences, which may be recent or remote. If these latter possibilities are considered, then clinicians are in a much more powerful position to appropriately explore the meaning of what has transpired.

Three of the vignettes presented illustrated a variety of sources of feelings arising from adherence to theory, from external events that led to boundary crossings, and from inexperience. Two of the vignettes illustrated countertransference responses in which the therapist's anxiety and frustration let to "errors" in response.

In most instances, patients do not directly communicate that they have been misunderstood or injured, and it is primarily through the clinician's feelings of unease or discomfort that the problem can be detected. Supervision or consultation may be useful in helping therapists gain a more complete perspective on the sources of their emotions.

When patients are direct about a therapist's misunderstanding, the clinician may be caught off guard, narcissistically injured, or not know what has transpired. A request for someone to repeat what has been said may provide sufficient space for the therapist to regain his or her balance and thereby be in a position to address the error.

In this essay, I have drawn attention to what I believe is an important task for all of us as clinicians—to try to find additional ways of helping us recognize when we misunderstand or err in our therapeutic endeavour.

SECTION III

SEVERE DISORDERS

CHAPTER TEN

Technique in group psychotherapy of narcissistic and borderline patients

Walter N. Stone and James P. Gustafson

Advances in theory regarding narcissistic and borderline disorders have reawakened interest in the group treatment of patients in those diagnostic categories. Even though theoretical points of view vary, often to the point of polarization, for the group therapist the translation of theory into technique remains in a nascent stage.

The interplay between theory and technique is seldom made explicit, but therapists use their theoretical base to organize the diverse material presented in the group and then intervene in accordance with theoretical understanding. Nevertheless, theory can be constricting for therapist, since it may offer the security of the familiar and therapists may thereby avoid the complexity of exploring new possibilities for understanding patients. In addition, there is a risk that patients will conform their responses to the theories of the therapist. A useful theory would provide the group therapist with ways of organizing the material and his approaches to his patients while minimizing the constrictions.

Here, we specify our technical approaches that suggest that a particular sequence of therapeutic steps will be useful in many of those patients who are labeled borderline or patients with narcissistic character disorders (Kernberg, 1975a, 1976; Kohut, 1971, 1997; Masterson, 1976). At present, no therapeutic approach is useful for all patients, as Gedo (1977) noted. Yet, there is merit in being as precise as possible about the techniques that are used so that others can examine them, see where they are useful, and see where further modification or a newer theory may be necessary.

Our approach, using a developmental model of anxiety and object relations proposed by Gedo and Goldberg (1973), focuses on the establishment of a therapeutic alliance. Gedo and Goldberg state:

> After the establishment of a stable cognitive differentiation between the infant's self and his primary object, the danger of overstimulation is succeeded by that of separation anxiety. The fear of object loss remains the typical danger situation as long as the object is primarily a required portion of the child's narcissistic world, that is, an archaic "self-object." This state of affairs comes to an end with the consolidation of a cohesive self, following which omnipotent control over the object is no longer needed much of the time (p. 78).

The technical implication of a developmental approach is to explore methods that enable a patient to tolerate the developmental anxieties and to differentiate between his or her own self and others. Masterson (1978), who approached the issue from a different theoretical position, emphasized a similar point in his discussion of the therapeutic alliance. That alliance is based on a real relationship in which both participants are aware of each other as completely separate figures. He continued, "in psychotherapy with the borderline patient the therapeutic alliance is a goal or objective rather than a precondition."

Our plan for the borderline or narcissistic patient is to enable him to develop his own individuality and sense of inner continuity, which in turn help him acknowledge others as separate persons and decrease his need for self-defeating or self-destructive solutions to problems. That plan encompasses, then, considerable therapeutic work on issues of separation, individuation, feelings of profound helplessness, disintegration, rage and the need to idealize.

Turning to the interplay between the individual and the group-as-a-whole constructs, Kernberg (1975b), exploring multiple non-concentric systems, argued that working through group resistances and basic assumptions is most compatible with the analysis of primitive object relationships in individual patients and is particularly suited for those with borderline conditions. In contrast, the exploration of individual transference and resistance is more compatible with further developmentally advanced psychopathology. Kernberg (1975b) believed that attention to group-as-a-whole phenomena enables the group psychotherapist to comprehend developmentally early levels of anxiety (whether it be overstimulation or profound helplessness) and the corresponding dangers in object relations. Horwitz (1977) modified his early extreme position by making the technical recommendation that attention be given to individual contributions to a group-centered conflict before the more generalized interpretation is offered. Malan, Balfour, Hood and Shooter's (1976) study of group therapy at the Tavistock Clinic, conducted along the lines recommended by Kernberg (1975b), suggested that strict analysis of the group-as-a-whole is useful only to highly motivated and tenacious patients, rather than to the more disturbed patients.

The organization of our discussion of technique follows the clinical path—that is, we discuss certain components of technique as they emerge sequentially within the developmental processes of a group. The following areas are examined: (1) noninterpretative therapist activity, (2) group idealization and group cohesion, (3) confrontation and empathy, and (4) unsolved problems.

Noninterpretative therapist activity

Considerable work is necessary for patients to recognize that their inner worlds are dominated by archaic needs and that they do not take others into account as separate, autonomous persons. Technically much of that recognition is gained from interaction between the therapist and the patient or among patients in a non-interpretative mode. Feldberg (1958), more than 20 years ago, emphasized that the therapist must be an active participant. The activity not only demonstrated the therapist's willingness to help but provides material for the patient to evaluate the therapist. Similarly, Glatzer (1978), in her essay on the working alliance, stated regarding the therapist, "He can limit his non-interpretive efforts to maintain a working alliance to the basic human influences his personality will have on the patients as he manifests qualities of courtesy, friendliness, human understanding, empathic neutrality and warm but not intrusive interest." Both authors implied that those interactions enable the patient to relate eventually to the therapist as a separate person.

Lateness and absences are often early group behaviors that contain important but unclear messages. Spotnitz (1957), recognizing that considerable resistance is stimulated on entering a group, suggested siding with the resistance by indicating that the patient has a right to be late and, if the topic is continued, offering the patient advice about how to avoid being late. That approach initially appears to be in sharp contrast to the more traditional recommendations to encourage group cohesion (Yalom, 1975) or protect group boundaries (Ganzarain, 1977). The focus on the group and its boundaries may ignore the individual transferences or transference resistances. Grobman (1978) working with aftercare patients, specifically counseled against the examination of fears of too much closeness but did not mean ignoring members and recommended actively reaching out to those who are late or absent. Spotnitz's (1957) advice regarding behavior change (how to come on time) primarily enabled the patient to avoid sanctions from others and clearly sided with the patient. Those recommendations avoid directly challenging patients to change behavior and implicitly respect individual boundaries.

A missing element in those techniques is the examination of each patient's plan for joining. Willingness to relinquish a part of oneself to truly join the group implies some sense of confidence by the person in his personal boundaries—that is, confidence that the boundaries may be permeable or expandable but will not dissolve. For instance, some patients may need to develop an individual ally before risking a more intense relationship with others. Another subgroup may dominate, control or monopolize the group in order to maintain their individual boundaries. Technically, the problem revolves around the task of recognizing those divers way of entering a group.

We see one approach to the task in the following way: The patient needs to enter the group at his own rate; he needs empathy and understanding of his problem of joining. At the same time, the therapist must attend to the responses of the other group members to the vicissitudes of entering a group. With the patients we are discussing, words may take on highly personal or idiosyncratic meanings, so the use of language may carry more meaning than it does with less neurotic or more developmentally advanced patients. The therapist then needs to attend closely to the patient's use of language as signals of progress or flight, not neglecting nonverbal ways of gathering data or receiving messages but using them as supplementary information on which to understand the patient's use of language.

Lateness often signifies a nonrecognition of others, and that nonrecognition may be reflected in how the patient uses language to describe his behavior. It is our therapeutic tactic to make it clear that the late member may need or fear the reactions of others and thereby have to keep them at arm's length. An interpretation to that effect does not need to have an immediate effect on the latecomer but is designed to help other members recognize how they are being used—that is, that they are selfobjects. That recognition, in turn, decreases the anger of the group members and enables them to be empathic with the latecomer. Such a plan on the part of the therapist may clash with some patient's method for entering the group, but it may be useful for others and have a group-wide calming effect.

A clinical example illustrates some of those points. Rita, one of several newcomers to an ongoing group, quickly established her pattern of feeling the outsider in all group situations and began to wonder about the usefulness of group psychotherapy. She would come slightly late to the meetings, a piece of behavior usually overlooked by the group members. Nevertheless, after several months, Rita commented that she was "beginning to feel better here." Rita's reference appeared to be to the setting, rather than to the other group members. The members, however, responded as if Rita had spoken to them personally. The resulting dissonance alienated Rita and members from one another. When the therapist clarified that "here" had been responded to as "me" and "us," the dynamics of the dissonance became clear: Rita was tentatively exploring relatedness, and the group members, who had attained more developed object relations, had expected Rita to respond at their developmental level. With the tension diminished, Rita's lateness stopped, and she was provided the necessary space for her plan to explore the less personal components of the treatment before going further (Cooper, and Gustafson, 1979a, 1979b; Gustafson and Cooper, 1979).

A similar approach is recommended when the lateness contains the dynamic meaning of a wish for attention or admiration. A non-scolding interpretation of that need that either explicitly or implicitly recognizes the universality of such needs enables all members to less judgmentally examine similar strivings within themselves. Havens (1978) addressed the same problem through what he labeled "simple empathic speech"—exclamations or translations that put the other's state of mind into words. The resulting universalization enables group members to be attuned empathically to early developmental needs. Experience in groups using that approach has enabled us to see that group members become less critical of aberrant behaviors and are then able to explore their own inner needs. Little change can be anticipated in the latecomer, and premature change might be considered a sign of compliance, which will need examination later.

In a long-term outpatient group one man was always prompt and missed meetings only after carefully explaining his reasons. He often threatened to quit the group because others were less invested, as evidenced by their lateness or absences. Only after he began to understand fully that his compulsive behavior had carried the message that others must behave identically and that he needed the others' prompt and unremitting presence was he able to reveal similar poignant external difficulties. He reported that, at the 10 year reunion of his high school class, the absence of one person destroyed the feeling of class solidarity and ruined the evening. Of course, such preoccupation with the absence underscored the need for the external environment to be perfect in order to calm the defective inner world.

A second common early group behavior is the request for the therapist to answer questions. Patients ask questions for a variety of reasons, usually linked to orienting themselves, containing anxiety or other safety-effecting mechanisms.

Nonresponse to questions produces two principal effects: It stimulates fantasy about the therapist, and it is frustrating, particularly when direct questions remain unanswered or are met with an aversion of the therapist's eyes. Reflecting questions back to the group is often experienced by the members as a nonresponse. Some authors have suggested that patients be told that questions will be answered after the group members have explored the meaning underlying the question (Rutan and Alonso, 1978). The patient's ability to work with such a response depends on the state of the alliance, since such therapeutic strategies are predicated on the patients' ability to collaborate. Without an alliance, delay may evoke compliance or frustration and rage. Blanck and Blanck (1974) addressed that issue in transferential terms: "Negative transference manifestations are also to be dealt with but always against a backdrop of just having built up positive self and object representations so that relatively unneutralized aggressiveness of the more disturbed patient does not threaten him with destruction of self and object" (p. 135).

The argument against the alternative of directly responding to questions has been that gratifying patients would interfere with the exploration of hidden motives. Kohut (1971) cogently argued that answering questions with tact is similar to the average expectable environment. The answer undercuts the cold, withholding, nonhuman element and potentially provides therapeutic leverage in the form of building an alliance.

Patients exhibit a variety of responses to the therapist's direct replies to questions. The therapist need not explore immediately the motivation for the question; instead, he may allow the group members to develop their own observing capacities. Early in the group process, patients frequently respond to direct answers by ignoring the process or the content, which in itself provides information regarding the state of the alliance. Another response from the patients may be to ask further questions. Here, timing is critical, since, after repeated questions, an exploration of the motivation may be readily undertaken.

It may be argued that specific transferences were missed because patients were gratified. Instead, we think that directly answering questions serves strategic purposes. Questions may be answered directly and simply, followed by a request from the therapist that the inquiring patient may want to consider why the question arose at that juncture, but in the early phases of therapy even that should be done judiciously. Later, it may be feasible to ask the group to take on the task of exploring the process either for the individual or for the group. The overall intent is to further the alliance without excessive frustration but to retain the stance of helping the patients to understand their interpersonal or intrapsychic needs as they emerge in the treatment process.

Questions regarding the therapist emerge frequently enough to deserve comment, yet specifics are difficult to discuss because questions arise in the therapeutic context. Inquiries regarding the therapist's age, training and orientation to group psychotherapy may be answered directly. Responses to questions of that nature are to be differentiated from providing opinions about events or interactions. It is similar to asking the therapist if he saw a movie or asking his opinions or feelings about the movie. The underlying therapeutic stance of neutrality and restraint in imposing the therapist's personal viewpoints is an essential element in enabling group members to grow and develop their own individuality.

The therapist often does not know the precise nature of the specific resistances that are embodied in a question. After a direct response to a question, the dynamics frequently emerge, and then a more complete interpretation is possible. A premature comment about a specific patient or group resistance may be perceived as an attack or, in reality, not be tactful. Both errors heighten resistances and interfere with the development of an alliance. Thus, the therapist, through direct responses to some questions, may gain time and additional information that will enable him to strengthen the alliance through understanding and empathy.

Responding to questions has often been construed to represent a countertransference behavior. The possibility exists that the intense affects of those developmentally arrested patients stir fears within the therapist of his own ability to maintain ego boundaries. Nonresponse retains a protective barrier for the therapist. The therapist, by not responding, may in a sense pick a battleground, since he has experience with interactions based on that mode of relating. He therefore fights on familiar ground.

Idealization and group cohesion

The ultimate aim of using the group atmosphere as an environment in which individual problems may be exposed and worked through is parallel to the development of a working alliance in dyadic treatment. A number of authors have stressed the need for cohesion and appropriate attention to boundaries. Yalom (1975) placed that task as a cornerstone in the interpersonal approach. Moreover, he actively emphasized the importance of the group members to one another by asking patients to ask others for feedback. However, despite superficial similarities, group cohesion is not the same as group idealization (Stone and Whitman, 1977; Wong, 1979).

We conceptualize the attainment of a cohesive group as attainment of a stage where individuals view one another as separate. It is an oversimplification to lump warm, positive feelings under the umbrella of group cohesion, when they may represent a diversity of developmental levels. Different technical management is required to respond to the patients struggling to protect themselves against the exposing their developmental arrest or ego defect, in contrast exposing painful conflicts at a level of separate object relations, such as trust or triangular conflicts.

The therapeutic process can be geared to allow idealization to develop within the group. With that plan in mind, the therapist's task centers on avoiding interference with the emergence of that archaic need and simultaneously observing the other members' response to idealization. The responses in the group may include premature debunking and scorn at the idealization or, alternatively, variations of withdrawal. Both responses are based in part on prior developmental experiences. No single therapeutic plan can be formulated, but attention to the process within the group should take precedence. Is there evidence for therapeutic movement within the multiple interactions related to idealization?

An illustration of the process arose in the complex interaction of group members with Joan. Joan, a woman in her late 50's, repeated in the group her habitual style of maintaining distance and proving that others used her or really didn't understand her. She was terrified of being alone but was more terrified of becoming involved, because she feared being dominated and controlled by men. Underneath those fears was the fantasy that the men knew everything and would care for her. Dynamically, Joan's position within the group was a series of defenses against an idealizing transference. The surface defense was a controlling domineering, distancing interaction that provoked others and reinforced her masochistic position. Joan was aware of one portion of the interaction—specifically, her distancing, which was fueled by her wish to avoid masochistic relationships such as she had endured with two alcoholic, abusive husbands.

Within the group, one pattern Joan exhibited was to ask for someone's opinion. That behavior represented a derivative of her idealizing transference but was a wish for contact as well. Joan would continue without pause, anticipating what the response would be and attacking the potential respondent for inflating his own ego by demeaning her. Of course, group members protested or became enraged with Joan. The therapist's strategy was to point out Joan's need for understanding from others in order to feel that she had the human contact she desperately wanted, but he added that the emergence of such wishes stimulated Joan's fear of being used by others, and, as a result, she drove them away. He did not comment on Joan's need for an ideal other who could always respond. Joan's response to the interpretation was to repeat tales of abuse from her husbands, which momentarily removed her from the group interaction. Joan unconsciously had found a way of maintaining herself within the group through displacement onto the past, thereby signaling in the group that they weren't totally responsible for her trouble. That initial unconscious communication from Joan, coupled with the therapist's comments on how the group members were needed and feared by Joan, diminished the members' induced reciprocal need to be perfect for Joan. In turn, they less frequently counterattacked, thereby furthering the emergence of Joan's idealizing transference to the group. The net result was progressive freedom to explore shameful and embarrassing archaic needs. Eventually, Joan was able to directly examine her loneliness. She said that she wanted to keep people away or to hurt them for not responding to her when they had not been what she needed at the moment—that is, members must be perfectly responsive. In that example, a sense of group involvement was fostered without emotionally or in reality extruding a difficult member. In our schema, one portion of the group had become cohesive, recognizing individual differences, whereas Joan remained at a predifferentiation but need-fulfilling phase.

Grandiosity and idealization often overlap, and members fluctuate between one and the other self-presentation. The grandiose stage in developmentally arrested members is psychologically played out in groups by direct expression of the need, withdrawal, or reaction to gratification through overstimulation with a pseudomanic state. Such members do not see others as having their own individuality; the other members are present only to fulfill needs. Fried (1979) distinguished between narcissistic wounds and defenses; narcissistic wounds are a product of insufficient or inappropriate mirroring, and defenses are a protection against the emergence of other affects. Exhibitionism, monopolization, and grandiosity may be a defensive structure against oedipal conflicts or, at the other end of the spectrum, against psychotic disorganization, but such diagnoses are usually not apparent until there has been overstimulation or injury to the narcissistic exhibitionistic needs (Stone and Whitman, 1977). Often the initial technical step is for the therapist to be empathically in tune with the grandiose needs and to help the group understand their function for the others. Understanding is not equivalent to gratification. Rather the response indicates the therapist's willingness to acknowledge the presence of those archaic needs. The despair of a patient who says that he can't stop pushing himself to be the center of attention, even though he know it isn't necessary, is considerable progress from an earlier stage, when the need was consistently reenacted. The step suggests a beginning differentiation has occurred, rather than acting as if others are present solely for the purpose of gratification.

Raw exhibitionism and demands for attention are often painful for others to see. They stimulate archaic affects and a variety of defensive maneuvers. The therapist is not immune to such stimulation, particularly when he has an attentive and interested audience. The potential for the group members to idealize the therapist may fit in with the therapist's own grandiosity, producing significant blocks in therapy. Accumulation of clinical experience within the framework of selfobjects and primitive grandiosity may provide clearer technical guidelines, but currently an awareness of countertransferential response may protect the therapeutic process.

Confrontation and empathy

Confrontation has been viewed as one of the most useful components of effecting change in group psychotherapy (Pines, 1975; Meyers, 1978; Roth, 1979). Conceptually, the group offers special advantages, since the confrontation or its handmaiden, feedback, comes from other group members, who are experienced as peers or less intensely invested parental transference figures. In addition, the weight of consensus is a further impetus for self-examination and change.

Confrontation is drawing attention to a behavior or describing an effect the behavior has on another person—for example, saying, "When you do that, it makes me angry." Greenson (1967) conceived of confrontation as working toward an agreement that a piece of behavior is problematic. An alliance is implied between the patient and the therapist. Traditionally, confrontation is used to make an ego-syntonic behavior ego-alien. However, not all confrontations are so benign. Frequently, they are a request to change behavior, so that the confronter will not hurt others.

A confrontation deals with behaviors, but it neglects the empathic component of the interaction. Often, the confronter does not attempt to understand the emotional position or state of the one being confronted. Rather, what is espoused is that, under the weight of group consensus or personal relationship, a person steps back and reflects on the particular behavior.

It would be inappropriate, if not fruitless, to proscribe confrontations. Within the emotionally charged group interactions, confrontations are bound to occur and, indeed, can have enormous impact. It is the therapist's task to maximize the therapeutic potential of the confrontations. That maximization can be accomplished within the developing therapeutic process in most instances if the therapist remains alert to the affective response aroused by the confrontation. It is at that point that important empathic connections can be made with the member who is confronted. In turn, it facilitates the development of an alliance based on the patient's repeated experience of being understood.

A clinical vignette illustrates some of the techniques. Bruce, labeled a borderline personality, was often angry with other members for what he judged to be their foolish, nonthinking manner of dealing with their problems. In addition, Bruce was ever critical of the therapist for stressing the examination of feelings and ignoring the intellectual side of life. Clarification of the context of that criticism and interpretative guesses as to the reasons for Bruce's provocativeness were to no avail, nor was insistence that he stop. The pattern began to dominate the group interaction, much to the despair of the therapist and the frustration of the members.

The intervention that proved most useful was identifying Bruce's surprise and confusion at the confrontations. What had been neglected in the heat of battle was an empathic contact with Bruce, for he genuinely felt that he was helpful with his cognitive approach, as well as correct in his critique of the therapist. The therapist's recognition and then appreciation of Bruce's affect of surprise enabled Bruce to feel that someone was genuinely in touch with some of his immediate feelings. After that, Bruce tried to listen to others say that they could agree with the need for balance between emotional and intellectual understanding. Bruce could also consider the point that communication occurs both emotionally and intellectually, often simultaneously.

Two years after entering group psychotherapy, Bruce began one meeting by repeating that he had been to the library, reading about group treatment. He read that successful groups both confronted and supported. He knew that confrontations occurred but wondered why support was absent in the group. The members perfunctorily agreed with Bruce's assessment but dropped the issue because the comment stimulated their fears of too much closeness. Later in the meeting Kate poignantly reflected on her own flight whenever someone was nice to her. Bruce, who had initially introduced the problem, was apparently unable to tolerate that avenue of exploring the problems of closeness and support, and he critically demanded that Kate explain her behavior. Several members then sharply criticized Bruce for attacking Kate. The potential for a donnybrook was present. The therapist suggested that Bruce was trying to make contact with and help Kate but was using the primary channel available to him—that is, he was asking that Kate explain her behavior. That recognition of a positive component of the interaction enabled Bruce to state directly that he felt helpless to solve Kate's problem. That response was a distinct change from Bruce's persistent, angry criticism whenever affective contact was established within the group. Such experiences will, of necessity, need to be repeated many times to help free Bruce of he is fears of losing control of his feelings.

That clinical example illustrates the following techniques revolving around confrontations. The technique avoided blaming the victim; in that instance a subtle judgment was made by the members that Bruce change his behavior in order to fit in with the group. Bruce because of his unconscious fears of being controlled or engulfed, responded as if that were the only meaning of the response he received from the members or the therapist (Stone and Whitman, 1980). The first shift came through the therapist's empathy with Bruce's only dimly recognized affect—his surprise. Bruce eventually reached a point at which he knew he was misunderstood and could quickly regain his inner balance, rather than continue his diatribe against affect. In essence, through empathic contact, Bruce was able to develop self-soothing functions. Generally, the group members could step back and see that they were caught up by Bruce's provocations. That level of emotional understanding promoted an increased sense of safety within the group and led to a more constant sense of others as separate persons with their own developmental and interpersonal problems. In that context then Bruce could tentatively reveal his feelings of helplessness, rather than falling back on his old solution of cognitive mastery.

The therapist can temporarily identify with the group members and join in their wish to stop or rejct frustrating or provocative behavior. There is probably no way of preventing that from happening, and it may be the cause of some dropping out (Stone, Blasé, and Bozzuto, 1980) Nevertheless, the therapist can monitor his own affect and step back to consider that even silence on his part may be countertransferential. The critical shift occurs when the therapist no longer considers the behavior solely as defensive, with its associated pejorative implications, and tries to understand the patient's efforts to solve a problem in a positive fashion. Those efforts may seem misguided, inappropriate or restrictive, but the therapist can convey an genuine respect for the patient's efforts.

Unsolved problems

Having surveyed the available technical recommendations about group therapy for narcissistic and borderline patients and having added several recommendations of our own, we see that little is known. We have nothing like the comprehensive recommendations by Kohut (1971, 1977), Kernberg (1975a, 1976) and Masterson (1976) for the individual psychotherapy for such patients. Instead, we have a few reported attempts to translate those ideas into the group context, with the modest success that is barely described in anecdotes.

The translation of ideas from individual to group psychotherapy concerning such patients, although useful for locating some way to start with those patients, takes almost no account of the complexities of the group context. Let us assume, for example, that a narcissistic member of the group does need an idealizing transference to become safely involved with the group. The task of the group therapist may be to allow the patient to idealize him and to analyze embarrassment and other resistances to letting that relationship emerge. Let us assume, on the other hand, that a borderline patient idealizes the therapist in a shallow way, out of fear that his envy and rage at the therapist will be discovered. The task of the group therapist may be to allow the patient to drop the pretense of idealization. Those two tasks are contradictory. A group formation that idealizes the leader, such as that recommended by Foulkes (1951), may leave the idealizing patient without his necessary security. If those two patients are to be treated in the same group, with each getting his necessary therapeutic conditions, some way of steering between those contradictory demands on the therapist must be negotiated. Although we believe it is possible to do so, there is not a single report of managing that kind of complex maneuver in group therapy (Gustafson and Cooper, 1979).

Another area of needed examination is the kinesics of therapy groups. Since the nonverbal climate of the group and the relationship to the therapist are so palpable to those patients, we should like to know the different possibilities for the different patients in that broad category. Surely, some of them appreciate the cool thoughtfulness of the analytic stance when they themselves get into turmoil in the group. Others, however, find that distance cold, even abandoning. They need the ready empathy, which we have described in several forms (Stone and Whitman, 1980; Stone et al., 1980). Still others are suspicious of either the neutrality or the closeness, and their negative projections are not cleared by empathic attempts; rather, they are worsened, as the patient feels in greater danger of being taken. The projections have to be actively countered, often displacing them away from the patient-therapist relationship. Havens (1976) defined those alternative relationships for individual psychotherapy. It is probably true that sophisticated group therapists make those nonverbal adjustments, but our theoretical accounts tend to prescribe a single kind of alliance as optimal.

The problems of getting a cooperative group when those disturbed patients are involved have been scarcely identified (Cooper, Gustafson et al., 1981). Roughly speaking, the likely dangers are withdrawal and ugly confrontation. We have noted the importance of the therapist's capacity for empathy. That capacity makes it less likely that any patient will be entirely alone against the rest of the group, for at least the therapist will be partly with him. However, empathy by itself will not save many of those situations, because a therapist cannot afford to alienate the rest of the group by staying with a single patient for too long. Those problems of steering between the contradictory needs of the different members can take many forms, which need to be identified clearly, so they can be taught. We have mentioned only one type thus far, the contradiction between the need of some narcissistic patients to idealize the therapist and some borderline patients to leave off the pretense of idealization. A second type occurs when some patients need to bring out their grandiose and sadistic qualities, while others desperately need to stop a pattern of moral masochism. Either side can be easily sacrificed. For example, a group that develops a feminist culture that is protective against patterns of moral masochism in its women members may make the disclosure of phallic grandiosity and aggression impossible, thus helping some members while blocking others. Those problems of the contradictory needs of those group therapy patients can often be solved, but they will not be solved unless they are admitted and posed clearly as problems. We propose that there are many other types of contradictions than the two we have outlined.

Conclusion

In summary, we have reviewed the issues of technique in group psychotherapy for borderline and narcissistic patients. We believe that the helpful lines of interpretation and the management of non-interpretative relationships are dimly understood and prescriptions so contradictory that they cannot be applied to specific cases with any reliability.

We have attempted to highlight some of the theoretical differences that affect clinical interventions and have suggested that a developmental approach to the individual patient with the fit between the individual and group development may be a useful paradigm to advance the specificity we require. We have examined the model of the working alliance, which highlights the cooperative components of separate patients working together. Thus, the working alliance represents a goal, rather than an intermediate step in group psychotherapy for borderline and narcissistic patients. Modifications in technique for therapist activity related to lateness, absences, and patient-posed questions were discussed. The concept of group idealization has been reexplored and separated from group cohesion.

Concomitantly, our technical suggestions highlighted one therapeutic plan in which we empathized with a patient's need to idealize but simultaneously helped the other members become aware that they were not experienced or needed for their own particular attributes; they were transference objects.

We have reviewed the place of confrontation in groups and have raised the following technical considerations. An initial step toward developing an alliance is to empathize with the surprise and hurt the patients experience as a result of their behavior before examining the source or the process leading up to a particular behavior. After that preliminary step, which may need to be repeated many times, the positive part of a patient's behavior, as well as the limiting or defensive components, need to be included in the interpretation. In addition, we have examined the unsolved problems in the area of patients with different plans for how they will be helped and the situation when contradictory plans are present.

CHAPTER ELEVEN

Affect and therapeutic process in groups for chronically mentally persons

Walter N. Stone

Abstract: A dynamic group treatment model for chronically ill persons allowing them to determine the frequency of attendance empowers the members and potentiates group development. This format respects patients' needs for space as represented by missed meetings. In this context, absences are formulated as self-protective and self-stabilizing acts rather than as resistance. In an accepting supportive environment, members can be helped to explore affects and gain insight into their behaviours. A clinical example illustrates patients' examination of the meaning of missing and attending sessions, with particular focus on intensity of involvement, autonomy, and control. In the process of the therapist and group, members show capacity to gain insight into recent in-group and extra-group behaviours.

The ravaging effects of schizophrenic and bipolar illness on though and affect remain a therapeutic challenge. The multiple biological, social and emotional needs that are the basis and consequence of severe and persistent mental illness defy simplistic solutions. Medication may alleviate some of the chaos but fails to reverse or halt impairment in essential areas of human functioning—relations with the self and with others from which come a sense of wellness and comfortable regard.

For many patients, the illness may have begun in childhood even before overt clinical features were present or were of sufficient intensity to justify a clinical diagnosis. Many first-person reports attest to patients' recollections of feeling different, estranged, or isolated from peer groups. Before the onset of a diagnosable illness, impairments may be expressed in the social domain as diminished interpersonal responsiveness, poor eye contact, and failures in expression of positive affect. Subtle motor symptoms add to these individuals' relational awkwardness (Walker & Lewine, 1990). After the onset of clinical illness, the personal and societal costs escalate.

Innovative psychosocial treatment approaches have been partially effective in alleviating patients' disabilities. Case management and assertive community treatment have focused on providing services to severely impaired individuals who require assistance in everyday living. Social skills training and vocational rehabilitation address aspects of social impairment. Psychoeducational programs including family management, are valuable additions to the overall treatment armamentarium. Amidst this plethora of interventions, the place of psychotherapy, and in particular long-term group psychotherapy aimed at assisting patients in their efforts to improve their psychosocial functioning, has been relegated to lesser overall importance.

Research findings for psychotherapy of schizophrenia have not been robust, and as a result research efforts in the area have nearly vanished. This has occurred in part because of the hypothesized lack of effectiveness of psychotherapy when compared to medications and in part because of problems inherent in funding and conducting psychotherapy research. The difficulties are magnified when it comes to research on group treatment.

Reviews of psychotherapy for schizophrenia suggest that outpatient group treatment may help patients improve social functioning (Mosher & Keith, 1980; Schooler & Keith, 1993). The treatment process is described as occurring in a two-step sequence: 1) a stabilization phase, which focuses on reducing and stabilizing positive symptoms and maintaining patients in the community; and 2) a rehabilitation phase, in which emphasis is on social adjustment relationships, interpersonal relationships, and vocational possibilities (Breier & Srauss, 1984).

In the stabilization phase, treatment emphasizes patients continuing their medications and becoming more informed about their illness through supportive and educational strategies. This approach is particularly salient with the current practice of brief periods of hospitalization.

In the rehabilitation phase, the emphasis shifts to exploration of patients' capacities to form and sustain social relations and to determination of vocational capacities. Change in these latter sectors takes place much more slowly and is more difficult to assess. Yet it is in the rehabilitation phase that long-term psychotherapy, including group therapy, can have a significant impact on interpersonal and intrapsychic functioning. In this process patients can slowly gain greater control over their affects and develop insights into aspects of their relationships with others and with self.

The salience of addressing the social and interpersonal sectors of functioning in chronic mental illness was reported in a survey by Coursey et al. (1993). Chronically ill patients in rehabilitation settings were asked to rate the importance of 40 therapeutic topics. The highest rated items clustered in a category described as "illness-intensified life issues" and encompassed independences, developing self-esteem, relationships, and feelings. Other categories rated important at least two-thirds of the time, included adverse secondary consequences of the illness, self-management of the disorder, and coming to terms with the disability. These findings bring into focus patients' awareness of a continuity in their life and an appreciation that their condition has added a particularly devastating dimension to difficulties that may have been present prior to the onset of their clinical illness.

In the context of a history of social disappointments and emotional injury or rejection, it would be unrealistic to expect patients engaging in treatment to rapidly reveal their inner experiences and risk being traumatized without thoroughly testing their environment. They will test and retest the therapist and the group to assess the safety of the situation. The clinician who "sticks with it" despite the personal difficulties—which may include both countertransferences and the real aspects of the relationships—will find opportunities to gain understanding of patients' efforts to cope, protect themselves, and work toward making positive changes in their lives.

The changing face of psychotherapy

The quality of the relationship between patient and therapist is recognized as the foundation on which the therapist can assist the patient in gaining self-awareness and psychological growth. Among the many theoretical advances there are two important strands: the consistent use of an empathic stance (Bacal, 1995; Kohut, 1977, 1984) and increasing attention to the therapist's affect (Garfield, 1993; Semrad & Van Buskirk, 1969; Stone, 1990).

Self psychology has enabled clinicians to gain greater understanding of the patient's "use" of the therapist as a selfobject to fulfill missing or incompletely formed psychological functions, including containment of affects. Therapists can experience considerable dysphoria when they feel depersonalized and treated as a function. Recognizing this phenomenon as an archaic selfobject transference helps clinicians maintain their emotional equilibrium. In turn, therapists, by maintaining their balance, can more effectively help patients understand themselves.

A second valuable theoretical contribution, the "higher mental functioning" hypothesis described by Weiss and Sampson, explicates patients' interactions as conscious and unconscious testing in the therapeutic encounter. The tests are "designed" to determine if pathogenic beliefs in childhood should be sustained (Weiss & Sampson, 1986, 1993). Skolnick (1994) working with psychotic and borderline individuals writes, "No matter how withdrawn or bizarre these individuals may seem, or how much they try to destroy links with others, often there remain disguised pleas for help and attempts to communicate about the agonies of becoming and relating" (p. 243). Apprehending the confusing and disturbing affects evoked in the clinician in response to the "test" provides information about the patient's therapeutic hopes.

These and other theoretical advances have contributed to changes in therapeutic technique. Writing primarily within a self psychological framework, Lichtenberg et al. (1996) note that they emphasize emotions as a guide for "appreciating self-experience and the desires, wishes, goals, aims and values that come to be elaborated in symbolic forms" (p. 9). In psychotherapy of psychosis, affect "serves as the 'handle' that the psychotherapist 'grabs' in the effort to help the patient tolerate unbearable feelings and subsequently to reorganize his or her behaviour in interpersonally productive ways" (p. 12) (Garfield, 1993). The clinician's capacity to examine his or her affects stirred in the treatment transactions and then to use these responses to advantage become a central element in the conduct of treatment.

The focus on affects contributes to therapy becoming a more collaborative venture in which clinicians no longer make interpretation as the "truth," but instead offer interventions that encourage patients to make necessary "corrections." This stance recognizes that the patient's self experience is central, and that each participant has important emotions that can mutually enhance understanding. Thus, a patient's rejection or incomplete acceptance of a therapist's interpretation is not considered solely as resistance, but as a potential message regarding the impact on the patient of the therapist's interventions.

In group psychotherapy the complexity of communication is multiplied in manifold ways. Interactions take place in relation to authority, to peers, or to the group-as-a-whole. Particularly salient for individuals with chronic mental illness are fears of being unable to maintain a sense of themselves in a potentially threatening situation with the possibility that they will experience further psychic disruption. The source of these potential injuries arises not only from the clinician, but from member-to-member interactions, or from member-to-subgroup or group-as-a-whole interactions.

In the process of emotionally joining a group, members may experience intense and potentially disorganizing affect stimulation that occurs in relation to others and within themselves. The group can come to represent or simulate life experiences, before or after the onset of the illness or in or outside the family. Old defensive and adaptive patterns will emerge, primarily as resistances or as tests to determine if the individual will be traumatized in the present as in the past. Thus the obvious cautious engagement and sense of mistrust displayed by most patients is understandable. Even with an optimal empathic response, change, if it is to occur, will take place slowly.

The model of the flexibly bound group is designed to collaboratively empower members and potentiate respect for each person's capacity to engage in treatment. The central element of the model is a group structure in which patients, after attending four sessions, choose the frequency with which they wish to attend meetings. This agreement, which reflects patient behaviour but diminishes the potential for patients to feel pressure to attend each session as well as lessening the clinician's concerns about attendance, results in a group formation of core and peripheral subgroups. Group development is delayed, but over time the group becomes cohesive, and members can begin to address their intragroup relationships. In this context, it becomes possible to explore absences and for individuals to examine the reasons they give for their absences and gain insight into their failures to attend in accord with their agreement.

The following illustration examines the impact of a treatment structure that builds in flexibility of attendance, but without precluding discussion of absence in members learning about themselves and their affect states in relation to others.

Illustration

The group, which has been in existence for over a decade, has achieved considerable stability, with a current census of 8 members. No persons have been added in the past two years. With the exception of Greg, who is diagnosed with mild mental retardation and a dependent personality disorder, all members have a diagnosis of schizophrenia, schizoaffective disorder, or bipolar disorder. The group structure has evolved with a core subgroup of 5 persons who attend more than 75% of the meetings; 2 members who attend intermittently; and 1 who appears at widely spaced intervals. Members had engaged sufficiently to interact with one another and were no longer turning almost exclusively to the therapist.

The vignette illustrates patients' capacity to work with affects related to group absences and to gain insight into aspects of their behaviour. Following a small meeting, with 2 or 3 persons present, it is possible to explore experiential aspects of group membership by focusing on subgroups (those who were present and those who were absent), thereby not isolating any single individual.

Sessions are 45 minutes long. All are videotaped, with the camera operator in the room and in view of the members. The vignette presented below was transcribed from the videotape and then edited for ease of presentation.

The session was particularly striking in members' movement of chairs. The seats had been set up in a horseshoe shape for videotaping but were pulled back by the patients in a manner that lessened the sense that they were sitting in a semicircle. However, within the first 12 minutes of the meeting, there were 4 instances of patients moving their seats more fully into their original position. At a point in the meeting at which the most distant member, Carl, seemed more engaged the therapist invited him to bring his chair closer, a request with which he complied.

The meeting took place in mid-December. Three weeks previously, the group had not met because of the Thanksgiving holiday. Additionally, members had been informed there would not be a meeting between Christmas and the New Year holiday. These circumstances created a sense of discontinuity, and in the session prior to that illustrated in the vignette only Rita and Greg had been present. The focus of that session had been Greg's fears that he would be separated from his mother whose deteriorating health made hospitalization appear imminent.

The following session began with 6 of the 8 members present. The therapist was 3 minutes late. After the therapist's entry into the room there was an initial subdued silence.

Therapist: What's been happening?

Lorna: You could say that we are all so sedated [*laughs*]

Rita: Well, it's the first time in a couple of weeks that everybody has been here, I think [*pulls in her chair*] It seems like the last couple of times a lot of people weren't here. Last week it was just Greg and me.

Jack: I had a bad cold last week. I could have come, but I didn't want to spread my germs. But I didn't feel good either.

Rita: I wouldn't either. That would have made you crabby

Jack: I'm crabby enough as it is

Greg: There was only Rita and I here.

Rita: We got a lot accomplished though

Following a brief interchange in which it is acknowledged that there have been prior meetings with only one or two members present the interaction continues

Jack: [*moves his chair into the circle*] So who did all the talking? Greg?

Rita: He had some problems at home he needed to talk about.

Jack: It was good that he had a chance to talk about them.

This comment seems to invite closure, but Rita (while moving her chair in more) continues the discussion of the previous week's topic, and Greg relates that his mother has improved and remains at home. Rick has wondered if prayer had helped her, and Greg responds that indeed they had preyed. When this discussion has run its course the therapist intervenes.

Therapist: We were talking about one side of it: what It's like for Greg and Rita to be here. What about the others? What's it like to miss?

Jack: I needed to miss because I was sick, but the reason, I mean, I'm here practically every week. I could say I'm here every week. I just want to get away from it for a while. Not that I didn't get away Thanksgiving, but there was no group Thanksgiving. I wanted to be away when there was a group once. So I was glad to get away for a while

Rita: I think it's good

Jack: Once in a great while

Rick: I was away for two or three weeks. I wanted to be here.

Greg: You didn't want to be here?

Rick: I did want to be here. I was having depression and stuff.

Rita: That's the worst part of it. When you want to be here and your depression keeps you away.

Rick: Yeah, well I wasn't doing anything else, either.

Therapist: What happens here? The two of you [Rita and Jack] are saying the same kind of thing. Though, I would expect in part that others feel the same, can you say what it is about the group that you want to get away from; or is it something inside you or something about yourself?

Jack: Well it's kind of equivalent to being on the job, every day for a year and just the pressure every day. Every day and the routine, not a boring routine; the routine of it all and it's just like ... I didn't go anywhere on vacation, but it felt like I was on vacation from the group, and I do feel better after I did that, and I do [*Greg pulls his chair closer into the group*].

Lorna: It's kinda like working on something. Each one of us has a different story.

Therapist: [*to Lorna*] Can you say more? Does it feel better to work on it at times alone or in the group? Can you identify when you might want to get away. What's happening inside you?

Lorna: Well, I never really want to get away, but I am asleep until 10:00 or 10:30 in the morning, which I have been doing lately. That kind of happens. It is good to get away at times. It is intense. All these ... you know, everybody is so different.

Therapist: To feel others' problems at times feels intense

Lorna: Yeah, I don't know exactly; it would be depression.

This theme related to missing meetings continues. Initially, Carl echoes the view that he "sort of likes missing," and he has so many things he is doing, but then he acknowledges that it is a relief not to have to listen to others. Rick indicates that the day he comes to the group is the only day he does anything, that otherwise his week is empty. Jack's ambivalence emerges, but he indicates that he would benefit from being away one time.

Therapist: It is different if one makes that decision [to be away] rather than the group not meeting. That is when you miss a week when you decide, rather than when there isn't a group scheduled.

Jack: It might be a week that there is no group scheduled, and you might really need one. And when you choose your own, maybe it's for a good reason. Maybe you are running away from something, but at least you are in control [*moves his chair further into the circle*]

Therapist: [*to Rita*] Where does this fit for you?

Rita: I might handle what they do the same way. I might not come once in a while. Also I might handle it another way in the group. You used to say I talked too much. Maybe I talked too much because ... what other people say upset me, and I ... it won't upset me so much.

Jack: So you didn't have to listen to somebody else

Rita: I might be saying that it could be

Rick: You don't talk too much anymore.

Rita: Maybe I'm getting better [*pause*] I felt bad because nobody was coming because [*referring to a prior meeting*] me and Rick were talking all of the time.

Carl: It's so hot in here. I'm getting hot.

Rita: You're not getting sick are you?

Not hearing the metaphor, the therapist refocuses back to feelings about regularly attending the meetings. Jack begins to express the idea that he wishes attendance were mandatory. He elaborates that he feels tension while in the group and that he is "forced to think harder in here than anyplace else." The therapist again intervenes, suggesting that each individual has his or her own 'internal monitor' that help regulate attendance, and asks again for descriptions of the inner feelings. Carl, who acknowledges that being busy is an excuse, says that the group is the place where he talks to people the most except when he is on the phone. At this point, the therapist invites Carl to move his chair into the group, and he complies. These interactions took place within the initial 15 minutes of the meeting.

Discussion

This vignette illustrates the capacity of some chronically ill persons to engage in a discussion of the intensity of their feelings stimulated by participating in group psychotherapy, and to gain insight into aspects of their self-protective behaviours. Participating in group therapy provides opportunities for patients to become more flexible in managing affects. A group also represents a threat, since patients fear that they will be unable to maintain their personal boundaries and will be flooded with their own and others' affects. The result is a tendency to miss sessions or terminate treatment (Yalom, 1985). However, absences can be understood not only a defense, but as a test as well. The test might be formulated, "If I assert my independence and decide not co come to a meeting, will I be criticized, punished, neglected, or ignored altogether?" If this and similar tests are passed, patients may increase their trust in others and being to tolerate and integrate their affects.

Rita begins with the bland statement that people have not been present for several weeks. The affective meaning of this is not initially apparent but emerges in the ensuing process. Jack indicates that his absence was due to his cold, but his gratuitous comment, "I didn't want to spread my germs," may be understood as a metaphor for his fears that he would emotionally infect others. The interchange focuses on being "crabby" as the uncomfortable emotion.

The emotionally salient central theme of separations and losses is illustrated by Rita's continued discussion with Greg of his mother's illness and the possibility of her requiring hospital care. The dyadic form of this discussion, as if only Rita and Greg were present, re-enacted the prior week's session. The therapist's inquiry framed members' enactment as belonging to one of two subgroups: those present and those absent the preceding week. The interpretation emerged from the therapist's listening "and not bother[ing] about keeping anything in mind" (Freud, 1912). Such interventions have been labelled "disciplined spontaneous engagements" and represent the therapist's "generative intent" emerging from knowledge of the patients (Lichtenberg et al., 1996). Contributing to the intervention was the therapist's experience with group treatment and his appreciation that patients were more willing to share feelings and engage in the group if they were part of a subgroup (Agazrian, 1993).

The model of the flexibly bound group does not preclude discussion of absences. Over time a rhythm of attendance becomes established, and members know, and respond, when others do not attend in accordance with their usual agreement. In this session, members' responses ranged from describing meetings as boring to describing them as intense. This latter feeling is addressed by Jack and by Carl, who indicates that it is a relief not to have to listen to others.

After the therapist differentiates between missing due to cancelled sessions and missing though a patient's personal decision, Jack is able to summarize the central theme as a conflict that "you have control even if you are running away." Lotterman (1996) reflects on the importance of control in the psychotherapy of patients diagnosed with schizophrenia:

> Schizophrenic patients are enormously sensitive to intrusion and what to them feels like coercion. If they feel invaded or violate, they will flee to describing them. (They) can travel far down the path of self-destruction with little concern, and can quickly bring themselves and their treatments to the brink of collapse … The therapist is caught between the Scylla of overactivity and intrusiveness, and the Charybdis of being lulled by the patient's bland denial until suddenly the treatment is destroyed (p. 115).

The flexibly bound group model enables the therapist to comfortably permit missing, which thereby allows patients to maintain a degree of sanction free control.

A paradox is involved in discussing patient's fears of being overwhelmed and accepting, if not encouraging, their choosing to distance themselves. The therapist, by verbalizing patients' needs to have control, accepts their needs to create personal space and distance. Members are then prepared to explore fears of losing control and being unable to manage personal boundaries. Out of this therapeutic stance emerged the patients' wish for involvement, which had been partially obscured. The members' wish for greater engagement is enacted in behaviour as they draw their chairs into the group circle.

Coursey et al. (1993) reported that 84% of the surveyed schizophrenic patients preferred; shorter, less frequent individual sessions (less that 30 minutes, less than once a month). With this treatment dosage, ¾ of respondents indicated that therapy had brought positive or very positive changes to their lives. Thus it is not surprising that attendance in a more complex social setting of a group will be linked to absences. Over time, absences may decrease and greater engagement take place. Moving one's chair outside the circle represent a mini-distancing. When patients have a sense of control and acceptance, they are freer to diminish that distance. Jack's comment equating running away with control was directly linked to his moving his chair into the circle.

The therapist, not consciously recalling Rita's history of monopolizing meetings, turned to her to ask where this fit in for her. Rita said that she used a different behaviour (talking) to achieve the similar goal of creating space. In this process, Rita's self-reflection demonstrated the paradox and represented a step in addressing a more difficult issues, her anxious fantasy that her excessive talking had been the cause of others' recent absences.

I would suggest that the integrative act (insight) of linking talking with control enhanced Rita's self-esteem. An experience of discovery and a concomitant experience of self-efficacy had taken place. In that context, Rita revealed her thought that she was the cause of the absences. This process reverses the more typical sequence in which insight in the present leads to insight into the past. The past and present are intertwined, and integration of the two does not follow a set formula.

For Carl, who had positioned himself on the group periphery, this sequence turned up the "heat" of involvement, and he complained. His position is echoed by Jack, who states how he is forced to think harder in the group than anywhere else. After the therapist frames the situation in terms of an "internal monitor," thereby diminishing the risk of group-wide criticism, Carl exposes his behaviour as an excuse. At this point Carl is able to accept the therapist's invitation to move his chair more into the group circle.

Comment

Schizophrenic patients are not prone to be introspective. Most individuals are content to seal over their psychotic experience, and only a small proportion are motivated to integrate the experience as part of their lives (McGlashan, Levy & Carpenter, 1975). An important contribution to patients' difficulties in engaging in treatment is their lack of insight into their illness behaviours. Deficits in insight exist even in stable outpatients and contribute substantially to their limited participation in social activities and interpersonal communication (Dickerson, Boronow & Ringel, 1997). By achieving insight into their illness, patients may lower barriers to engagement. Involvement in the group process may induce a positive, reinforcing spiral of insight and an increasingly emotionally satisfying engagement both in and out of the group setting.

Acknowledging that others are important and meaningful is a risky business. Many experiences preceding the onset of the illness have been perceived as emotionally toxic. With the establishment of a chronic course, patients are subjected to further trauma as aspects of their illness further alienate them and disrupt social relationships. The lack of insight is often manifested as denial of need for others. Thus, the process of testing to determine the nature of others' responses is an expectable interpersonal process.

Additional major components of the schizophrenic illness are the negative symptoms of apathy, low motivation, and disengagement, which may be an amalgam of biological and emotional elements. As demonstrated in studies of expressed emotion, these affective experiences, which often become particular targets for family hostility, may override the therapeutic benefit of medication (Kuipers, 1979; Runions & Prudo 1983). Patients' vulnerability to injury represents a significant therapeutic challenge as they place barriers to forming potentially therapeutic relationships, and they are particularly alert to any transaction that criticizes their distancing and self-protective mechanisms.

Clinicians face a formidable task of helping shape a milieu in which patients will abandon their preferences for sealing over and for brief, widely spaced session and move to a position in which they will risk reflecting and searching for meaning in their interactions. A central element in achieving these goals is emotional affirmation that will sustain patients through the inevitable affective stimulation intrinsic to group interactions.

Bacal (1992) asserts that patients are seeking "optimal responsiveness" not optimal frustration. Similarly, Teicholz (1996) notes that "frustration becomes not a positive developmental principle in its own right, but an inevitable concomitant of the human condition, to which specific environmental response is required in order to help the developing child or the patient master otherwise overwhelming affective experience" (p. 144). The intensity of an individual's response to a "hurtful" interaction (as experienced by the individual, even if the interaction is considered "appropriate" by the observer) is a product of the person's biological heritage, his or her developmental influences, and the current environment. Experiences of optimal responsiveness, particularly to affectively significant transactions, affirm the value of the injured person, a process that stabilizes the individual and encourages growth.

The clinical example illustrates a therapist's interventions that are based on valuing the establishment of a positive therapeutic climate and appreciating patients' communicative efforts as transmitted by missing sessions. These behaviours are understood not merely as resistances, but as self-protective and self-stabilizing responses, particularly in the sector of managing affect. Within the framework of the therapist's recognizing the behaviours as tests, members may feel appreciated and empowered, and they may be able to explore affects that were previously walled off and achieve insight into aspects of their interactions.

We have incomplete knowledge of the pathophysiology of schizophrenia. Current treatment models are sufficiently broad to take into account biological vulnerability and psychosocial stress. Inevitably, there will be fluctuations in patients clinical state as they experience stress arising from intrapsychic or interpersonal conflicts. With their presumed biological deficits, patients with schizophrenia appear to need extended periods of treatment, requiring therapeutic persistence, patience, tolerance of ambiguity and strong affects and a willingness to stick with the patient (Fenton & Cole, 1996). One session in which patients exhibit self-reflection and insight into their behaviour represents only a small step on their road to improved functioning. Many fluctuations will occur in the treatment process and therapeutic persistence is essential. The rewards for both therapist and patient, however, are substantial.

CHAPTER TWELVE

Strivings and expectations: An examination of process in groups for persons with chronic mental illness

Walter N. Stone

In the past half-century, models for treating schizophrenia have traversed a path from a primary reliance on psychotherapeutic intervention to one that emphasizes medication as the first line of treatment. Concern for patients' quality of life has been submerged as research became focused on finding medications that alleviated the major (positive) symptoms. A significant breakthrough in pharmacotherapy occurred with the recognition that clozapine impacted upon negative symptoms, providing increased hope for cure. However, the overall outcome for schizophrenia has not altered appreciably, with patients continuing to have considerable deficits in ability to fulfil expectable roles and to engage in emotionally meaningful discourse (Bustillo, Lauriello, Horan, & Keith, 2001).

No single factor can account for the multiple and varied aspects of patients' deficits. Most likely biological, developmental and social elements contribute to patients' failures to achieve an average expectable life trajectory. Viewed through a psychosocial/developmental lens, many children who subsequently will be diagnosed with schizophrenia exhibit developmental peculiarities that evoked aversive responses within the family, school and play, leaving the person emotionally scarred (Walker & Lewine, 1990). When overt symptoms appear, often necessitating hospitalization, adolescents or young adults become further alienated from their peer group and further impaired in their ability to fulfil usual role expectations.

With such a background, persons diagnosed with schizophrenia have learned to protect themselves from further subjective trauma. They create defenses that emotionally and physically distance themselves and others. However, emerging data suggests that schizophrenic patients retain a more active emotional life than they present in ordinary discourse (Myrin, Germeys, Delespaul & deVries, 2000). Yet, if a portion of a person's psychopathology arose from social interactions, a treatment exploring the emotions and ideas that are stimulated when people attempt to engage with one another may provide an arena for healing.

Expert consensus guidelines consider psychodynamic psychotherapy a third line treatment choice. However, supportive/reality oriented therapies, either individual or group, are rated as on the border between high first and second or high second line treatments. (McEvoy, Scheifler, & Frances, 1999). Group treatment research mostly dates back to the 1970's. There is some evidence that group therapy can be effective in improving social adjustment (American Psychiatric Association Practice Guideline for the Treatment of Patients with schizophrenia, 1997). Nevertheless, clinical decisions often are based on availability and ease of referral to particular treatments and not on research findings.

Individual therapy for persistently and severely mentally ill persons has evolved from treatment based primarily on drive theory to more flexible adaptive approaches based on more recent models privileging "relationships." Kohut's theory of the self (1977) and subsequent relational/intersubjective modifications have served as the basis for these changes.

Advances in theory have been accompanied by newer perspectives on the therapeutic process. Kohut, in his seminal work with narcissism and disorders of the self, altered the basic psychotherapy paradigm from one of conflict resolution to one of exploring and ameliorating self-deficits, which derailed development. Through consistent empathic listening and responding, Kohut suggested that patients would establish selfobject transferences, which serve to stabilize a fragmenting or disorganizing self. Psychic development would eventuate from patients' experiences of narcissistic injury followed by restorative, stabilizing responses that are empathically understood and explained. In optimal circumstances patients slowly internalize the therapist's functions, and through this process patients acquire the capacity to more effectively perform self-soothing, self-stabilizing functions.

Embedded in self psychology is a notion that patients very cautiously explore the possibility to change and to grow. They hope for a response different from their past experience; one that will facilitate their sense of safety and being understood and will let them risk attempting new ways of dealing with their emotions and their responses in interacting with others. This process has been described by A. Ornstein (1992) as a curative fantasy, which contains both conscious and unconscious elements, and conceptualized as "organized sets of hopes and expectations for recovery that have to be recognized by psychotherapists as essential aspects of the treatment process" (p. 21). Tolpin (1998) describes listening to patient's associations as containing "forward edge tendrils—normal aspects of development extended toward an analyst" with the hope that these efforts will be met with a phase-appropriate empathic response. Tolpin contrasts the "leading edge" [forward strivings] as a searching for the empathic response that will lead to new experiences, with the "trailing edge," which focuses on the pathology [expectancies that trauma will be repeated]. Similarly, The Higher Mental Functioning Hypothesis (HMFH) (Weiss, Sampson et al. 1986) focuses on patients' unconsciously testing the environment to determine if previously acquired pathogenic beliefs should be sustained, or if they can be modified and more adaptive functioning attempted.

Self psychological formulations, which assume an intrinsic [biologically based] developmental thrust, emphasize patients' attempts, to achieve more than restoration of prior emotional balance. They represent a forward-looking developmental perspective. An improvement in quality of life through increased relational capacities, even with residual symptoms, may be a small but meaningful achievement for individuals with persistent and severe illness.

In this manuscript I will attempt to illustrate clinical applications of these recent theoretical advances in the group treatment of chronically ill individuals.

The flexibly bound model

This model, developed for outpatient group treatment of persons with persistent mental illness, primarily those diagnosed with schizophrenia, has evolved over the past three decades (Stone, 1996a). Recognizing the problems associated with patients attending sessions regularly, a group structure was developed in which, after attending an initial four weekly sessions, members could collaboratively, with the therapist, determine the frequency with which they chose to attend meetings. Choices were limited to a range from weekly to monthly. This innovation empowered patients, in a setting ordinarily characterized by power differentials. We found that patients generally adhered to their agreement (Stone, 1995). We also explicitly indicated that members could talk about difficulties with hallucinations, paranoid thinking, social relationships and problems in everyday living (See also Kanas, 1996). In practice, this "normalizes" major positive symptoms of schizophrenia, and thereby has the potential for patients to share their experiences and coping strategies. However, clinically, most of the treatment time is used by patients to address their interpersonal problems as experiences in problems of everyday living and in social relationships.

Groups formed along this model generally are larger (10 to 14 members) and meet for briefer duration (45–60 minutes) than traditional outpatient groups. Over time, members develop a sense of cohesion with a core subgroup of regular attendees and a peripheral subgroup of those who come monthly or irregularly. Patients can move from one subgroup to the other, but most sessions are attended by 6–8 individuals.

Clinical illustrations

Illustration #1: Ben

This composite example typifies a group's responses to a member's apparent beginning decompensation into overt paranoia. Ben's story of a family conflict likely represents a displacement from an unexamined group conflict. Aspects of Ben's illness are enacted in the group setting.

Ben, diagnosed with chronic paranoid schizophrenia and a ten year core member, received haloperidal injections biweekly, generally prior to the meeting At Ben's insistence, the nurse, who gave the injections, called me to say that Ben complained of increased nervousness and wanted his injections given weekly.

As I entered the group room, Ben rather rapidly approached me saying that if I did not do something, he would find a new doctor. We sat down, and I asked him to discuss what had happened. In a rambling and agitated fashion, he began to describe conflict with his widowed mother, who was asking him to cut the grass, take out the garbage, and do errands. He said she didn't realize that he was ill and tired. I inquired if there had been any recent changes in the home, and he said no. Almost immediately the members began to suggest that he move out and find another place to live. Ben reminded them that his mother was his payee. He said that she would always give him his money, but that he had an argument with her about it this month. He added that he had failed in his previous efforts to live independently. He didn't want to leave home. Nevertheless, the others continued to recommend that he go to the Social Security office and have his monthly check sent directly to him; he could then move out. Ben became more agitated and grandiose as the session continued.

I intervened, addressing members' efforts to be helpful to Ben. I suggested that they were attempting to help solve the problem that they heard Ben describing. They too had experiences of conflict that were never easy for them. I did not offer an interpretation that would address a projective meaning for their behaviour, i.e., their projecting their passivity and conflict avoidance into Ben. The members responded by associating to their own experiences that illustrated their difficulties asserting themselves and their propensity to withdraw and avoid conflict. They indicated that these responses helped calm themselves. Ben became quieter. My unspoken concerns that I might need to see Ben for several brief individual sessions or of his needing hospitalization decreased. Although it is hoped that most patients can be treated with the combination of medications and group treatment, during periods of crises individual sessions are arranged in an effort to help maintain the patient in the community. In most instances two to five sessions suffice.

At the close of the session, when medications are managed, I chose to supplement Ben's haloperidal injections with a week's supply of (oral) olanzapine, which I provided for him from clinic samples. Ben departed the group smiling and said he would be back next week.

The following week, the session began with members responding to my announcing an upcoming vacation. This included concern regarding airline safety (this session occurred within a month of the attack on the World Trade Center). Ben said that he was much better. He went on to say that he hoped he hadn't upset people too much last week. I indicated that I was pleased that he felt better and added that he wouldn't need any additional olanzapine. He said that he hadn't taken it all. I made it clear that it was all right with me that he had made decisions about how best to use his medication. He continued that his brother had come to the house and they had worked together, as their mother had requested, but the yard work was begun but not completed. I said that he had found a way to feel that he could do tasks in the way he wanted. Ben agreed.

Comment

This vignette illustrates the frequent process in which members attempt to manage their own inner anxieties, often stimulated by a story about conflict and potential for family hostility, by suppressing another's problem. Exploration of any implied transferences or transference disruptions to the therapist or to the group take second place to the immediate task of creating holding space to prevent a member's fragmentation into overt psychosis (Ben, several years previously in a different group, had an experience of having his conflicts challenged, leading to uncontrolled grandiosity and sudden withdrawal from the group). The therapist's empathizing with members' efforts to be helpful led to spontaneous discussion of expectations of and defenses against feared emotional trauma. These were associations Ben could identify with, or as a twinship experience, merge with. Twinship (alter ego) experiences are conceived of as gaining positive coping mechanisms. As formulated by Detrick (1985) they are experiences of sameness or likeness to others that link individuals to a human group. In this instance, members with severe pathology provided an adaptive strategy that served to modulate tension and help Ben regain internal balance.

Ben's improvement, most strikingly signalled by his concern for others, could be attributed to the extra medication. I would suggest however, that his show of concern was a unique display of awareness of others, which I would not attribute solely to medication. Rather, I believe it to have been a response to the process in which I mirrored members' efforts to help—their forward strivings—rather than exposing repetitive resistances or defenses. This intervention provided Ben a potential for twinship experiences and strategies for adaptive, stabilizing behaviours. These experiences were translated into working with his brother and performing the task at his own pace. My subsequent response was aimed at mirroring Ben's achievement and his nascent show of autonomy. I further "mirrored" his pattern of managing the olanzapine—that is, I accepted his "independent" behaviour, in accord with my efforts to empower patients.

This sequence was not without some "negative" effects. One woman, a core member, missed her first meeting in three months following the first session in this sequence. Even though members exhibited overt signs of discomfort in the first session, those who returned for the second were unable to acknowledge their discomfort. Thus, even though Ben had provided "positive" feedback of feeling better, and he expressed concern for their emotional state, others were reluctant to expose their negative affect, both of discomfort, and presumably of any resentment at Ben for upsetting them.

Illustration #2: Richard

This example, in a well-established group, illustrates a patient's confronting me with my irritability and my acknowledgement of his accuracy. The "mirror" response, focusing on his forward move, led to members' associations of previously unreported family experiences of empathic failures and less obvious efforts to master trauma.

The session occurred while the entire nation remained focused on the World Trade Center (WTC) attack and the "war" in Afghanistan. There were four men and one woman present. All but Greg had a diagnosis of schizophrenia. Greg was a passive/dependent man mildly mentally retarded. The group had been videotaped from its inception.

I entered the group in an irritated state, having been involved with an administrative conflict in the preceding hour. The meeting began with Greg wondering if others had heard of the previous days widely publicized incident in which a bus driver had been attacked and had his throat slashed with a knife. Although the driver had survived, six passengers were killed in the ensuing wreck. This had been followed by what seemed a lengthy silence (upon review of the tape of the session, the time period was about 15 seconds). I found myself further annoyed with the members seeming inability to respond to such a prominent public event. In what I experienced as a rather delayed response, Leon said he didn't want to talk about negative things, and wanted to discuss something "good." The session proceeded in starts and stops, with the members overtly not responding to one another, but reacting by recounting events in their own lives. I was aware that I was asking questions to try to engage them (later, I appreciated that this was a displacement from my irritability with the external situation and an enactment of intrusion focused on the group of my irritation with their "response time" and generally limited engagement). Richard discussed his fluctuating anger, at first saying he didn't know the cause, and then ascribing his moods as reactions to other tenants in his apartment building noisily partying, and his landlord asking him to do favours. He had left a message on the landlord's voicemail asking him to stop "bugging" him to do chores around the building. He wanted the landlord to stay away from him. Leon then said that he also experienced unexplained periods of anger with his wife. He didn't know when they would begin or end.

I tried to engage Diane, the most severely ill of the members. She spoke of the past and fearing death and the end of the world coming. I linked her thoughts about the future with the anticipatory thoughts expressed by Richard and Leon, but Diane responded concretely speaking of difficulty controlling her weight and smoking. When I tried to engage Joe, he responded by reiterating an old theme of his father's irritability being a major cause of his problem, and his repeatedly failed wish to make peace with him.

I turned back to Richard to see if he could add more to his continuing perplexity at his mood changes. Richard initially responded that he felt better not hearing from his landlord, who was not "bugging" him. He paused, and then abruptly said to me. "You're not impatient with the group today are you?"

I was somewhat taken aback, because I believed that I was keeping these feelings in check. I initially responded by acknowledging that he was right, but in my countertransference, questioned the members about the "difficulty" talking. Richard responded that he couldn't figure out what upset him. I then "corrected" my initial response, indicating again that Richard was accurate and direct in stating what he said to me.

The process evolved in which members spoke about letting little things slide, and then worrying that they would blow up, a reference similar to Diane's end of the world and the WTC context. I drew attention to Richard's calm demeanour as he spoke to me. Richard, with some pride, spoke of anticipating future calls from his landlord. He said: "I've already rehearsed what I'm going to do in certain situations, and that strengthens me a little bit." I chose not to address the probable transference reference to myself as a landlord because I felt that Richard was pleased and experiencing himself as effective.

The focus, but not the theme, then shifted with Joe speaking about his fear of confronting authority, followed by recalling that during his first "breakdown" he was so confused he could not find the handle on the front door when he was leaving home to go to the hospital. His mother had put his hand on the handle, but father had grabbed it away. He never understood father's action. (I heard this as an indirect criticism of me, but I was still trying to sort out how I had exposed my irritability). Joe then followed with associations to when he was younger and father would ask him to help with household repairs which he (Joe) could not perform Somewhat later in the session he commented that his father treats him as "property." Diane associated to her father frequently interrupting her and not letting her finish her thoughts, which led to an inquiry and an exchange between Joe and Diane about their wish to forgive their parents. Gregg, with a bit of humour and a sense of power, described withholding information from his father. Leon then revealed how he and his siblings all hated their father, who treated them "like crap," even as adults. Joe then wondered why the parents were so totally blind. I commented, agreeing that they seemed consistent in saying that their parents "didn't get it." Continuing, I said that their experiences and attitudes carried over into the present, and yet Richard had taken a risk and spoken directly to me. My agreement with his assessment was likely different because in the past their experiences seemed to be that those in authority didn't know what they were talking about. To which Joe said, "you don't talk back."

In the final minutes, Richard worried that people would be uneasy about what he had said. Joe replied that they would have to continue to think about the meeting during the week.

Comment

This example highlights a confluence of culture and personal experiences of a therapist crossing the group boundary, entering the meeting and contributing to a countertransference enactment (Hopper, 1996; E Stone, 2001). The culture was suffused with responses to the terror of the destruction of the World Trade Center, and subsequent acts of violence only further stimulated deep concerns of personal safety and of personal self-control. Within this context it should not have been surprising that patients would have difficulty addressing violent acts[1]. (It is noteworthy that the topic was introduced by the only member not diagnosed with a psychotic illness.) Indeed, the entire session can be viewed as co-constructed by therapist and members, with the discussion primarily taking place in metaphor (Gans and Alonso, 1998).

My affect was primarily channelled in the manner in which I questioned the members, although I believed I had hidden my emotional state. However, my concern about not exposing my emotions interfered with hearing rather telling metaphors, including Diane's "psychotic" response fearing the end of the world, which, in retrospect, was an allusion to the WTC bombing, and literally an end of the world of the United States' invulnerability. Joe seemed to have spoken about my "display" of feelings in describing his chronic frustration with his irritable father. Likely this was "heard" by Richard who directly and courageously confronted me.

I initially responded to Richard's confrontation with a comment from my background in drive theory that represented a one-person model with myself as a blank screen: they were repeating old patterns of hesitancy. I recognized that I had "blamed" them, and "corrected" my comments, mirroring Richard's forward move, which he reinforced by describing the meaning of his speaking directly to me (not leaving a phone message) which by association was a result of his practicing responses to his landlord. My "corrected" intervention shifted away from a focus on archaic patterns of hesitancy and resistance, and instead mirrored Richard's forward progress.

These two interventions represent ends of a spectrum, in which first, the trailing edge, focused on repetitive maladaptive behaviour acquired in childhood and the second, the leading edge, focused on progress and forward movement. This latter approach mirrors patients' strengths and supports hope that patients can alter established interpersonal behavioural patterns.

I believe there was some support for the hypothesis that my corrected intervention created space for some tendrils of forward progress, although cloaked with prior fears and expectations. These forward moves were contained in Richard's "practicing" responses, and Greg's sense of power in "withholding." The trailing themes were omnipresent: fathers ask too much, are abusive, treat them as property, or are blind. However, following again my expressing appreciation of Richard's risk taking, Joe's final comment that he would continue to think about the meeting suggests that not everyone would "wall off" what had transpired.

Ilustration #3 Rochelle

This illustration, from the same group in illustration #1, took place at the final meeting before Christmas; there was to be no interruption of the regularly scheduled sessions. The meeting illustrates a shift in a member's response to the therapist's empathic attunement, and the subsequent impact within the meeting. Five members were present, three women, and two men. Ben, however, who arrived late, was present for only one half the session. One of the women, Rochelle, was diagnosed with recurrent major depression and personality disorder; the other four members were diagnosed with schizophrenia.

The meeting began with Arlene giving Christmas cards to everyone, including myself. She beamed in response to the positive "thank you's". The session continued with a depressive tone, as the women spoke about the emptiness of Christmas and how the excitement was really only for children.

Sam, then, spoke vaguely of being upset. He did not bring up, nor did I initially recall that a likely basis for his distress was the anniversary of his wife's death the previous year of a drug overdose. Her death was particularly problematic because, following a separation, they had been trying to reconcile. Sam felt that he should have been more aware of his wife's drug addiction, alert to signs of overdose and saved her life. He had never disclosed any of the facts surrounding her death to the group. He had requested a single individual session, at which time he related the details, but he had refused to return for additional "crises" treatment or to address the event in the group.

The conversation in the group was strikingly "reactive," in that Rochelle and Patricia spoke about their own distress, and neither inquired of Sam as to the basis for his upset. I intervened and asked Sam if he could say more about what had led to his upset. He continued with vague generalizations. However, following an additional inquiry, Sam commented that he had a disagreement with his mother who wanted him to put flowers on his sister's grave. (It was at this point that I clicked with my memory of the death of Sam's wife.) Initially he had been angry and was fearful that he would "put his mother in the hospital." However, he realized he was not angry with his sister, and because he was going to put flowers on his wife's grave, he acquiesced to his mother's wishes. I commented that it was difficult going to the cemetery because it brought up many painful memories.

Rochelle said it was difficult to go to the cemetery because this was the time of year her daughter had been murdered, and that memory makes Christmas difficult for her. Sam asked Rochelle how long it took for her to become comfortable at the thought of her daughter's death, and she replied, "about five years." Patricia then commented that her brother, who lived with her sister, still wanted Patricia to visit him, but she wasn't certain she would go because he never paid a return visit. I suggested that Patricia, like the others, wanted contact with people, but they were cautious because they fear that there would not be much in return, like Patricia's brother's unwillingness to visit her. I added that it was like putting a toe in the water to see how it felt. If the temperature was ok they might proceed with telling something about themselves. I suggested that it was usual human behaviour to check things out. To this, Rochelle told of going to her sister's and revealing that she was in therapy. Her sister had said, "Why would you do that, you don't need therapy." Rochelle said that she determined not to tell her sister anything personal she had been thinking about. She further emphasized the "correctness" of her decision, because she subsequently learned that her sister gossiped with others in the family that she was in treatment. I commented that I understood from what she had told us that she wanted to tell her sister more about herself, and that is why she had begun by telling her she was in therapy. Rochelle, with some sadness, said yes, and she hasn't told her anything about herself since then.

About this time Ben entered. He explained that he had lost his money and had to return home to get bus fare. I said that I was glad he made it. Arlene then gave him a Christmas card. She stared at him intently when he opened it, and as Ben studied the card, she seemed tense. However, after only a brief delay he graciously thanked her, and Arlene broke into a smile. Sam wondered how she had thought to bring a card for him, since his pattern of attendance was inconsistent. Arlene said she just thought of the regular members of the group, and somehow expected him to be present; with that Sam smiled broadly.

Rochelle then spoke to Arlene, saying that "Boots" (her cat) hadn't signed the card. Arlene laughed. The mood of the group brightened, and Arlene, who seldom spoke, said that Boots wouldn't be upset. I said he might feel left out, and Arlene again smiled and said she loved the cat, and he would jump up in bed and she could put her hand on him when she went to sleep. The members wished each other a merry Christmas as the meeting ended.

Comment

This session highlights members' attachment to the group (Arlene's distribution of Christmas cards, and Ben's reason for late arrival), and some of the fears and cautiousness with which members become engaged with one another. The initial portion of the meeting is characterized by a reactive, rather than a responsive, mode of interacting. Bacal (1998) states, "When reactiveness predominates, the experience of others is registered in terms of a sense of how the experience affects one's self" (p. 177). In contrast, responsiveness is acknowledging the emotional position of the other. Previously I have described this as the sandbox metaphor: each person might be building a castle, but he/she only furtively glances at the other, but proceeds by working on his own construction (Stone, 1996a).

The therapist's task is to appreciate members' tentative efforts at engagement (the leading edge) and help to create an environment in which patients' experiences can be mirrored or they can feel protected by (merged with) an idealized other.

Schematically I understood the process as begun by Arlene who conveyed her attachment to the group by distributing Christmas cards, including bringing one for a peripheral member. Arlene is an isolated woman, who had her phone disconnected because she felt harassed by a neighbour, thereby further isolating herself from ordinary contacts. Initially, Sam did not comment on receiving a card, but indicated that he had been upset. Sam's failure to respond to Arlene was echoed by the two other women who also responded in a "reactive" manner. Countering the potential injury to Sam, I intervened and was "rewarded" with Sam's cautious, but revealing, story of the precipitant for his conflict, his mother's request to go to the cemetery. I offered an empathic response regarding the "pain" of going to cemeteries. This led to a deepening of the dialogue with Sam almost directly indicating the source of his trouble was his continuing grief.

Patricia seemed to join a main theme of the session by commenting about her brother injuring her. This provided a bridge for my suggesting that there were cautious wishes for engagement. This led to Rochelle's story describing interaction with her sister, a "model scene," (Licthenberg, Lachmann, & Fosshave, 1992; Correale & Celli, 1998) in which she presented the paradigmatic experience for herself and most likely for others. Model scenes may be referred to by members or the therapist as a way of highlighting particular affective laden transactions that represent core dynamics for the members, i.e., members expectations and self-protective responses.

With resolution of the unexpressed brief tension between Ben and Arlene, signalled by Ben's appreciative (mirroring) response, Sam risked inquiring of Arlene how she thought to bring him a card. Her prescient response, anticipating his attendance, seemed to enhance the growing sense of responsiveness and safety within the meeting. In turn, as if in an upward spiral of increasing emotional contact, Rochelle playfully reached out to Arlene, empathically implying she understood the stabilizing nature of the selfobject connection between Arlene and her cat. The session, I believe illustrates the shift from reactive to responsive mode, in which members directly addressed one another, forward moving, risk-taking in the context of confidence that a self-enhancing reply would be forthcoming.

Discussion and summary

Clinical examples merely illustrate the complex interactions and the nature of the discourse that occurs in groups with chronically mentally ill persons. In this paper, I have illustrated applications of self-psychological formulation focusing on patients' strivings as an effort to enhance the relationship between the group and therapist and increase a sense of trust and safety. This is not a linear process, but filled with detours and backtracking. No single theory addresses the complexity of the work, and references to other perspectives in viewing material that emerged in the treatment process are included to illuminate the process as I understood it.

In example #1, my focus was on the members' response to Ben. Everyone seemed to be experiencing anxiety (including myself). Members' initial response to Ben increased his tension, although he tried to communicate that their suggestions would be ineffective. My intervention, acknowledging what they were trying to accomplish (a response to their strivings), shifted the responses to "reactive" stories, which lessened the pressure and provided Ben space. Ben then seemed to identify with aspects of their solutions, regain his equilibrium and move to a place where he could inquire of others' emotional state. This represented a move away from others as merely selfobjects, but as separate persons.

Example #2 illustrates a member's ability to accurately identify and label a countertransference enactment, in which I communicated my irritability by pushing members to participate. When I acknowledged the accuracy of the observation (after a faltering start) members associated to conflicts with fathers. Two "tendrils" of more personally satisfying strivings were embedded in the associations. My efforts to provide a mirroring experiences focused on Richard's ability to assertive speak up without being enraged. The session had ended with Joe indicating he would continue to think about the session, rather suppress the experience.

In example #3, Arlene exposed her attachment to the group as a positive experience by giving out Christmas cards, and Ben in his effort to attend the meeting even if late. Moreover, the session exemplified the very common "reactive" rather than "responsive" mode of interacting, which I understood as self-protective in the sense that too great intimacy evokes expectations of greater personal vulnerability. Efforts at exposing attachment were followed by distancing. Considerable risks were taken, and the shift to very personal engagement reflecting a deepening of the engagement that included some light play and humour. The banter also recognized the deeper (selfobject) meaning of Arlene's cat.

My focus in these three examples was primarily to illustrate the value of shifting from a position of focusing on patients' repeating old patterns (exploring expectations) to one of trying to address strivings and new modes of interacting. Ornstein (1991) quotes a patient saying, "My efforts to please others know no bounds, but I never feel the job I do is good enough. I resent that … I know that these are *my* (emphasis in the original) expectations, but I still want others to recognize that I am doing a good job" [strivings] (p. 390). Ornstein continues, "Phase appropriate selfobject responsiveness assures development of a well structuralized and cohesive self which is capable of experiencing affects of various kinds with various levels of intensity …." (pp. 395–6). With chronically mentally ill, individuals confirming the self's abilities may be a new experience. Patients with a more consolidated self appear to forgive their therapist's misunderstandings and shortcomings, and do not repeat with the same intensity or duration self-protective withdrawal or psychotic fragmentation.

Monitoring the discourse as "reactive" and "responsive" illuminates patients' ability to achieve a balance of experience-distant or experience-near responses. In situations where there seems to be increasing tension within the session, as illustrated with Ben (example #1), the transactions could be formulated as the members' projecting their discomfort into Ben. With the intervention focusing on the positive aspects, members moved to a position of "re-owning" their projections and decreasing the pressure on Ben. He was then in a position to identify with the solutions suggested in their "reactive" stories. In example #2 my counter-transference pressure was experienced and directly addressed by Richard. This eventuated in a discussion of the experience and danger of confronting authority. The members appeared to associate to expectations with minimal evidence of strivings. In example #3 the "model scene" story of Rochelle (the only member not diagnosed with schizophrenia), which I interpreted as strivings for greater intimacy, led to a very unusual segment of playful teasing and greater engagement than ordinarily experienced in this group.

Traditional psychodynamic interpretations are often experienced by chronically ill patients as beyond their integrative capacity. Weegman (2001) comments, "It could be argued, for example, that until a person is assured through a selfobject experience that his/ her self is supported or cohesive enough, it is unlikely he/she will be able to tackle psychic conflict in a safe manner" (p. 526). In my evolving view of work with this population, I believe that patients need (require) the experience of being understood in how they are trying to manage their interpersonal (and therefore their intrapsychic) problems in a new way, a way that had been previously misunderstood or thwarted. If the process is successful, members have an experience of another recognizing their desire to overcome prior developmental sticking points and to grow. These are affirmative and respectful experiences of members' strengths. Within a milieu sustained by the therapist's empathic understanding, patients will take new risks, deepen their engagement, and shift to a greater balance between "reactive" and "responsive" modes of interacting. The main emphasis in this model is assisting members in improving the quality of their relationships and learning to tolerate greater intimacy of increasing duration. Perhaps in the future, biological interventions will be found that can correct an underlying psychopathological component of persons diagnosed with schizophrenia. However, many individuals will have been traumatized during their formative years. The deleterious impact of such experiences is most amenable to psychotherapeutic intervention. Focusing on what patients are trying to achieve provides a pathway to a better quality of life.

Note

1. The literature on expressed emotions (EE) is the basis for this statement. It is one of the most consistent findings in the literature for schizophrenia, in which in families with high levels of EE the relapse rate is elevated. By analogy, the group comes to represent a family.

CHAPTER THIRTEEN

Saying goodbye: Exploring attachments as a therapist leaves a group of chronically ill persons

Walter N. Stone

Abstract: This clinical report highlights some of the processes arising in a therapy group of persons with persistent and chronic psychiatric illnesses as they cope with the stress of their long-standing therapist's impending retirement. Members' were initially disbelieving that the therapist would leave and were also concerned about their future care, particularly in terms of medications. Gradually they were more able to experience their feelings of loss and their genuine caring for the therapist and the group, using higher-level defenses and increasing their ability to tolerate strong affects. They became increasingly able to demonstrate empathy, notably in their ability to consider the therapist's emotions. The clinical material also illustrates the therapist's personal involvement, countertransferences and expressions of concern.

Introduction

"Now schizophrenics proper ... are able as long as they are not too disturbed to relate themselves meaningfully to others. They have early gained experience in looking introspectively at inter-personal processes and gathering and reporting correct, mean-ingful data" (Fromm-Reichmann, pp. 52–53).

207

In the more than 30 years of my clinical practice and supervision of groups for seriously and persistently disturbed persons, I have experienced many goodbyes. Now, in the context of my own saying goodbye, retiring and closing my practice, I began to reflect upon these experiences with leave taking. What had I learned in supervising trainees and mental health centre staff about their patients' and their own responses to departures. Ending relationships had almost invariably been problematic, for the patients, the trainees and staff, and for me. I reflected on how infrequently real opportunities to say goodbye had occurred. Patients would abruptly move from the catchment area, become physically ill and unable to attend sessions, they would die, or just simply disappear, many times with minimal or no advance warning. While trainees would depart on predetermined schedules, the process of their leaving would almost always seem attenuated, incomplete, or sometimes even rote, for both clinician and patient. Not infrequently, they resisted—perhaps due to guilt—exploring and experiencing the impact of their leave-taking on themselves and their patients. Some "demonstrated" their discomfort by planning vacations shortly before the time of their departure. A particularly frequent source of shame and guilt was exposed when patients would comment that the therapist was leaving to enter private practice or take high salaried position. Departing residents would initially underestimate their impact upon the group, only to gain understanding of their significance in the final session or two before their leave taking (Mikkelsen & Gutheil, 1979). Those staff who co-led groups with trainees would express grief and resentment at losing a clinician they had worked with or relief to be rid of a trainee who had been disinterested in the work. As supervisor, I had some of the same feelings: both a sense of loss and relief in ending the task of teaching neophytes. At times working with multiple terminations, even aware of parallel processes of patient, trainee, staff and my own way of saying goodbye, I appreciated that my capacity to manage my feelings was not optimal.

As I reminisced about various terminations, I recalled two poignant experiences dating back almost forty years, both memorable, both illustrating the capacity of these chronically ill patients to experience real affects as I left their groups. The first example occurred when, as chief resident at the VA, I was asked by a research team studying effectiveness of group treatment to lead a six month, time-limited, after-care group of patients with schizophrenia. During the final session, the patients reminisced about life dreams that had been destroyed by their illness. Grady, a 27-year-old man, spoke about his dashed hopes of becoming a major league baseball player. He had had talent, having been a star on his high school team. Grady's sense of loss was profound, as he talked about the impact of his illness on his hopes and ambitions. Not surprisingly, he touched on some of my own childhood fantasies of being a major league baseball player. I certainly understood Grady's story as an association to the loss of the group and myself, and as a very moving goodbye.

The second vignette is quite different. As a neophyte VA faculty member, I had been asked to lead a hospital group of patients diagnosed with schizophrenia for four 75-minutes sessions across two days.[1] Staff members were to observe and then discuss these sessions as part of their group training. In the final meeting, the patients began fantasying about having a goodbye party, stimulating an excited, hypomanic response. They imagined a barbecue, in which I would be roasted on a spit, cut up and eaten. I had little difficulty appreciating a concretization of primitive oral incorporation impulses, and I recall feeling awed at the imagery and the power of affect contagion. These early cogent experiences impressed me with the intensity and depth of very ill patients' capacity to engage in a treatment process and express their sense of loss when it ended.

Termination and leave taking

One model for conceptualizing the process by which an individual leaves a therapy group is that of the separation/individuation phase of human development (Kauff, 1977; Fieldsteel, 1996). Departing individuals feel as if they are leaving home and are going out on their own. They are losing the support and understanding of the therapist and peers, and even though they feel prepared to leave, invariably they feel a degree of ambivalence. Some core problems may re-emerge for the departing individual, although usually felt less intensively and lasting for shorter periods when compared to earlier periods in the treatment (Rubovits-Seitz, 1998). This revisiting of earlier issues is akin to the coda at the end of a symphony, when the main themes are stated again. Strong and varied affects are stimulated throughout the group by the departure of a valued member, including envy, sadness, or anger at the therapist for not being equally effective in the therapy of the others (Lothstein, 1993). These forces may impact upon the group developmental level, and earlier forms of relating may reappear, such as advice giving or previously addressed and worked though enactments. Therapists are not immune to intense feelings. They may experience pride in what they have helped accomplish, discomfort with the loss of a valued member, and fearful or excited anticipation of the changes that will follow. Yalom (1995) emphasizes that the termination is final; the group is forever changed; and, a patient cannot return to the same situation. Nevertheless, with individual terminations, the group continues and there is time to further examine the responses of those remaining to the leave taking.

The processes are different when the entire group is to terminate, as starkly illustrated in time-limited formats. When the whole group is scheduled to end, the dynamics articulated by Kubler-Ross (1967) in coping with impending death (denial, anger, bargaining, depression and acceptance) are often evident (Bostic, Shadid & Blotcky, 1996; MacKenzie, 1996). The process has also been conceptualized as bereavement (Rice, 1977). The overall developmental level of the group and the inevitability of members' differing readiness to end treatment (based on achievement of goals) strongly influence the group interactions. In the process of saying goodbye, considerable benefit may accrue from exploration of members' differences in readiness for termination.

A variation on the themes evoked in time-limited groups arises from a decision to terminate an on-going group. This may take place when the attendance/census is low and new prospects too few or non-existent. Joyce and colleagues (Joyce, Duncan, et al., 1996) describe setting a termination date for previously open-ended groups based on administrative considerations. The authors highlight the disruption of a fantasy of timelessness, and immortality stimulating dynamics of betrayal, and loss of trust. Affect contagion further amplifies members' emotions.

Therapists who leave their groups evoke other dynamic processes. While their departures signify the end of their therapeutic work, therapy for the patients continues. The decision of the therapist to leave may be based on a variety of reasons: illness, change of job responsibilities, relocating one's residence, retirement or death. Alternatively, terminations may be administratively dictated, common in clinic/training settings where trainee rotations and staff turnover occur with a degree of regularity.

Prominent themes in these situations typically involve parental abandonment or death or the view of authority figures as unreliable and corrupt. The particulars of the therapist's departure (assuming reasons have been provided) may impact upon the patients' associations, although there are no reasons that are 'good enough' in the unconscious of the patient to avoid painful affects. In clinic settings, long-term patients anticipate and try to manage their feelings about the periodic trainee rotations. One prominent defense against these predictable losses is for members to reduce their investment in successive leaders through distancing and devaluing. Some clients, who have had a repeated experience of losing a therapist, will gain a greater capacity to truly say goodbye. Penn (1990) reviewing the literature on "forced terminations" in dyadic settings observes that "therapist and patient need to work toward feelings of closure in their relationship while not prematurely closing off important therapy issues that could be worked on with a future therapist" (p. 379). She summarizes common patient responses as initial reluctance to express feelings and subsequent expressions of anger, anxiety and loss, self-blame, and grief. Often various members threaten to stop their treatment either before or at the time the departing therapist leaves. Such wishes are commonly expressed, and when acted on, add to the complicated dynamics of saying goodbye and of anticipatory grieving the departing therapist.

As noted previously, trainees, often driven by guilt over leaving or difficulty experiencing patients' heart-felt appreciation, tend to minimize their importance to the group. The opposite error occurs when neophyte therapists *over* estimate their significance to the group they are leaving. "No one could possible take care of *my* group as well as I."

My groups for persons with chronic illness: Structure and orientation

I have led many groups for people with chronic illness since the days of my residency, one group lasting over 25 years, another for more than a decade and a third for eight years, these in addition to supervising four or five groups throughout the period. One consistent and salient observation in all of these situations is the irregular attendance of the chronically mentally ill individual across group meetings. Having struggled for a number of years with this phenomenon, I came to appreciate that more than intrapsychic/relational resistance to engagement was involved. Reality issues were present, including limited access to transportation, prohibitive costs of coming to treatment, and higher priorities of attending to personal medical illnesses or caring for family members.

I also recognized that significant countertransference problems were stimulated as a result of the generally irregular attendance, involving therapists' frustration and diminished self esteem. If one were to "act like a therapist" (Friedman, 1988) then considerable time and energy would be spent exploring members' tardiness and absences. If one failed to address these behaviours, the clinician would likely feel diminished. My solution to this conundrum was to alter a basic element of the traditional group psychotherapy structure in which patients agreed to attend every session. The key to this "Flexibly Bound" model (Stone, 1996) was altering the patient agreement. On entering a group patients were asked to attend four sessions in succession. At the end of the fourth session, patients were provided the opportunity to choose the frequency with which they would attend, ranging from weekly to monthly. This results in groups which form with a core subgroup of regular attendees and a peripheral subgroup of individuals participating less frequently (Stone, 1995). Over time, members develop a sense of group cohesion. Individuals could flexibly change the frequency of attendance, choosing to attend more or less frequently, and as they achieved greater stability, they could decrease the frequency of attendance and maintain indefinite contact with peers and a therapist.

This format provides patients a more active, empowering say in their treatment; and, perhaps more importantly it relieves the therapist of needing to attend to "tight" group boundaries in which members are expected to be present at each session. I believe that groups organized in this manner provide a respectful dynamic treatment for severely ill persons.

With regard to therapeutic orientation, I was originally trained in a very traditional psychodynamically oriented residency, in which psychoanalysis was seen as the most valued approach to understanding human psychology. My initial training experience in group therapy emphasized a rather rigid focus on the group-as-a-whole, with a de-emphasis on the individual (Whitman & Stock, 1957; Whitaker & Lieberman 1964; Bion 1961). Theory and practice has undergone considerable since my training some forty years ago.

Self Psychology and intersubjectivity with attention to concepts of empathic attunement, self reparative responses to narcissistic injury, and the therapist's co-construction of the process has enabled clinicians to assume a more dynamic stance in the context of providing traditional supportive interventions (Pinsker, 1997). Of particular importance, in my view, is attending to patients' attempts to grow, to change (Tolpin, 2002). These efforts may be only vaguely hinted at, yet if the therapist can recognize such attempts, the patient feels understood, leading to greater sense of self cohesion. Takahshi, Lipson et al; (1999), from an object relations perspective, state: "Positive interpretation of negative behaviour can mobilize a patient's inner resources....because patients may experience significant containment and hence find a new object in the therapist and the group ..." (p. 243). The authors describe commenting to a patient, " That by walking around you tried hard to keep yourself in the group in spite of your anxiety" (p. 244).

My theoretical shifts have been accompanied by shifts in the manner I conceptualize the relational aspects of treatment, including the handling of terminations. Through the 1960's, reports of therapists' terminations of dyadic treatments emphasized strict adherence to an interpretative stance. Provision of support or reality information was seen as a deviation or signs of countertransference. In some situations where the therapist was leaving the city for another position, patients were not informed of the new location (DeWald, 1966) or the information was delayed (Weiss, 1972). These technical decisions were based on the premise that reality would interfere with the patient's working through of the transference. Change in technique was signalled by Beatrice (1982) who observed that noninterpretive comments addressing the working relationship facilitated patients' ability to hear interpretations. Martinez (1989) expressed similar sentiments, "My patients had an intensified focus on me and issues related to my leaving. It was in response that I found the non-interpretive interventions useful. It seemed from their associations that my patients were struggling to find a way to solidify a helpful internal image of me, rather than trying to dilute the transference" (pp. 108–109).

I have found in working with groups of chronically ill individuals that grounding in reality has been useful in working with the transference at a pace they seemed able to manage. Thus I answer many questions, trying to remain alert to the impact of that information on the process—a difficult task as illustrated in one of the vignettes below.

My leaving

The eight member out-patient group, conducted using the flexibly bound model, had existed for 15 years; I was therapist the final 12 years. The group meets weekly for 45 minutes in the late morning. Patients signed a release prior to entering the group allowing videotaping and the tapes used for educational purposes. The video camera was in open view as was the graduate student operator. I also functioned as the psychopharmacologist for half the members.

I informed the group of my retirement six months in advance of my departure. The group had been quite stable, with the most recent addition arriving two and a half years earlier. A core existed of four persons who attended sessions very regularly. Except for one member, all were diagnosed with schizophrenia or schizoaffective disorder. The members' initial responses to my retirement announcement provided a template on which to assess changes. Their various self-stabilizing efforts and ability to experience loss and grief appeared early, and continued through the period prior to my departure. I was aware that ideal grieving is seldom achieved and the work could not be completed until I actually departed. Still, to the greatest extent possible, I hoped to help the members (and myself) stick with and experience feelings of loss. Following the lead of Rubovits-Seitz (1998), I recognized that "defenses" against the pain and poignancy of a loss persist, but that their intensity would be diminished and duration lessened, as members worked individually and as a group to manage the feelings of loss.

An early response, and a continuing theme during the terminal phase, was the sense of shock that I would ever retire. It was as if I would not age—a commentary on the sense of timelessness of the group. Members never seemed to consider that I might choose to leave—a thought apparently too painful to imagine. As long-term clinic patients, they had experienced the many annual rotations of trainees and intermittent staff departures. And while they would offer comments about these leavings, I could not remember having ever been asked if I too was leaving. It was almost as if I had become my name, a permanent place in their life, a large stone.

A second theme was members' worries about their future care. They knew clinic groups were seldom discontinued, but who would take over the group? Particularly intense was their concern regarding medication management. Would a doctor (resident) take my place? Would they have to enter the more costly private sector for care? I heard these concerns with mixed reactions—I was pleased that they recognized the importance of medications, but at the same time I felt this focus of concern to be a depreciation of the psychotherapy. I thought too that perhaps this was a way of expressing their anger at me. Assurances that care would be provided were never sufficient. Although their "distrust" was understandable, I found this difficult because of my own wish to clarify planning for the group's future. My lame-duck status was brought sharply into focus, and despite their fantasy that I was all-powerful, I realized I no longer impacted on decision making in the clinic. Uncertainty is a powerful emotion in the intersubjective field (Brothers, 2003), and as I reviewed the videotapes and saw periods when I seemed to "prematurely" intervene, I wondered if I was attempting to regulate my own emotions, turning passive into active.

A third theme might be categorized as their increasing interest in me, a significant issue in patients' emotional development. Not only is it useful to be able to self-reflect and consider one's own motivations, but importantly in developing fully authentic relationships is the capacity to mentalize, that is to imagine the emotional state of another (Fonagy, Gergely, et al. 2002). Thus questions about my behaviour and my mental state provided opportunities for members to consider my emotional state. Could they imagine what retirement meant for me? They tried to learn more about me, presumably to

assist in the mentalization process. Learning that I was moving to
California, they queried if I was going to continue practicing. Evolving from this type of inquiry, patients began asking more personal
questions. Did I have family there? What would I do with my time?

A fourth element in addressing patients responses to the process
of saying goodbye salient to working with individuals diagnosed
with schizophrenia is their ability to cognitively process information
(Green, 1996 Green, Kerns et al., 2000; Bagner, Melinder et al., 2003).
Deficits in cognitive processing including verbal memory, vigilance
and executive functions, are an important portion of the syndrome
separate from the psychotic elements. I was aware of the need to
repeat information about dates and timing of any schedule changes.
However, members seemed to more quickly integrate such information when comparing the early sessions following my announced
retirement with those later in the process. This suggests that emotional elements compounded the cognitive difficulties.

Over the six months addressing saying goodbye, members
seemed to achieve greater capacity to "stick with" their feelings
about my departure or the anticipated changes in the group. If someone derailed a discussion about feelings about my leave-taking or
new therapists, there was increased likelihood that another member
would shortly return to the original affect laden topic.

Clinical illustrations

From the final six months of my therapeutic work, I have chosen
three vignettes to illustrate salient dynamics of attachment and loss.

Vignette 1

The first session in May, six months in advance of my planned
retirement, I began with a simple announcement, "I will be
retiring at the end of October, so there will be six more months
before I stop." I added that I would be missing some sessions
in the interim, and that I would keep them informed of when
I would be away. The immediate response focused on who
might be taking my place. Keeping with my general approach
to answer certain questions directly, I responded that I did not
know, but that I could assure them that new therapists would
take the group. Members expressed a strong preference for having a psychiatrist who could also prescribe their medications.

The topic shifted to an extended discussion initiated by Davida, the most obviously ill member, who wondered if she should call a man she had met at a Recovery Inc meeting. She was encouraged by others to take a risk. Tim interjected, saying he wished women would call him. Davida worried that she might be harassing this man; and, further, that she would not want a sexual relationship. I commented about risks involved in meeting new people and how, understandably, people are cautious, not wanting to get hurt. I also noted that Davida had described the man as sending her encouraging signals. Jack wished women would be more forthcoming, and a Rita added that she would take her boy friend out when she had money.

Reflecting on my anxiety and guilt in initially announcing my retirement, I heard this discussion as metaphorically expressing their wishes for me to say more about my retirement. This self-scrutiny helped me appreciate that I had been cryptic in my initial announcement, different from my usual style. I remarked, "I wondered if there was any feelings you had to my response—that didn't tell you enough about what was going on or that I left questions unanswered."

Tim replied "I think you're talking about relationships, having a bond with you. No matter if it's a man and woman, or friend and friend, or patient to doctor, you know, there's still that bond, and I think Davida in essence would like to have that bond with a person. We would like to have that bond with you continue. It is kind of difficult." Jack added, "Yeah, I'd go along with that. There's a bond and I hate to not see you again for the rest of my life after six months, you know. And I have to get used to that, so it's going to be a loss." George, the non-psychotic, but mildly mentally retarded man, interrupted, saying, "I mean, I've just kind of grown close to you. Real close. You've helped me a lot. You understand. You've corrected me and I'm going to miss that. The medication, oh everything."

At this point Tim reiterated his position that Davida should call the man. She expressed fear that she smoked too much, implying he wouldn't like that. Rita said that if her boy friend abandons her, no other man will have her. She emphasized that she couldn't do everything for herself. Jack added that that is just another blow to being sick. I then commented, "Would anybody want to take a group of sick people. I wonder if that's your concern." Tim mumbled, "Definitely, definitely." Davida anxiously remarked that another man wouldn't like her because she smoked. Several suggestions were made to her about how to not smoke around him. The discussion became animated, and I started to talk several times, only to be spoken over. Finally, in the context of the smoking conversation, I commented, "If you are different from others, they won't accept you." Jack said he wouldn't know how he might entertain a new girl friend, and Davida resolved her dilemma, saying that she would ask the man to go for a cup of coffee after a Recovery meeting.

Commentary

The patients' initial focus on arrangements for their continuing care seemed to represent both a denial and a wish for continuity. They're feeling unacceptable and fearing risk taking aroused a sense of insecurity about the future. In the context of the "other" doing more, I recognized that I had co-constructed the discussion by presenting this startling information too cryptically, thereby injuring them (Gans & Alonso, 1998). Boss (2003) comments, "Speaking is a relational act in its own right, forged in the earliest interactions of human life, and the complex elements of such an act are always shaping the meaning of the message" (p. 660). The members had heard my anxiety in the way I told them I was leaving. Their message to me finally seeped through to my consciousness, and I was able to verbalize my understanding of the process. In turn, they understood my comment and briefly but poignantly focused on their attachment to me. As the affective intensity increased, they returned to concerns that they were unacceptable. My question about their being acceptable to a new therapist was diverted, but my next intervention (in the displacement) about fears of exposing differences, eventuated in Davida's proposing going for coffee. This "solution" carried the message of a willingness to take limited risks—an initial indication that they could manage their emotions.

Vignette 2

In the sixth session following my announcement, only Davida, George and Tim were present. The preceding week had been "difficult" as a theme emerged focusing on increased impulsivity and fears of losing self-control. Davida wondered if she might look for work. Tim, progressively dominating the session, offered suggestions to Davida about how to find work. The advice reflected his "successful" experiences of hustling work, but seemed unrelated to Davida's disabilities. Rather expansively, Tim explained the possibility of a new job: He would be selling merchandise on the street, others would supply the merchandise, and his business could expand across the state. When he mentioned that he would need a vendor's license, I expressed concern because he was usually paid for his work in cash (which carried the understanding that he did not report these earnings). I noted that a public record of his working would exist. Tim said that wouldn't matter. I repeated my apprehension that he might jeopardize his benefits. George described how Medicaid limited how much money he could keep in the bank. Tim became pensive, worrying about dying, and then in a seeming abrupt change of topic, noted that a lot of members were missing the session. He then briefly fell quiet.

In a rare bit of humour, Davida, commenting on the small attendance, said, "if it gets any smaller, I'm going to get a shrink." The four of us laughed, lightening the mood. She then commented about men being small, and that her boy friend was small, and "he knows it too." Her voice had an unusual liveliness, and she seemed more animated. After a pause, I asked George, who had not worked for over 20 years, what it was like for him during the earlier discussion. He said it made him nervous. Tim used a question about George's age to segue into my retirement, and expressed fears that the next therapists might only stay with the group a very short time. He then mentioned that he might begin to travel (he had not left the city in almost two decades) followed by musings about members who had left in the past, noting that the group still moved on. I said that he could still have feelings about the change. He continued, "I have feelings cause I feel I've learned a lot from you, ... but then too, I have to show love more. I'm not afraid to tell someone I love them, you know, from the heart. It's kind of tough for a man to say that. It's kind of difficult, I'm still working on it, but I want to get that out of me a little bit more, you, love,

I love you. I want to say I care, but you know, I mean it's kind
of difficult getting that out for a man." He added that he had
thought about this when Davida had commented about men
being small, and he would work on these feelings. Tim's associations came just at the end of the session, leaving no time to
address this poignant moment any further.

Commentary

I understood Tim's over-stimulated discussion of work as his efforts
to maintain self-esteem in the face of loss. My countertransferen-
tal state was to protect Tim from what I believed to put him at risk
of jeopardizing his benefits (in actuality, I did not know whether
getting a license would put him at any risk!). Perhaps I could have
waited to see what the others had done, or I could have inquired
about any risks he saw in this, but my response was spontaneous
and even with Tim's initial denial, I persisted. In retrospect, I believe
this enactment gives voice to my caring and wish to protect the members. Whether I would have responded in this fashion not under the
conditions of my departure is unclear to me. Perhaps my comments
were heard as genuine concern.

In retrospect, Davida's unusual display of humour and her put-
down of men likely reflected her anger with me for leaving and with
Tim for his insensitivity regarding her difficulty in working. Most
striking was the change in Davida's affect as she became playful
and her usual stilted speech gave way to more spontaneous teasing. Tim, apparently "hearing" Davida criticize him, in a sophisticated displacement expressed his attachment and appreciation of
my involvement. The session had a much greater "real" feeling and
I certainly found myself influenced and pleased with the interactions, even though I had incompletely understood them during the
session.

Vignette 3

At the first meeting in October, the final month before I retired, all
the members were present. In response to Tim's question about
new doctors, I said that two new doctors would be starting in
November, and they would need to change the meeting day from

Thursday to Friday. I also reminded them that three patients from another group would be starting on the same date.

Following a flurry of questions clarifying the date of the first Friday meeting in November, Tim began talking about work, clearly conveying that this kept him from thinking about the forthcoming changes. He mentioned that he had to get a lot of work in before the weather changed. I used his reference to focus not only on changes in the weather, but also in the group. This was followed by members questioning how long the new doctors would remain, would they be prescribing medicines, would I orient them to the group, and finally where were the new patients coming from. I briefly answered each of these questions.

Tim interrupted this by asking Jack about work, but Davida immediately switched back to asking if I had plans to work in California. I responded saying that I would not be seeing patients, but I would be doing some teaching. Rita asked if I would send them a postcard describing the first earthquake! Rather surprised, I paused and responded, "I would be all shook up." Rita replied, "Elvis Presley!" This was precisely what I had thought of when the phrase came to my mind.

After a pause, I asked Davida to further explore her question about my working in California. She then led the group in a surprising direction, saying, "People can say too much about themselves sometimes; people should be quiet and not talk so much about themselves." Davida continued, saying that a girl in her group home did not fit because she was too young. Yet she was unsure if she wanted her to leave. I wondered if she also was concerned about people leaving the group. She replied that she might not be able to come on Fridays because of her work in a sheltered workshop. I directly responded asking if she could switch work days, and told her I would hate to see her stop coming to the group.

The response was dramatic as four members spoke about significant recent depressive feelings. They focused on being rejected for complaining and whining. I inquired how it had been for them as children complaining to parents, which led initially to further sharing of the parental suppression of complaints. Tim made a distinction between speaking up in circumstances where one had an awareness of how others would respond, and there were places where he could complain. Jack added that "if you don't speak up, people will walk over you." Tim brought the session to a close by talking about looking forward to spring when he would start a new job and make a lot of money.

Commentary

I began this meeting with considerable anxiety, as I suddenly was unable to recall the names of the two residents who were taking my place. I was also anxious about their need to change the day and the members' response to "one more change." Strikingly, Davida successfully cut short the usual defensive flight into discussions of work by turning the discussion back to my plans. I understood this shift as the group's growing capacity to more directly address intense feelings and an acceptance of the forthcoming change.

Rita's inquiry about sending a note following an earthquake startled me. I was momentarily confused, a response I am certain they observed. I had a flood of thoughts as I tried to respond in some manner that would be useful to them. I was feeling guilt, wondering whether I had injured them by implying that I was happy no longer seeing patients. I wondered if the playful "I'm all shook up" remark might suppress anger. Perhaps Davida's association to people talking too much was such a message. For an extended period I was perplexed by this association. I seemed unable to consider it as an association to me. Indeed, it was only as I was working on a draft of this manuscript that a colleague pointed out its obvious transference implications, that I understood her comment as a reference to my talking about my plans. In retrospect, I believe that Davida's association had touched upon an aspect of my views that my sharing of information would enhance the treatment alliance, and I could not, so close to my retirement, afford to have that belief challenged.

Davida, characteristically in a displacement, exposed her fears about possibly having to leave the group. When this became explicit, I directly said that I hoped she would stay. I believe that this intervention was experienced as my caring and resulted in members feeling freer to report depressive feelings. My question relating their experiences back to early family experiences was in the service of increased sharing and deepening of the in-group attachments, rather than a search for a "genetic" basis for their inhibitions. Indeed, Tim showed an awareness of others' mental states, an infrequent sign of mentalization. I silently responded to Tim's comment about looking forward to spring with an association to Bion's (1961) "pairing" basic assumption—things will be better in the future, when they have gotten to know the new therapists.

Countertransferences and conclusions

I found myself working very hard to manage my own feelings about saying goodbye to patients I had known for more than a decade. In part, I was able to handle some of the more difficult countertransference elements in my leave-taking with my weekly review of the videotapes. This review process was aided by a talented psychology graduate student, who had been in charge of the camera work for over a year and was quite familiar with the members and my usual style. His comments and observations often assisted me in looking closer at some my behaviours, both explicit interventions and non-verbal communications.[2] I felt that these informal "supervisory" sessions along with my own opportunity to review my work served the recommended and necessary consultative function in addressing inevitable countertransference reactions(Martinez, 1989, Weddington & Cavenar, 1979). Illustrative of the value of the videotape review was a session in mid-October, in which I realized that I was intervening without allowing the usual pauses after someone spoke. It was subtle change, but it became was very clear to me that I wanted to be very giving in the context of my leave taking.

Another contribution to my emotional state was relief at ending a longstanding struggle of keeping the group therapy program afloat, feelings reinforced by my sense that the future plans for the program were not promising. One manifestation of this organizational problem was that, despite persistent inquiries over an extended period, I was unable to learn who would be assigned to lead the group. When I was informed in late September of those residents who would be taking the group, I was unable to remember their names. My stumbling over my announcement without providing names left me temporarily more shamed and guilty about how I was handling my departure.

I was also sad that I was giving up my work, particularly as I had grown very fond of people in the group[3]. I greatly admired the tenacity with which they hung on to a life that often seemed devoid of genuine intimacy and which so much of the time seemed so empty. I often experienced this emptiness myself. At times the barrier between us seemed impenetrable. Nevertheless, as I learned, if I could only really hear their efforts to link and to change, we could make contact. Some of my personal pleasure came when they risked expressing care for one another.

I became particularly attuned to Davida whose seemingly psychotic interjections were more appropriately understood as salient metaphoric commentary on the treatment process. Yet, I did not understand the transference implications of her important message that people talk too much. On another recent occasion, she vaguely said that she had had a dream and, contrary to my usual style, I did not inquire about the content. It was only when reviewing the videotape that I became aware of my failure. I believe that my avoiding hearing about her dream was my countertransference wish to seal the process over and not address depth emotions—I was experiencing an overload of which I was only partially aware. Tim often frustrated me with his braggadocio presentation, and yet, I was aware that he had some capacity for self reflection and mentalizing despite a deep sense of inferiority. Indeed as I reflected upon the entire experience and reviewed in my mind all the members, I could see each person's assets and deficits, their sensitivities and vulnerabilities, their humour and ability to tease.

My experiences with this group helped me understand that therapist's can only "arm" themselves with theoretical overviews. This group did not follow any particular pattern in how the members dealt with my departure. While they certainly expressed many of the feelings described by Kubler-Ross, the sequencing did not follow that model. Although viewing the videotapes was very helpful as was the student's observations and questions, I believe that I would have benefited from a more formal consultation as I think that I was at times overly protective and feeling too much guilt and anxiety over my retirement.

As I reviewed the videotapes and the transcripts in the process of writing this paper, I re-experienced how much I miss the group. At times, watching the sessions many months after my official retirement, I felt embarrassed by what seemed to be my sophomoric work, but I also recognized that members were resilient and forgiving. I feel that I have learned so much from them. When, as described in the third vignette, they talked about their depression, I felt that this was so ordinary and expectable. In the words of one of my colleagues, "they blew their cover." We all were deeply attached.

Notes

1. In the early 1960's, the average length of stay at the VA hospital in Cincinnati was about 42 days.
2. Although the graduate student, Ian Pritchard had encountered a scheduling conflict, and for a portion of the period was unable to manage the camera (it was merely left on fixed focus) we were able to work out weekly time to view the sessions.
3. Originally I had written this sentence ... in MY group. While editing the manuscript, I realized that this construction further expressed my attachment to these people I had worked with over so many years.

REFERENCES

Abse, W. (1983). Some Complimentary Functions of Group-analytic Psychotherapy and Individual Psychoanalysis, In: M. Pines (Ed.), *The Evolution of Group Analysis*, pp. 17–28 London: Routledge and Kegan Paul.

Agazarian, Y.M. (1992). Contemporary theories of group psychotherapy: A systems approach to the group-as-a-whole. *International Journal of Group Psychotherapy*, 42: 177–203.

Agazarian, Y.M. (1997). *Systems-Centred Therapy for Groups.* New York: Guilford Press.

Agazarian, Y.M. & Janoff, (1997). Systems theory and small groups. In: I. Kaplan & B.J. Sadock (Eds.), *Comprehensive Textbook of Group Psychotherapy (3rd Ed.)* Baltimore: Williams & Wilkins.

Agazarian, Y. (1993). Systems theory and small groups, In: H.I. Kaplan & B.J. Sadock (Eds.), *Comprehensive Group Psychotherapy, 3rd* edition. Baltimore, Williams and Wilkins, pp. 32–33.

American Psychiatric Association (1997). Practice guidelines for the treatment of patients with schizophrenia *American Journal of Psychiatry 154* (Supplement).

Arensberg, F. (1998). A consideration of Kohut's views on group psychotherapy. In: I.N.H. Harwood & M. Pines (Eds.), *Self Experiences in Group: Intersubjective and Self Psychological Pathways to Human Understanding*. London: Jessica Kingsley, (pp. 19–23).

Atwood, G.E. & Stolorow, R.D. (1984). *Structures of subjectivity: Explorations in psychoanalytic phenomenology*. New York: The Analytic Press.

Austin, J.L. (1962). *How to do things with words*. Oxford: Oxford University Press.

Bacal, H.A. (1985). Object-relations in the group from the perspective of self psychology. *International Journal of Group Psychotherapy, 35*: 483–501.

Bacal, H.A. (1985). Optimal responsiveness and the therapeutic process. In: A Goldberg (Ed.), *Progress in Self Psychology, (Vol. 1)*. A. Goldberg (Ed.) Hillsdale, NJ: The Analytic Press, pp. 202–226.

Bacal, H.A. (1992). Recent theoretical developments: contributions from self psychology theory, In: R.D. Klein, H.S. Bernard & D.L. Singer (Eds.) *Handbook of Contemporary Group Psychotherapy*, Madison CT, International Universities Press, pp. 55–85.

Bacal, H.A. (1995). The essence of Kohut's work and the progress of self psychology. *Psychoanalytic Dialogues, 5*: 353–366.

Bacal, H.A. (1998). Notes on optimal responsiveness in the group process. In: I.N.H. Harwood and M. Pines (Eds.) *Self Experiences in Group: Intersubjective and Self Psychological Pathways to Human Understanding*. (pp. 175–180). London and Philadelphia: Jessica Kingsley.

Bagner, D.M., Melinder, M.R.D. & Barch, D.M. (2003). Language comprehension and working memory language comprehension and working memory deficits in patients with schizophrenia. *Schizophrenia Research, 60*: 299–309.

Basch, M.F. (1992). *Practicing psychotherapy: A casebook*. New York: Basic Books.

Beatrice, J. (1982–1983). Premature termination: A therapist leaving. *International Journal of Psychoanalytic Psychotherapy. 9*: 313–316.

Bennis, W.G. & Shepard, H.H. (1956). A Theory of Group Development. *Human Relations, 9*: 415–437.

Berger, M.M. & Rosenbaum, M. (1967). Notes on the Help-Rejecting Complainer. *International Journal of Group Psychotherapy, 17*: 357–370.

Bion W.R. (1959). *Experiences in Groups*. New York: Basic Books.

Blanck, G. & Blanck, R. (1974). *Ego Psychology: Theory and Practice*. New York: Columbia University Press.

Blum, H.P. (1992). Affect theory and the theory of technique. In: T. Shapiro and R.N. Emde (Eds.) *Affect: Psychoanalytic perspectives* (pp. 65–89) Madison, CT: International Universities Press.

Boris, H.N. (1986). The "other" Brest: Greed, Envy, Spite and Revenge. *Contemporary Psychoanalysis 22*(1): 45–59.

Boss, A. (2003). "E" enactments in psychoanalysis: Another medium, another message. *Psychoanalytic Dialogues, 13*: 657–675.

Bostic, J.Q., Shadid, L.G. & Blotcky, M.J. (1996). Our time is up: Forced terminations during psychotherapy training. *American Journal of Psychotherapy, 50*: 347–359.

Breier. A. & Strauss, J.S. (1984). The role of social relationships in the recovery from psychotic disorders. *American Journal of Psychiatry, 141*: 949–955.

Brothers, D. (1983). The search for the hidden self: A fresh look at later ego transferences. In: A. Goldberg (Ed.), *The widening scope of self psychology: Progress in self psychology* (pp. 191–207). Hillsdale, NJ: The Analytic Press.

Brothers, D. (2003). Clutching at certainty: Thoughts on the coercive grip of cult-like groups. *Group, 27*: 79–88.

Brownbridge, G. (2003). The group in the individual. *Group Analysis, 36*: 23–35.

Bustillo, J.R., Lauriello, J., Horan, W.P. & Keith, S.J. (2001). The psychosocial treatment of schizophrenia: An update. *American Journal of Psychiatry, 158*: 163–175.

Cohen, B.D. & Ettin, M.F. (2002). Personal group-self and transpersonal groupobject. *GroupAnalysis, 35*: 287–300.

Cooper, L. & Gustafson, J.P. (1979). Toward a general theory of group therapy. *Human Relations, 32*: 967–981.

Cooper, L. & Gustafson, J.P. (1979a). Planning and mastery in group therapy: A contribution to theory and technique. *Human Relations., 32*: 689–703.

Cooper, L., Gustafson, J.P., Lathrop, N.C., Ringler, K., Seldin, F. & Wright, M.K. (1981). Cooperative and clashing interests in small groups: Part I. Theory. *Human Relations. 34*: 315–339.

Correale, A. & Celli, A.M. (1998). The model-scene in group psychotherapy with chronic psychotic patients. *International Journal of Group Psychotherapy, 48*: 55–68.

Coursey, R.D., Keller, A.B. & Farrell, E.W. (1993). Individual psychotherapy and persons with serious mental illness: the clients' perspective. *Schizophrenia Bulletin, 21*: 283–301.

Detrick, D. (1986). Alter-ego phenomena and the alter-ego transferences: Some further consideration. In: A. Goldberg (Ed.), *Progress in self psychology* New York: Guilford. (pp. 299–304).

DeWald, P. (1966). Forced termination of psychoanalysis: transference, countertransference and reality responses in five patients. *Bulletin of the Menninger Clinic, 30:* 98–110.

Dickerson, F.B., Boronow, J.J. & Ringel, N. et al. (1997). Lack of insight among outpatients with schizophrenia. *Psychiatric Services, 48:* 195–1999.

Durkin, H.E. (1964). *The Group in Depth.* New York: International Universities Press.

Durkin, H.E. (1981). The group therapies and general system theory as an integrative structure. In: J.E. Durkin (Ed.), *Living Groups: Group Psychotherapy and General System Theory* New York: Brunner/Mazel (pp. 5–23).

Durkin, J.E. (1981). (Ed.), *Living Groups: Group Psychotherapy and General System Theory* New York: Brunner/Mazel.

Epstein, J. (1991). A few Kind Words for Envy, In: J. Kaplan and R. Alwan (Eds.), *The Best American Essays 1990,* pp. 83–09 New York: Ticknor and Fields.

Ethan, S. (1978). The Question of Dilution of Transference in Group Psychotherapy. *Psychoanalytic Review* 65(4): 569–578.

Feldberg, T.M. (1958). Treatment of "borderline" psychotics in groups of neurotic patients. *International Journal of Group Psychotherapy, 8:* 76–84.

Fenton, W.S. & Cole S.A. (1996). Psychosocial therapies of schizophrenia: individual, group, and family, in *Synopsis of Treatments of Psychiatric Disorders,* 2nd edition, edited by Gabbard GO, Atkinson SD. Washington DC, American Psychiatric Press, pp. 425–438.

Fieldsteel, N.D. (1996). The process of termination in long-term psychoanalytic group therapy. *International Journal of Group Psychotherapy. 46:* 25–39.

Fonagy, P., Gergely, G., Jurist, E.L. & Target, M. (2002). *Affect Regulation, Mentalization, and the Development of the Self.* New York: Other Press.

Fosshage, J.L. (1997). The organizing function of dream mentation. *Contemporary Psychoanalysis, 33:* 429–458.

Fosshage, J.L. (2002). Love and anger within the analytic relationship: A Clinical workshop. Presented at International Conference on the Psychology of the Self Washington DC.

Foulkes, E.H. (1951). Concerning leadership in group analytic psychotherapy. *International Journal of Group Psychotherapy, 1*: 319–329.

Foulkes, S.H. (1973). The group as matrix of the individual's mental
life. In: L.R. Wolberg & E.K. Schwartz (Eds.), *Group Therapy 1973*.
New York: Intercontinental Medical Book Corporation.

Foulkes, S.H. & Anthony, E.J. (1957). *Group Psychotherapy: The Psychoanalytical Approach*. Harmondsworth: Penguin Books.

Freud, S. (1900a). The interpretation of dreams. *Standard Edition, 6*: 1–627.
London, Hogarth Press, 1953.

Freud, S. (1912e). Recommendations to physicians practicing psych-
analysis *Standard Edition 12*: 109–120. London, Hogarth Press, 1958.

Freud, S. (1914c). On narcissism: An introduction. *Standard Edition, 14*:
67–104. London Hogarth Press, 1955.

Freud, S. (1917e). Mourning and Melancholia. *Standard Edition, 14*: 237–260.
London, Hogarth Press, 1955.

Freud, S. (1921c). Group Psychology and the Analysis of the Ego. *Standard Edition, 18*: 69–143 London: Hogarth Press, 1955.

Fried, E. (1955). Combined Group and Individual Therapy with Passive Narcissistic Patients. *International Journal of Group Psychotherapy,
5*: 194–203.

Fried, E. (1973). Group Bonds, In *Group Therapy 1973: An Overview*, L.R.
Wolberg and E.K. Schwartz (Eds.), New York: Intercontinental Medical Book Corp., pp. 161–168.

Fried, E. (1979). Narcissistic inaccessibility, *Group, 3*: 79–87.

Friedman, L. (1988). *The anatomy of psychotherapy*. Hillsdale, NJ: Analytic
Press.

Fromm-Reichmann, F. (1990). The assets of the mentally handicapped:
The interplay of mental illness and creativity. In: A.-L.S. Silver & M.B.
Cantor (Eds.), *Psychoanalysis and severe emotional illness*. New York
Guilford, pp. 47–72.

Gadamer, H.G. (1960). *Truth and Method*. London: Sheed & Ward (1989).

Gans, J.S. & Alonso, A. (1998). Difficult patients: Their construction
in group therapy. *International Journal of Group Psychotherapy, 48*:
311–326.

Ganzarain, R. (1977). General systems and object relations theories:
Their usefulness in group psychotherapy. *International. Journal of
Group Psychotherapy, 27*: 441–456.

Garfield, D.A.S. (1993). *Unbearable Affect: A Guide to the Psychotherapy of
Psychosis*. New York, Wiley, 1993.

Garland, C. (1982). Taking the non-problem seriously. *Group Analysis,* 15: 4–14.

Gedo, J.E. (1977). Notes on the psychoanalytic management of archaic transferences. *Journal of the American. Psychoanalytic Association,* 25: 787–803.

Gedo, J.E. & Goldberg, A. (1973). *Models of the Mind: A Psychoanalytic Theory.* Chicago: University of Chicago Press.

Gibbard, G.S. & Hartman, J.J. (1973). The Significance of Utopian Fantasies in Small Groups. *International Journal of Group Psychotherapy,* 23: 125–147.

Glatzer, H.I. (1962). Handling Narcissistic Problems in Group Psychotherapy. *International Journal of Group Psychotherapy,* 12: 448–455.

Glatzer, H.T. (1978). The working alliance in analytic group psychotherapy. *International Journal of Group Psychotherapy,* 28: 147–161.

Glover, E. (1932). A Psycho-Analytic Approach to the Classification of Mental Disorders. In *On Early Development of the Mind.* New York: International Universities Press, 1956, pp. 161–186.

Goldberg, A. (1998). Self psychology since Kohut. *Psychoanalytic Quarterly,* 67: 240–255.

Goldstein, W.N. (1991). Clarification of projective identification. *American Journal of Psychiatry,* 148: 153–161.

Green, M.F. (1996). What are the functional consequences of neurocognitive deficits in schizophrenia? *American Journal of Psychiatry,* 153: 321–330.

Green, M.F., Kerns, R.S., Braff, D.L. & Mintz, J. (2000). Neurocognitive deficits and functional outcome in schizophrenia: Are we measuring the "right stuff"? *Schizophrenia Bulletin,* 26: 119–136.

Greenberg, J.R. (1986). Theoretical models and the analyst's neutrality. *Contemporary Psychoanalysis,* 22: 87–106.

Greenson, R.R. (1967). *The technique and practice of psychoanalysis.* New York: International Universities Press.

Grobman, J. (1978). Achieving cohesiveness in therapy groups of chronically disturbed patients. *Group,* 2: 141–148.

Gustafson, J.P. & Cooper, L. (1978). Collaboration in small groups: Theory and technique for the study of small-group processes, *Human Relations,* 31: 155–171.

Gustafson, J.P. & Cooper, L. (1979). Unconscious planning in small groups. *Human Relations,* 32: 1039–1064.

Gustafson, J.P. & Cooper, L. (1981). Cooperative and clashing interests in small groups: Part II. Group narratives. *Human Relations,* 34: 367–78.

Harwood, I.N.H. (1983). The application of self-psychology concepts to group psychotherapy. *International Journal of Group Psychotherapy, 33*: 469–487.

Harwood, I.N.H. (1998). Can group analysis/psychotherapy provide a wide angle lends for self psychology. In: I.N.H. Harwood and M. Pines (Eds.), *Self perspectives in group: Intersubjective and self psychological pathways to human understanding*) London: Jessica Kingsley, pp. 155–174.

Harwood, I.N.H. (2002). Discussion of Martin Livingston's working playspace. In: C. Neri, M. Pines & R. Friedman (Eds) *Dreams in Group Psychotherapy: Theory and Technique*. London, Jessica Kingsley, pp. 191–196.

Havens, L.L. (1976). *Participant Observation*. New York: Jason Aronson.

Havens, L.L. (1978). Explorations in the use of language in psychotherapy: Simple empathic statements. *Psychiatry, 41*: 336–345.

Hearst, L. & Sharpe, M. (1991). Training for Trainees in Group Analysis, In: J. Roberts and M. Pines (Eds.), *The Practice of Group Analysis,.* London: Routledge. pp. 148–154.

Hopper, E. (1996). The Social Unconscious in Clinical Work, *Group, 20*: 7–42.

Hopper, E. (2003). *The Social Unconscious: Selected Papers*. London and Philadelphia: Jessica Kingsley.

Horner, A.H. (1975). A Charaterological Contraindication for Group Psychotherapy. *Journal of the American Academy of Psychoanalysis, 3*: 301–305.

Horwitz, L. (1977). A group-centered approach to group psychotherapy. *International Journal of Group Psychotherapy, 27*: 423–439.

Horwitz, L. (1983). Projective identification in dyads and groups. *International Journal of Group Psychotherapy, 33*: 259–279.

Johnson, H. (1991). *Sleepwalking Through History: America in the Reagan Years*. New York: Anchor Books.

Joyce, A.S., Duncan, S.C., Duncan, A., Kipnes, D. & Piper, W.E. (1996). Limiting time-unlimited group psychotherapy. *International Journal of Group Psychotherapy, 46*: 61–79.

Kanas, N. (1996). *Group Therapy for Schizophrenic Patients* Washington, DC: American Psychiatric Press.

Karterud, S. (1992). Group dreams revisited. *Group Analysis, 25*: 207–221.

Karterud, S. (1998). The group self, empathy, intersubjectivity and Hermeneutics: A group analytic perspective. In: I.N.H. Harwood &

M. Pines (Eds.), *Self Experiences in Group: Intersubjective and Self Psychological Pathways to Human Understanding*. London: Jessica Kingsley, pp. 83–98.

Karterud, S. (1999). *Gruppeanalyse og psykodynamisk gruppepsykoterapi*. Oslo: Pax forlag.

Karterud, S. & Stone, W.N. (2003). The group self: A neglected aspect of group psychotherapy. *Group Analysis, 36*: 7–22.

Kauff, P. (1977). The Termination Process: Its Relationship to the Separation-Individuation Phase of Development. *International Journal of Group Psychotherapy, 27*: 14–22.

Kennard, D. (1993). The first session—an apparent distraction. In: D. Kennard, J. Roberts & D.A. Winter (Eds.), *A work book of group-analytic interventions* London: Routledge, pp. 21–28.

Kernberg, O.F. (1975a). *Borderline Conditions and Pathological Narcissism*. New York: Jason Aronson.

Kernberg, O.F. (1975b). A systems approach to priority setting of intervention in groups. *International Journal of Group Psychotherapy, 25*: 251–275.

Kernberg, O.F. (1976). *Object Relations Theory and Clinical Psychoanalysis*. New York: Jason Aronson.

Kibel, H.D. (1990). The inpatient psychotherapy group as a testing ground for theory. In: B.E. Roth, W.N. Stone & H.D. Kibel (Eds.), *The difficult patient in group*. Madison CT: International Universities Press. pp. 245–264.

Kieffer, C.C. (2001). Phases of group development: A view from self psychology. *Group, 25*: 91–105.

Klein, M. (1957). *Envy and Gratitude*. New York: Basic Books.

Kohut, H. (1966). Forms and transformations of narcissism. *Journal of the American. Psychoanalytic Association, 14*: 243–272.

Kohut, H. (1968). The Psychoanalytic Treatment of Narcissistic Personality Disorders. *The Psychoanalytic Study of the Child*, New York. International Universities Press, *23*: 86–113.

Kohut, H. (1970). Moderator's opening and closing remarks. In: Discussion of D.D. Levin's "The Self." *International Journal of Psycho-Analysis, 51*: 175–181.

Kohut, H. (1971). *The Analysis of the Self*. New York: International Universities Press.

Kohut, H. (1972). Thoughts on Narcissism and Narcissistic Rage. *The Psychoanalytic Study of the Child, 27*: 360–400. New York: Quadrangle Books.

Kohut, H. (1976). Creativeness, charisma, group psychology. In: J.E. Gedo and G.H. Pollock (Eds.) *Freud: The Fusion of Science and Humanism.* New York: International Universities Press, pp. 379–425.

Kohut, H. (1977). *The Restoration of the Self.* New York: International Universities Press.

Kohut, H. (1984). *How Does Analysis Cure?* Chicago: University of Chicago Press.

Kohut, H. (1985). *Self Psychology and the Humanities.* New York: W.W. Norton & Company.

Kohut, H. & Seitz, P.F.D. (1963). Concepts and Theories of Psychoanalysis. In: P.H. Ornstein (Ed.) *The Search for the Self, Vol. 1.* New York: International Universities Press (1978).

Koseff, J.W. (1990). Anchoring the self through the group: Congruences, play and the potential for change. In: B.E. Roth, W.N. Stone & H.D. Kibel (Eds.), *The difficult patient in group: Group psychotherapy and borderline and narcissistic disorders* Madison, CT: International Universities Press, pp. 87–108.

Krystal, H. (1974). The Genetic Development of Affect and Affect Regression. *The Annual of Psychoanalysis, Vol. 2,* New York: International Universities Press, pp. 98–126.

Krystal, H. (1975). Affect tolerance. *The Annual of Psychoanalysis, 3:* 179–219.

Kubler-Ross, E. (1967). *On death and dying.* New York: Macmillan Press.

Kuipers, L. (1979). Expressed emotion: a review. *British Journal of Social and Clinical Psychology, 18:* 237–243.

Lewin, K. (1951). *Field Theory in Social Science* New York: Harper & Row.

Lichtenberg, J.D. (2005). *Craft and Spirit: A Guide to the Exploratory Psychotherapies.* Hillsdale, NJ: The Analytic Press.

Lichtenberg, J.D., Lachmann, F.M. & Fosshage, J.L. (1992). *Self and motivational systems: Toward a theory of psychoanalytic technique.* Hillsdale, NJ: The Analytic Press.

Lichtenberg, J.D., Lachmann, F.M. & Fosshage, J.I. (1996). *The Clinical Exchange: Techniques; Derived from Self and Motivational Systems.* Hillsdale, NJ Analytic Press.

Lichtenstein, H. (1961). Identity and Sexuality. *Journal of the American Psychoanalytic Association, 9:* 179–260.

Livingston, M.S. (1999). Vulnerability, tenderness and the experience of selfobject relationship: A self psychological view of deepening curative process in group psychotherapy. *International Journal of Group Psychotherapy, 49*: 19–40.

Livingston, M.S. (2001). Self psychology, dreams and group psychotherapy: Working in the playspace. *Group, 25*: 15–26.

Lothstein, L.M. (1993). Termination processes in group psychotherapy. In: H.I. Kaplan & B.J. Sadock (Eds.), *Comprehensive Group Psychotherapy (3rd edition)*. Baltimore, MD: Williams & Wilkins, pp. 115–124.

Lotterman, A. (1996). *Specific techniques for the Psychotherapy of Schizophrenic patients*. Madison CT, International Universities Press.

MacKenzie, K.R. (1996). Time-limited group psychotherapy. *International Journal of Group Psychotherapy, 46*: 41–60.

Malan, D.H., Balfour, F.H.G., Hood, V.G. & Shooter, A. (1976). Group psychotherapy: A long-term follow-up study. *Archives of General Psychiatry, 33*: 1303–1315.

Malcolm, J. (1981). Psychoanalysis: The impossible profession. Northdale, NJ: Jason Aronson.

Martinez, D. (1989). Pains and gains: A study of forced terminations. *Journal of American Psychoanalytic Association, 37*: 89–115.

Martinez, D. (1993). The bad girl, the good girl, their mothers and the analyst; The role of the twinship selfobject in female oedipal development. In: A. Goldberg (Ed.), *The widening scope of self psychology: Progress in self psychology*. Hillsdale, NJ: The Analytic Press, pp. 87–107.

Masterson, J.F. (1976). *Psychotherapy of the borderline adult*. New York: Brunner/Mazel.

Masterson, J.F. (1978). The borderline adult: Therapeutic alliance and transference. *American Journal of Psychiatry, 135*: 437–441.

McEvoy, J.P., Scheifler, P.L. & Frances, A. (Eds.) (1999). The Expert Consensus Guideline Series: Treatment of Schizophrenia 1999. *The Journal of Clinical Psychiatry, 60* (Supp. 11).

McGlashan, T.H., Levy, S.T. & Carpenter, W.T. (1975). Integration and sealing over: clinically distinct recovery styles from schizophrenia. *Archives of General Psychiatry, 32*: 269–272.

Meyers, S.J. (1978). The disorders of the self: Developmental and clinical considerations. *Group, 2*: 131–140.

Meyers, S.J. (1996). Group therapy and disorders of the self *Group Analysis, 29*: 219–227.

Morrison, A.P. (1990). Secrets: A self-psychological view of shame in group therapy, In: B.E. Roth, W.N. Stone and H.D. Kibel (Eds.), *The*

Difficult patient in group, Madison, CT: International Universities Press, pp. 175–189.

Michels, R. (1999). Psychoanalysts' theories. In: P. Fonagy, A.M. Cooper & R.S. Wallerstein (Eds.), *Psychoanalysis on the move: The work of Joseph Sandler* London: Routledge, pp. 187–200.

Mikkelsen, E.J. & Guthehil, T.G. (1979). Stages of forced termination: Uses of the death metaphor. *Psychiatry Quarterly, 51*: 15–27.

Mosher, L.R. & Keith S.J. (1980). Psychosocial treatment: individual, group, family, and community support approaches. *Schizophrenia Bulletin, 6*: 110–141.

Myin-Germeys, I., Delespaul, P.A.E.G. & deVries, M. (2000). Schizophrenia patients are more emotionally active than is assumed based on their behavior. *Schizoprhenia Bulletin, 26*: 847–851.

Newman, K. (2007). Therapeutic action in self psychology. *Psychoanalytic Quarterly, 76*: 1513–1546.

Ornstein, A. (1974). The Dread to Repeat and the New Beginning— A Contribution to the Psychoanalysis of the Narcissistic Personality Disorder, *The Annual of Psychoanalysis 2*: 131–148.

Ornstein, A. (1990). Selfobject transferences and the process of working through. In: A. Godlberg (Ed.), *The realities of transference: Progress in self psychology* (pp. 41–58). Hillsdale, NJ: The Analytic Press.

Ornstein, A. (1991). The dread to repeat: Comments on the working-through process in psychoanalysis. *Journal of the American Psychoanalytic Association, 39*: 377–397.

Ornstein, A. (1992). The curative fantasy and psychic recovery: Contribution to the theory of psychoanalytic psychotherapy. *Journal of Psychotherapy Practice and Research. 1*: 16–28.

Ornstein, P.H. (1974). On narcissism beyond the introduction, highlights of Heinz Kohut's contributions to psychoanalytic treatment of narcissistic personality disorders. *The Annual of Psychoanalysis, 2*: New York: International Universities Press, 127–149.

Ornstein, P.H. (1987). On self-state dreams in psychoanalytic treatment process. In: A. Rothstein (Ed.), *The interpretation of dreams in clinical work*. Madison, CT: International Universities Press, pp. 87–104.

Ornstein, P.H. (2003). The elusive concept of the psychoanalytic process. *Journal of the American Psychoanalytic Association, 52*: 15–41.

Ornstein, P.H. & Kay, J. (1990). Development of psychoanalytic self-psychology: A historical perspective. In: A. Tasman and S.M. Goldfiner & C. Kaufman (Eds.), *American psychiatric press review of psychiatry* (pp. 302–322) Washington DC: American Psychiatric Press.

Ornstein, P.H. & Ornstein, A. (1985). Clinical understanding and explaining: The empathic vantage point. In: A. Goldberg (Ed.), *Progress in self psychology*, New York: Guilford, pp. 43–61.

Ornstein, P.H. & Ornstein, A. (1993). Assertiveness, anger, rage and destructive aggression: A perspective from the treatment process. In: R. Glick & S. Roose (Eds.), *Rage, power and aggression*. New Haven, Yale University Press, (pp. 102–119).

Ornstein, P.H. & Ornstein, A. (1996). Some general principles of psychoanalytic psychotherapy: A self-psychological perspective. In: L.E. Lifson (Ed.), *Understanding therapeutic action: Psychodynamic concepts of cure*. Hillsdale, NJ: Analytic Press, pp. 87–101.

Ornstein, P.H. & Ornstein, A. (2003). The function of theory in psychoanalysis: A self psychological perspective. *Psychoanalytic Quarterly, 72*: 157–182.

Penn, L. (1990). When the therapist must leave: Forced termination of psychodynamic therapy. *Professional Psychology: Research and Practice.* 21: 379–384.

Pine, F. (1985). *Developmental theory and clinical process*. New Haven: Yale University Press.

Pines, M. (1975). Group therapy with "difficult" patients. In: L.R. Wolberg & M.L Aronson (Eds.), Group Therapy 1975: An Overview New York: Stratton Intercontinental Medical Books, pp. 102–119.

Pinsker, H. (1997). *A primer of supportive psychotherapy*. New York: Guilford Press.

Rice, C.A. (1977). Observations on the unexpected and simultaneous termination of leader and group. *Group, 1:* 100–117.

Rioch, M.S. (1970). The Work of Wilfred Bion on Groups. *Psychiatry, 33:* 55–66.

Roth, B.E. (1979). Problems of early maintenance and entry into group psychotherapy with persons suffering from borderline and narcissistic states. *Group, 3:* 3–22.

Rubovits-Seitz, P. (1998). *Depth-psychological understanding: The methodologic grounding of clinical interpretations*. Hillsdale, NJ: The Analytic Press.

Rubovits-Seitz, P.F.D. (2001). *The interpretive process in clinical practice: Progressive understand and communication of latent meanings*. Northvale, NJ: Jason Aronson, Inc.

Runions, J. & Prudo, R. (1983). Problem behaviors encountered by families living with a schizophrenic member. *Canadian Journal of Psychiatry, 28*: 382–386.

Rutan, J.S. & Alonso, A. (1978). Some guidelines for group therapists. *Group, 2*: 4–13.

Rutan, J.S. & Stone, W.N. (1984). *Psychodynamic Group Psychotherapy.* New York: Macmillan.

Rutan, J.S. & Stone, W.N. (1993). *Psychodynamic Group Psychotherapy,* (*2nd Ed.*), New York: Guilford Press.

Rutan, J.S. & Stone, W.N. (2001). *Psychodynamic Group Psychotherapy,* (*3rd Ed.*), New York: Guilford Press.

Sartre, J.P. (1943). *Being and Nothingness.* New York: Washington Square Press (1966).

Scheidlinger, S. (1974). On the concept of the "mother group." *International Journal of Group Psychotherapy, 24*: 417–428.

Scheidlinger, S. (1982). On scapegoating in group psychotherapy, *International Journal of Group Psychotherapy, 32*: 131–143.

Schermer, V.L. & Pines, M. (Eds.) (1999). *Group psychotherapy of the psychoses: Concepts, interventions and contexts.* London: Jessica Kingsley.

Schooler, N.R. & Keith, S.J. (1993). The clinical research base of the treatment of schizophrenia, in *Health Care Reform for Americans with Severe Mental Illnesses: Report of the National Advisory Mental Health Council* (US Dept of Health and Human Services). Washington DC, US Government Printing Office, pp. 22–30.

Schwaber, E.A. (1995). Towards a definition of the term and concept of interaction. *International Journal of Psycho-Analysis, 76*: 557–564.

Schwartz, E.K. (1972). Group Process Laboratories as a Teaching Method, *International Journal of Group Psychotherapy 22(1)*: 16–21.

Segalla, R.A. (1996). "The unbearable embeddedness of being": Self psychology, Intersubjectivity and large group experiences. *Group, 20*: 257–271.

Semrad, E. & Van Buskirk, D. (1969). *Teaching Psychotherapy of Psychotic Patients.* New York, Grune and Stratton.

Shapiro, S. (1995). *Talking with patients: A self psychological view.* Northvale, NJ: Jason Aronson.

Siegel, A.M. (1999). The optimal conversation: A concern about the current trends within self psychology. In: A. Goldberg (Ed.), *Pluralism in Self Psychology: Progress in Self Psychology Vol. 15.* Hillsdale, NJ, The Analytic Press.

Skolnick, M.R. (1994). Intensive group and social systems treatment of psychotic and borderline patients, In: V.L. Schermer & M. Pines (Eds.), *Ring of fire: Primitive affects and object relations in group psychotherapy*, pp. 240–274.

Slater, P.E. (1966). *Microcosm: Structural, psychological and religious evolution in groups*, New York: Wiley.

Spotnitz, H. (1957). The borderline schizophrenic in group psychotherapy. *International Journal of Group Psychotherapy, 7*: 155–174.

Stern, D.N. (1985). *The Interpersonal World of the Infant*. New York Basic Books.

Stern, D.N., Sander, L.W., Nahum, J.P., Harrison, A.M., Lyons-Ruth, K., Morgan, A.C., Bruschweiler-Stern, N. & Troncik, E.Z. (1998). Non-interpretive mechanisms in psychoanalytic therapy: The 'something more' than interpretation. *International Journal of Psycho-Analysis, 79*: 903–921.

Stolorow, R.D. (1984). Aggression in the psychoanalytic situation: An intersubjective viewpoint. *Contemporary Psychoanalysis. 20*: 643–651.

Stolorow, R.D. (1995). An intersubjective view of self psychology. *Psychoanalytic Dialogues, 5*: 393–399.

Stolorow, R.D., Brandchaft, B. & Atwood, G. (1987). *Psychoanalytic treatment: An intersubjective approach*. Hillsdale, NJ: Analytic Press.

Stone, E. (2001). Culture, politics and group therapy: Identification and voyeurism. *Group Analysis, 34*: 501–514.

Stone, W.N. (1985). The curative fantasy in group psychotherapy. *Group 9(1)*: 3–14.

Stone, W.N. (1990). On affects in group psychotherapy. In: B.E. Roth, W.N. Stone & H.D. Kibel (Eds.), *The difficult patient in group: Group psychotherapy and borderline and narcissistic disorders* Madison, CT: International Universities Press, pp. 191–208.

Stone, W.N. (1991). Treatment of the chronic mentally ill: An opportunity for the group therapist, *International Journal of Group Psychotherapy 41(1)*: 11–22.

Stone, W.N. (1992). A Self Psychological Perspective on Envy in Group Psychotherapy, *Group Analysis 25*: 413–431.

Stone, W.N. (1992). The clinical application of self psychology theory. In: R.H. Klein, H.S. Bernard & D.L. Singer (Eds.), *Handbook of contemporary group psychotherapy: Contributions from object relations, self psychology and social systems theories* Madison, CT: International Universities Press, pp. 177–208.

Stone, W.N. (1992a). The place of self psychology in group psychother-apy: A status report. *International Journal of Group Psychotherapy, 41*: 335–350.

Stone, W.N. (1995). Frustration, Anger and the significance of alter-ego transferences in group psychotherapy. *International Journal of Group Psychotherapy, 45*: 287–302.

Stone, W.N. (1995). Group therapy for seriously mentally ill patients in a managed care system. In: K.R. MacKenzie (Ed.), *Effective use of group therapy in managed care.* Washington, DC: American Psychiatric Press, pp. 129–146.

Stone, W.N. (1996a). Group Psychotherapy for Persons with Chronic Mental Illness. New York: Guilford.

Stone, W.N. (1996b). Self psychology and the higher mental functioning hypothesis: Complementary theories. *Group Analysis, 29*: 169–181.

Stone, W.N. (1998). Affect and therapeutic process in groups for chroni-cally mentally ill persons. *Journal of Psychotherapy Practice and Research,* 7: 208–210.

Stone, W.N. (2001). The role of the therapist's affect in the detection of empathic failures, misunderstandings and injury. *Group, 25*: 3–14.

Stone, W.N. (2003). Strivings and Expectations: An Examination of Proc-ess in Groups for Persons with Chronic Mental Illness. *Psychoanalytic Inquiry, 23*: 678–696.

Stone, W.N., Blasé, M. & Bozzuto, J. (1980). Late dropouts from group therapy. *American Journal of Psychotherapy, 34*: 401–413.

Stone, W.N. & Gustafson, J.P. (1982). Technique in group psychotherapy of narcissistic and borderline patients. *International Journal of Group Psychotherapy, 32*: 29–47.

Stone, W.N. & Stevenson, F.B. (1991). Seeking perspective on patients' attendance in group psychotherapy. In: S. Tuttman (Ed.), *Psycho-analytic group theory and therapy: Essays in honor of Saul Scheidlinger.* Madison, CT: International Universities Press, pp. 339–356.

Stone, W.N. & Whitman, R.M. (1977). Contributions of the Psychology of the Self to Group Process ad Group Therapy. *International Journal of Group Psychotherapy, 27*: 343–359.

Strozier, C.B. (2001). *Heinz Kohut: The Making of a Psychoanalyst.* New York: Farrar, Straus and Giroux.

Sullivan, H.S. (1953). *The interpersonal theory of psychiatry.* New York: Norton.

Takahashi, T. (1994). Object Relations Group Psychotherapy with Chronic Schizophrenic Patients, paper presented at XIth International Symposium for the Psychotherapy of Schizophrenia, Washington DC.

Takahashi, T., Liipson, G. & Chazdon, L. (1999). Supportive-expressive group psychotherapy with chronic mental illness, including psychosis. In: V.L. Schermer & M. Pines (Eds.), *Group psychotherapy of the psychoses: Concepts, interventions and contexts.* London: Jessica Kingsley, pp. 221–250.

Teicholz, J.G. (1996). Optimal responsiveness: its role in psychic growth and change, In: Lifson LE (Ed.), *Understanding therapeutic action: Psychodynamic concept of cure*, Hillsdale, NJ, Analytic Press, pp. 131–161.

The Expert Consensus Guideline Series (1999). Treatment of Schizophrenia. *The Journal of Clinical Psychiatry, 60* Supplement 11.

Tolpin, M. (2002). Doing psychoanalysis of normal development: Forward edge transferences. In: A. Goldberg (Ed.), *Postmodern self psychology: Progress in self psychology* 18, Hillsdale: NJ: Analytic Press, pp. 167–190.

Tuckman, G.B.W. (1965). Developmental sequence in small groups. *Psychological Bulletin, 63*: 384–399.

Wahba, R. (1991). Envy in the transferences: A specific selfobject disruption. In: A. Goldberg (Ed.), *The evolution of self psychology: Progress in self psychology* Hillsdale, NJ: The Analytic Press, pp. 137–154.

Waldinger, R.J. (1993). The role of psychodynamic concepts in the diagnosis of borderline personality disorder. *Harvard Review of Psychiatry, 1*: 155–166.

Walker, E. & Lewine, R.J. (1990). Prediction of adult-onset schizophrenia from childhood home movies of patients. *American Journal of Psychiatry, 147*: 1052–1056.

Weddington, W.W. & Cavenar, J.O. Jr. (1979). Termination initiated by the therapist: A countertransference storm. *American Journal of Psychiatry, 136*: 1302–1305.

Weinstein, D. (1987). Self psychology and group therapy. *Group, 11*: 144–154.

Weinstein, D. (1991). Exhibitionism in Group Psychotherapy In: A. Goldberg (Ed.), *The Evolution of Self Psychology: Progress in Self Psychology, Vol. 7*, Hillsdale, NJ: Analytic Press, pp. 219–233.

Weiss, J. (1993). *How psychotherapy works: Process and technique.* New York, Guilford.

Weiss, J. & Sampson, H. (1986). The Mount Zion Psychotherapy Research Group. *The Psychoanalytic Process: Theory, Clinical Observations and Empirical Research.* New York: Guilford Press.

Weiss, S. (1972). Some thoughts and clinical vignettes on translocation of an analytic practice. *International Journal of Psychoanalysis 53*: 505–513.

Wells, L. Jr. (1985). The group-as-a-whole perspective and its theoretical roots. In: A.D. Coleman and M.H. Geller (Eds.), *Group relations reader 2*. Washington DC: A.K. Rice Institute (pp. 109–126).

Whitaker, D.S. & Lieberman, M.A. (1964). *Psychotherapy through the group process.* New York: Atherton Press.

Whitman, R.M. (1973). Dreams about the group: An Approach to the problem of group psychology. *International Journal of Group Psychotherapy, 23*: 408–420.

Whitman, R.M. & Bloch, E.L. (1990). Therapist envy, *Bulletin of the Menninger Clinic 54*(4): 478–487.

Whitman, R.M. & Stock, D. (1957). The group focal conflict. *Psychiatry, 21*: 269–276.

Wolf, E.S. (1988). *Treating the self: Elements of clinical self psychology.* New York: Guilford.

Wolf, E.S. (1993). Disruptions of the therapeutic relationship in psychoanalysis: A view from self psychology. *International Journal of Psycho-Analysis, 74*: 675–687.

Yalom, I.D. (1966). Problems of neophyte group therapists. *International Journal of Social Psychiatry, 12*: 52–59.

Yalom, I.D. (1970). *The theory and practice of group psychotherapy.* New York: Basic Books.

Yalom, I.D. (1975). *The theory and practice of group psychotherapy,* (2nd ed). New York Basic Books.

Yalom, I.D. (1985). *The theory and practice of group psychotherapy,* (3rd ed). New York: Basic Books.

Yalom, I.D. (1995). *The theory and practice of group psychotherapy,* (4th ed). New York: Basic Books.

INDEX